S.A.F.E.
Play Areas

Creation, Maintenance, and Renovation

Donna Thompson
Susan D. Hudson
Heather M. Olsen

Human Kinetics

Library of Congress Cataloging-in-Publication Data

Thompson, Donna.
 S.A.F.E. play areas : creation, maintenance, and renovation / Donna Thompson, Susan D. Hudson, Heather M. Olsen.
    p. cm.
 Includes bibliographical references and index.
 ISBN-13: 978-0-7360-6003-5 (soft cover)
 ISBN-10: 0-7360-6003-0 (soft cover)
 1. Play environments--Safety measures. 2. Playgrounds--Safety measures. 3. Recreation areas--Safety measures. I. Hudson, Susan D. II. Olsen, Heather M. III. Title.
 GV424.T47 2007
 790'.068--dc22

                                    2006020900

ISBN-10: 0-7360-6003-0
ISBN-13: 978-0-7360-6003-5

The Web addresses cited in this text were current as of November 2006, unless otherwise noted.

Acquisitions Editor: Gayle Kassing, PhD; **Developmental Editor:** Ray Vallese; **Assistant Editor:** Derek Campbell; **Copyeditor:** Alisha Jeddeloh; **Proofreader:** Kathy Bennett; **Indexer:** Sharon Duffy; **Permission Manager:** Dalene Reeder; **Graphic Designer:** Bob Reuther; **Graphic Artist:** Dawn Sills; **Photo Manager:** Laura Fitch; **Cover Designer:** Keith Blomberg; **Photographer (cover):** Brenda Williams; **Photographer (interior):** © Human Kinetics, unless otherwise noted; **Art Manager:** Kelly Hendren; **Illustrator:** Tammy Page; **Printer:** United Graphics

Printed in the United States of America   10   9   8   7   6   5   4   3   2   1

Human Kinetics
Web site: www.HumanKinetics.com

United States: Human Kinetics
P.O. Box 5076
Champaign, IL 61825-5076
800-747-4457
e-mail: humank@hkusa.com

Canada: Human Kinetics
475 Devonshire Road Unit 100
Windsor, ON N8Y 2L5
800-465-7301 (in Canada only)
e-mail: orders@hkcanada.com

Europe: Human Kinetics
107 Bradford Road, Stanningley
Leeds LS28 6AT, United Kingdom
+44 (0) 113 255 5665
e-mail: hk@hkeurope.com

Australia: Human Kinetics
57A Price Avenue
Lower Mitcham, South Australia 5062
08 8372 0999
e-mail: liaw@hkaustralia.com

New Zealand: Human Kinetics
Division of Sports Distributors NZ Ltd.
P.O. Box 300 226 Albany
North Shore City
Auckland
0064 9 448 1207
e-mail: info@humankinetics.co.nz

This book is dedicated to Dr. Frances Wallach, who represents the wisdom of the past in relation to playground safety,

and

Lyle Frank Olsen, who represents the children of the future.

Contents

Preface

Playgrounds are a common denominator in almost every child's life. Whether at home, schools, community parks, apartment complexes, churches, child care centers, or other public gatherings, children have the opportunity to interact with various types of play equipment. However, too often these interactions lead to a visit to the emergency room. The U.S. Consumer Product Safety Commission (CPSC) estimates that over 200,000 children suffer serious playground-related injuries each year that require emergency medical treatment (1997). The Academy of Orthopedic Surgeons puts that number even higher at 500,000 (1999). In addition, the U.S. Office of Technology estimates that each year over $1.2 billion is spent on playground-related injuries (1995). Tragically, an average of 15 children die each year simply because they want to do what children do best—play.

For many communities, the answer to this problem is to remove play equipment from the children's play environment. This approach to playground safety may save an agency or community from a lawsuit but does little to enhance the development of children. We would never close a public golf course due to fear of being sued when someone is hit by a golf ball; to do so would deny the majority of residents the opportunity for recreation. Using the same reasoning, it would be irrational to pull out play equipment for children. Just as golf courses can be designed to mitigate the risks involved in playing the course, so too can play areas be designed to reduce risks but promote challenge.

Yet, for all the research that has been conducted, play equipment and play areas have not radically changed in over a century. Since the 1980s, national organizations such as the CPSC, the National Program for Playground Safety (NPPS), the International Playground Safety Manufacturers (IPEMA), and others have made us more aware of the need for play areas that are better planned—but in too many cases, we have 21st-century children playing on 20th-century equipment. Part of the problem is that we have not applied what we know from research about playgrounds in our daily practices.

S.A.F.E. Play Areas: Creation, Maintenance, and Renovation is an attempt to bridge this gap between research and practice. The acronym *S.A.F.E.* embodies a model of playground safety that focuses on four components:

S = Supervision

A = Age-appropriate design

F = Fall surfacing

E = Equipment maintenance

By adhering to these components when creating or renovating play areas, we can reduce the chance of death or debilitating injury for children who use them.

Using the Book

The introduction sets the stage by looking at different definitions of the term *public playground* and clarifying the designation used in this book. In addition, we present and debunk 10 common myths about playgrounds to show that it's important to reconsider assumptions and be open to new design ideas and techniques.

In chapter 1, we describe the four components of the S.A.F.E. model (supervision, age-appropriate design, fall surfacing, and equipment maintenance) and explain how they interact to provide a safety net for children at play. We also investigate how play areas can be designed to provide maximum challenge or play value while limiting risk factors. The chapter concludes with a look at the efforts of various organizations to promote playground safety.

In chapters 2 through 9, we examine in detail the four components of the S.A.F.E. model. Each component is explored in two linked chapters; the first presents the research on the topic, and the second shows how to put that knowledge into practice. We feel it's important to discuss *why* the components are essential before we look at the specific methods of *how* to implement them. This combination should provide a comprehensive guide for developing play areas for the 21st century that are both challenging and safe.

Chapters 2 and 3: Supervision

- In chapter 2, we delve into the research that explains why supervision is so crucial to safe play environments.
- Chapter 3 follows up with specific supervision methods and techniques to provide maximum security for children.

Chapters 4 and 5: Age-Appropriate Design

- In chapter 4, we cover the importance of the various developmental stages of children.
- Chapter 5 explores the implications of these stages and explains how to make wise choices in selecting appropriate equipment.

Chapters 6 and 7: Fall Surfacing

- In chapter 6, we examine the need for adequate surfacing under and around play equipment.
- Chapter 7 looks at how to select and maintain this cushion of safety.

Chapters 8 and 9: Equipment Maintenance

- In chapter 8, we discuss the elements of a sound maintenance policy to prevent play areas from falling into disrepair.
- Chapter 9 shows how to put such policies into practice with assessment and inspection procedures.

In chapter 10, we explore the future of play areas and offer practical ways to become involved in the process of creating and renovating S.A.F.E. environments.

Finally, four appendixes provide

- information about safety-related organizations,
- a Student Injury Report that you can use to document injuries,
- six checklists to help you put the S.A.F.E. model into practice, and
- details about the NPPS and its resources (including videos, training kits, and workshops).

A note about the case studies and incidents mentioned in this book: Most chapters feature cautionary tales, which show what can happen when a component of the S.A.F.E. model is not followed, and success stories, which celebrate more positive outcomes. In addition, we describe other incidents throughout the book to illustrate important points. All are real examples that have occurred in the United States since 1995. Many of them come from legal cases in which we have served as expert witnesses, and others reflect incidents we studied during our employment with the NPPS. Due to legal concerns, we don't always provide full citations for the examples, and we've changed the names, locations, and other identifying details.

Using the CD-ROM

The accompanying CD-ROM offers a presentation package of slides (using Microsoft PowerPoint®) to help you understand the key chapter concepts and to make it easy for you to share this information with others. By highlighting the significant points of the four components of the S.A.F.E. model, the slides serve as a handy learning and reference tool for essential details on supervision, age-appropriate design, fall surfacing, and equipment maintenance.

In addition, the CD-ROM includes the reproducible forms from this book so that you can easily print, reproduce, and use these materials. All forms are in portable document format (PDF) and are designed to fit on letter-sized paper.

See page 218 for technical details on using the CD-ROM.

Keeping Children Safe

The information in this book is based on 12 years of research and writing by the authors and more than 70 combined years of professional practice in the area of playground safety. In bringing together theory and practice in an easy-to-read resource, we hope that you will find the concepts useful as you work with children in play environments, whether you're a child care provider, a classroom teacher, a landscape architect, park personnel, a physical education instructor, a youth agency worker, or simply a person concerned about the safety of kids. In addition, we hope that the number of serious injuries suffered in play areas will decrease because people like you care enough to create challenging, innovative environments that enhance the developmental abilities of children while minimizing their risk of injury.

Acknowledgments

This book is the culmination of 12 years of work in the area of playground safety. During that time, there have been many individuals who have provided their expertise and guidance in our work. It is with extreme gratitude that we acknowledge these people for the help that they have given us through the years.

Sincere appreciation goes to our colleagues at the University of Northern Iowa (UNI) who have supported our work. They include people who have provided secretarial services through the years, including Donna Mokricky, Jane Clark, Phyllis Boelts; former NPPS staff, Dr. Mick Mack and Sharon Regenold; our great undergraduate and graduate student workers; and members of the UNI administration, Dr. Christopher Edginton, Dr. Robert Koob, Dr. Pat Geadelmann, Mr. Ed Ebert, Dr. Tom Switzer, and Dr. Jeffrey Cornett.

Special acknowledgment goes to U.S. Senator Tom Harkin, U.S. Senator Charles Grassley, and U.S. Congressman Jim Nussle, who have helped with federal appropriations for the National Program for Playground Safety (NPPS). We also recognize the support and help from our colleagues at the Centers for Disease Control and Prevention (CDC), particularly the injury-prevention unit, including Dr. Jeffrey Sacks, Tim Groza, Dr. Julie Gilchrist, Kim Blindauer, Sandy Coulberson, and Dr. Christine Branche.

Acknowledgment also goes to Ann Brown, former chair of the U.S. Consumer Product Safety Commission (CPSC); John Preston; Debbie Tinsworth; Joyce McDonald; George Shushinsky; Hope Johnson of the CPSC; and Kathie Morgan of the American Society for Testing and Materials (ASTM), who have fought the battles for children's safety at the national level.

A special thanks to Mike, Judy, Andrew, and John Kidd—our playground-safety family in Indiana. We are also indebted to other members of our NPPS family, safety school instructors and board members Larry Bruya and Jean Schappet, and former or current board members Louis Bowers, Annie Clement, Lyn Kalinowski, Sharon Mays, John Preston, Ken Ritchie, Beth Roberts, Safe Kids Worldwide, Jeanne Sanders, Eric Strickland, Fran Wallach, Tim Ahern, Melinda Bossenmeyer, Earl Colella, Tom Norquist, Mark White, Angela Mickalide, Mike Moran, Jane Moorman, Bobby Newell, Debbie Sampson, Judy Finkelstein, Carl Gabbard, Walt Henderson, Al Jackson, Jan Sutkus, Mario Schootman, Deb Beving, Kim Newman, Judy Payne, Robert Shiffer, Sue Wortham, Ken Kutska, Karla Henderson, and Toni Netusil.

Last but not least, we thank the people who have personally supported us through the years and continue to give us help and encouragement in our work: Ben Olsen, Sarah Rich, and Shirley Shogren.

Introduction

Ten Myths of Playgrounds

Playgrounds are something that we all take for granted. Just mention them to a group of adults at a party, and you'll soon hear about daring exploits that may or may not have ended in injury. Talk about monkey bars, double dares, and jumping out of swings fills the room. The problem with this type of talk is that it leads to many misconceptions that are hurting today's children. Unintentional injuries should not be a rite of passage in our children's lives. Before we break down the four components of the S.A.F.E. model in the following chapters, it seems appropriate to not only define what we mean by playgrounds but also examine 10 myths that we hope to debunk.

Definitions and Legality

The U.S. Consumer Product Safety Commission (CPSC) first published guidelines concerning public playgrounds in 1981. In its *Handbook for Public Playground Safety*, the CPSC has defined public playground equipment as "equipment for use in the play areas of parks, schools, child care facilities, institutions, multiple family dwellings, restaurants, resorts and recreational developments." The handbook goes on to state that the guidelines "are not intended for amusement park equipment, equipment normally intended for sports use, soft contained play equipment, or home playground equipment" (Consumer Product Safety Commission [CPSC], 1997, p.1).

The National Program for Playground Safety (NPPS) has defined public playgrounds as "designated areas located at public use sites such as schools, community parks, and child care centers where stationary and manipulative play equipment is located to facilitate a child's physical, emotional, social, and intellectual development" (Thompson and Hudson, 1996, p.1).

These definitions differ slightly, but they both concern playgrounds in the public domain—those at child care centers, schools, and parks. Such play areas are the focus of this book. Of course, some concepts from the public domain also carry over to the private domain, as in the case of play areas offered to members of private schools, churches, and so on. However, from a legal standpoint, the standards and guidelines discussed throughout this book pertain only to play areas in the public domain.

Ten Myths of Playgrounds

Whether in the public or private domain, certain myths have developed over time concerning playgrounds. In chapters 2 through 9, we explain why it's important to be open to new ideas about the design of play spaces for children. Here, we begin this attitude realignment by debunking 10 of the most common, entrenched beliefs in the United States about what makes a good or safe playground.

Myth 1: Playgrounds Supervise Children

Many adults seem to think that they can send children to play areas and the equipment will somehow supervise the kids. But children need guidance to determine whether or not the play area or a specific piece of equipment is safe. In addition, they need to be supervised when they play with others in case they have different opinions regarding play choices. And of course, adults should be present to cheer children's success when they accomplish something particularly challenging, such as traveling all the way across the horizontal bars or pumping the swing a certain number of times. In short, adults must be available to assist and encourage children. We'll study the importance of supervision in chapters 2 and 3.

Myth 2: One Size Fits All

If you consider only the physical appearance of children, it is easy to see that a 2-year-old is not the same size as a 12-year-old. It would stand to reason, then, that children in these age categories would have very different grip strengths and upper-body strengths. The next logical conclusion would be that the equipment and design of the play area should be different to meet the different sizes and developmental needs of children. These developmental needs are physical, but they are also emotional, social, and intellectual. Thus, play environments should be shaped to meet the needs of the specific children who will be using the space. Standards and guidelines since 1981 have stated that equipment should be present and separated for ages 2 to 5 years and 5 to 12 years. In 2005 a new standard was added for ages 6 to 23 months.

However, the majority of playgrounds in the United States are still developed for ages 2 to 12 years. Part of this is due to financial considerations, but a larger reason is that the public doesn't realize that play equipment comes in three sizes, not one. Chapters 4 and 5 will take a closer look at the topic of age-appropriate design.

Myth 3: Children Develop at the Same Rate

We categorize children into groups by age simply because it's easier to deal with large numbers than with individuals. However, children develop according to their own genetic clocks. They're more likely to be similar by age group than by any other criteria, but this is not absolute. All children vary in physical, emotional, social, and intellectual abilities, so equipment and play areas should allow for those variations.

For example, equipment for younger children (ages 2 to 5 years) should be lower to the ground, should not contain stand-alone climbers, and should not have move-able parts. On the other hand, equipment for children over the age of 5 years will be higher and larger and will require more complex movement. Again, we'll consider age-appropriate design in chapters 4 and 5.

Myth 4: Children's Play Matches Manufacturer's Design

Play is the work of children. During play, they feel free to explore, test, and challenge their surroundings and their place in the environment. It is a time when creativity and curiosity are stimulated. Thus, while the manufacturer of equipment might have a specific idea about how certain pieces should be used, children come up with other, inventive ways to create challenges. Who hasn't seen a child climb up a slide chute from the bottom, or swing as high as possible and then leap out into the air? It would be more instructive for manufacturers and other adults to watch children use equipment and then decide how to modify existing designs or create new designs. After

Figure I.1 Play equipment for young children should be low to the ground.

all, it's easier to redesign equipment than to reconfigure children. We'll explore this topic further in chapters 4 and 5.

Myth 5: Children With Disabilities Can't Use Playgrounds

Children with disabilities are usually more similar to children without disabilities than they are different. They have the same needs to develop physically, emotionally, socially, and intellectually to the best of their abilities. It shouldn't take an act of Congress to get a child with disabilities onto the playground, but it has. The Americans with Disabilities Act of 1990 states that children with disabilities must have the opportunity to play with children without disabilities in the same play areas. As we'll see in chapter 5, we can follow specific design guidelines to enable this integration. All children have the right to play.

Myth 6: Higher Equipment Is More Fun

There is no research to support the idea that children have more fun on higher pieces of equipment and less fun on lower pieces. However, as we'll discuss in chapter 6, there *is* a growing body of research that points to a greater risk of serious injury due to falls from higher equipment. Most people would be horrified to see a child jump out of a second-story window, yet adults think nothing of putting equipment on the playground that is equal to or greater than this height. As studies have shown, this problem is compounded by the lack of adequate surfacing under the majority of play equipment found in the United States.

A second consideration about height involves perception. Some children, especially those in preschool, are afraid of heights. If they perceive a danger in changing location from one level to another, they might not make the move. For example, until children are about 7 years old, they are reluctant to leave the security of a deck to reach for a pole to slide down to the ground. Therefore, adults need to approach design from a child's perspective, not from their own idea of what would be fun.

Myth 7: Grass and Dirt Cushion Falls

Falls to inappropriate surfaces are the major contributing factor of injuries to children (Mack, Hudson, and Thompson, 1997). Turf does not provide a constant amount of resiliency; its impact absorption varies according to climatic conditions and the compaction of the dirt underneath the grass. As we'll discuss in chapters 6 and 7, pea gravel, sand, wood products, rubber products, and unitary surfaces are much more likely to cushion falls and prevent injuries. Grass is good for golf courses, but it shouldn't be used under and around playground equipment.

Myth 8: Playgrounds Maintain Themselves

Wood rots, plastic cracks, and steel rusts. As a result, adults must maintain and repair materials to keep them safe and make them last as long as possible. For example, screws, nuts, and bolts can loosen at points where pieces join, and other parts wear out and need to be replaced. Someone must take charge of maintenance and ensure that manufacturer's directions for maintaining the equipment are followed on a regular basis. In chapters 8 and 9, we'll cover equipment maintenance in more depth.

In addition, surface materials need regular maintenance. Rubber mats, tiles, and other poured-in-place materials need to be replaced periodically. This is especially true of loose fill surfaces, which might be at the proper depth at the start of the day but become displaced during the course of play. Adults must replace or redistribute loose fill materials as needed to ensure an adequate supply. Children can do this, too, when they've finished playing—a quick kick of the loose fill surfacing under a swing or slide can help put surfacing materials back in place.

Myth 9: Equipment Lasts Forever

Nothing's built to last forever, but some adults think that playground equipment is the exception. It's true that equipment made of steel can last 50 years, but many playgrounds in the United States have pieces that are already this old or older. Similarly, wooden equipment will rot, and plastic equipment will crack.

We also need to approach this myth from the other direction. Sometimes equipment should be replaced even when it's in good condition so that we can take advantage of new technology and new insights into child development. We must modify older playgrounds to keep up with advancements. We will address this topic in chapters 8 and 9.

© NPPS

Figure I.2   Playground equipment does not last forever.

Myth 10: A New Playground Is a Safe Playground

Old or new, a playground isn't safe unless it's properly supervised, it's designed to match the ages and abilities of the children who play there, it has adequate and appropriate surfacing, and it's maintained regularly. After a new playground has been opened and the celebrations and community pride have faded, the work begins of making sure the environment remains safe. Without constant vigilance, a new playground can quickly become a dangerous place for children.

Reflection and Change

As you read this book and learn more about the four components of the S.A.F.E. model, reflect back on these myths. Are any held by members of your own community? Have children in your town or neighborhood been injured because the community clung to those myths?

We hope that *S.A.F.E. Play Areas: Creation, Maintenance, and Renovation* will help change your understanding of what constitutes appropriate play environments for children. Together, we can debunk these 10 myths and other misconceptions about playgrounds and instead develop play areas that both challenge our children and keep them safe.

The S.A.F.E. Model for Play Areas

If you want to know what a child is, study his play:
If you want to affect what he will be, direct the form of play.

Luther Gulick

© MarinMedia.org

Jacob was a curious 6-year-old who was full of energy and spunk. Not surprisingly, his favorite time at school was recess, when he got to explore the nature area behind the school, play tag with friends on the grassy fields, and climb on the playground equipment. On a chilly November day, Jacob put on his coat headed out to recess. On this day, he decided to spend his time on the playground equipment.

When the bell rang to go back inside, 99 out of 100 children who had been out for recess lined up to go back inside. The two teachers who were in charge of supervising the four classes did a quick head count and the children headed back inside. Jacob's teacher looked up as the children started to file back into the classroom, and she noted that he was missing. She assumed that he had stopped at the bathroom, but when he didn't appear in a few minutes, she went next door to the classroom of one of the teachers who had been out on the playground.

Ten minutes of frantic searching took place before Jacob was found, but it was too late. Jacob had strangled to death when the drawstring of the hood on his coat had become lodged in a gap at the top of a tube slide. The momentum of his body going down the slide forced the coat up under his neck, and in his panic, Jacob failed to unzip his coat. Because the tube slide was old and had no side openings, no one saw Jacob until it was too late.

Each year more than 15 children die in playground-related incidents (Tinsworth and McDonald, 2001). More than half of these deaths are due to strangulation. In addition, every two and a half minutes a child is injured seriously enough on playgrounds to seek emergency medical assistance (National Program for Playground Safety [NPPS], 1996). It shouldn't take the death of a child to realize the importance of playground safety.

In this chapter, we'll discuss the elements of playground safety that should be present in all play environments. Specifically, we'll investigate what we know about playground injuries, how playground injuries occur, the four components of the S.A.F.E. model, and the differences between risks and challenges. We'll also look at the efforts of safety organizations in helping to design safer play areas for children.

Playground Injuries

Why are children injured on playgrounds? This is a complex question that requires a complex answer. A study conducted by the U.S. Consumer Product Safety Commission (CPSC) found the following (Tinsworth and McDonald, 2001):

1. In 1999, an estimated 205,850 injuries related to playground equipment were treated in U.S. hospital emergency rooms. This translates to a rate of about 7.5 injuries per 10,000 children in the United States.
2. Approximately 75.8 percent of the injuries in 1999 occurred on equipment designed for public use, 22.8 percent occurred on equipment designed for home use, and the remaining 1.4 percent occurred on homemade equipment.

3. Fractures were the most commonly reported injury, accounting for 39 percent of all injuries on home and public equipment. Almost 80 percent of fractures involved the wrist, lower arm, and elbow.
4. About 79 percent of injuries that occurred on public playground equipment involved falling, primarily to the surface below the equipment.
5. From January 1990 through August 2000, the CPSC received reports of 147 deaths of children younger than 15 that involved playground equipment. Over half (56 percent) of these deaths involved hanging, primarily from ropes, shoestrings, cords, leashes, clothing, strings, and other items tied to or entangled in the equipment. Other causes of death included equipment tipping over on top of children and falls from equipment or onto equipment pieces. (Note that not all playground-related deaths are reported to the CPSC.)

In addition, the CPSC study conducted by Tinsworth and McDonald revealed the following injury patterns.

1. Children under the age of 4 years old tend to receive more facial and head injuries than older children. This is because they have a higher center of gravity (their heads are proportionately heavier than their torsos) and tend to fall face first. In addition, they usually don't brace the fall with their arms.
2. Children aged 5 years and older usually break arms or legs in falling off equipment. Most arm fractures are long-bone breaks because, unlike younger children, children older than 5 years have learned to use their arms to cushion falls.
3. Females are injured slightly more than males (55 percent versus 45 percent).
4. Children aged 5 to 9 years are injured more frequently (56 percent) than children younger than 4 years old (30 percent) or children aged 10 to 12 years (12 percent).

The data also shows that climbing equipment, swings, and slides are involved in the majority of playground injuries (approximately 88 percent) in both public and home settings. In the public setting, most injuries occur on climbing equipment, followed by injuries on swings and slides. However, in the home setting, swings are the biggest problem, followed by slides and climbers.

While this data describes the type and extent of playground injuries, it does not give much insight into how playground injuries occur. For a better understanding of the mechanisms that trigger playground injuries, we should examine risk factors in the play environment.

Defining Risk and Challenge in the Play Environment

The word *risk* has different connotations. Many times, adults remark that children should be able to take risks while playing—after all, that's supposedly what makes it fun! Some have attacked the work of safety experts during the last 12 years for making play areas too sterile by taking all the risk out of the environment. These critics range from people in the media to landscape architects who bemoan that getting rid of equipment such as monkey bars, 12-foot (3.7-meter) slides, and swing sets over concrete takes the thrill out of the play experience. Many argue that they survived such equipment and conditions, so their kids can do the same.

The response to this criticism is twofold. First, we know more about the play experience and safety than we knew 30 years ago. For instance, more people now wear seat belts in cars and advocate bicycle helmets for children because we know that they save lives. Likewise, as you will see throughout this book, the research is fairly conclusive that unsafe equipment, height, and surfacing lead to the majority of injuries on playgrounds.

Second, it is entirely possible that the critics have not really examined the differences between risk and challenge. In recent years, the most common definition of risk is that it is the "probability of loss or injury" (Edginton, Hudson, and Scholl, 2005). Thus, anyone who says that children should be able to take risks in the play environment is implying that children should be able to get hurt in the play environment.

On the other hand, the word *challenge* is defined as a difficulty in undertaking a task, or something that is arousal seeking (Hudson and Thompson, 1999). Before industrialization, most children were easily able to find exciting and challenging play areas. Trees, natural areas, and open spaces provided a wealth of opportunities to climb, explore, run, and socialize. However, as these natural areas have been taken over by housing and factories, it has become important to try to capture their essence in planned areas. To do so, we need to understand how to challenge children in the play environment.

Play environments that follow the S.A.F.E. model should include areas that challenge children's physical, emotional, social, and intellectual skills and abilities (PESI—see figure 1.1). A 2-year-old does not have the same abilities as a 5-year-old, and a 5-year-old does not have the same abilities as a 10-year-old. As a result, an area designed for a 2-year-old should be different from an area for a 5- or 10-year-old.

We must remember that "playgrounds are places for children to safely explore experiences that are out of the ordinary. . . . The playground is there to allow for further exploration, in the context of play, that which will help children stretch their physical and intellectual abilities, social and emotional skills, and learn some basic principles that can be applied to life in the world" (Owens, 1997, p. 56). However, it is equally important that the challenge does not impose an increased risk of injury.

For instance, trying to walk a straight line is a difficult task for 2-year-olds because their balancing abilities are not fully developed. However, 4-year-olds generally have mastered this ability, so it doesn't pose much of a challenge for them. If you take that same line and convert it to a 2-by-4-inch (5-by-10-centimeter) board resting on the ground, it becomes a more difficult and stimulating task as now the children have

---

Physical challenges: Fine and gross motor skills, movement awareness, range of movement

Emotional challenges: Feelings of success and mastery

Social challenges: Opportunities for interaction and cooperation

Intellectual challenges: Experimentation with cause and effect, use of imagination, and manipulation

Figure 1.1 PESI (physical, emotional, social, and intellectual) challenges.

to move their body through space, and the risk of injury is minimal because falling off the board poses little probability of injury. For children aged 5 years and older, however, this task does not pose a great deal of challenge. What is needed is another modification, such as a curved beam, an inclined beam, or a moving beam. Whatever the modification, though, you would not have to elevate the beam higher than 12 inches (30.4 centimeters), because this would significantly increase the probability of injury but does nothing to increase the challenge.

The Link Between Risk and Challenge

The point is that risk and challenge are linked but are not necessarily the same. As shown in figure 1.2, risk and challenge are separate dimensions. A high score in one dimension does not necessitate a low score in the other; a play area that is high in risk is not necessarily high in challenge, or play value. The play environment thus can be explained as a mix of both dimensions.

A low-risk and low-challenge area is one where all play components are in compliance with national standards and guidelines but where little variation in tasks or activities is offered (see figure 1.3). For example, an area containing two pieces of stand-alone equipment would not offer much of a challenge. At the opposite extreme is a complex play structure that offers several interlocking pieces. However, while providing high play value, the play pieces may be arranged such that head entrapments, blind spots, and other safety risks also raise the probability of injury (figure 1.4).

The ideal play area contains high play value and low risk. Thus, the challenge for playground designers and developers is to create play spaces that enhance play value but decrease risk. In order to do this, they must understand the developmental characteristics of children so that they can create play areas that match children's abilities. They also must understand the risk factors in the play environment. Finally, they need to be aware of how these risk factors lead to injuries.

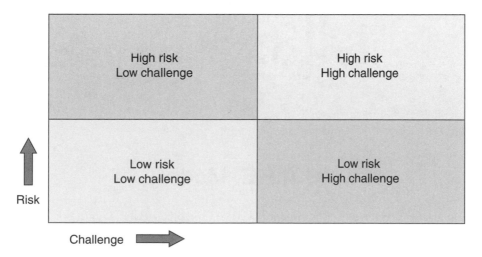

Figure 1.2　The risk–challenge model shows that risk and challenge are not the same.

Figure 1.3 A low-risk, low-challenge play area.

Figure 1.4 A high-risk, high-challenge play area.

S.A.F.E. Model

If you ask 20 people why children get injured on the playground, you may well get 20 different answers. Each person may have a story about how someone they know got injured. While these anecdotes are interesting, they provide no guidelines for those interested in making the play environment safe for all children. What is needed is a framework or conceptual model that helps us visualize the play environment and possible risk factors in that environment.

The model must represent the specific variables in the environment and indicate the possible relationships and interactions of those variables in producing safe play areas. In other words, to build this model, first we must ask the question, "What are the risk factors within the play environment?" Then we must understand how the risk factors might interact with one another to raise the probability of injury.

In 1995, the Centers for Disease Control and Prevention (CDC) funded a project at the University of Northern Iowa, which created the National Program for Playground Safety (NPPS). The mandate of the program was to raise awareness about playground safety and the need for injury prevention. One of the first tasks undertaken by the NPPS was to create a conceptual model for playground safety. The NPPS accomplished this task by calling together leaders in the fields of early childhood, elementary, and physical education; parks and recreation; and safety to answer the following question: What constitutes a safe play area? The conceptual model was published in 1996 in the *National Action Plan for the Prevention of Playground Injuries* (Thompson and Hudson, 1996), which was released during a national news conference in Washington, D.C. The purpose of the model is to provide a blueprint for the creation of safe play areas.

The model consists of four elements that lay the foundation for safe play areas:

S = Supervision

A = Age-appropriate design

F = Fall surfacing

E = Equipment maintenance

Rather than being hierarchical in nature, these four elements interact with one another to create a safe play environment (see figure 1.5). In other words, working on one element alone, such as surfacing, will not prevent all injuries unless supervision, age-appropriate design, and maintenance are also considered.

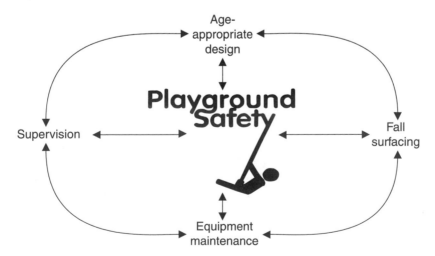

Figure 1.5 The S.A.F.E. model for playgrounds.

Reprinted, by permission, from NPPS, 2005, *National action plan for the prevention of playground injuries* (Cedar Falls, IA: National Program for Playground Safety), 3.

For example, let's say a 3-year-old child fell from a horizontal ladder onto a grass surface under the equipment and broke her arm. The hard ground under the equipment (inappropriate surface) will be cited as the cause of the injury, but was it really the only cause? Was it not also a lack of supervision, since it is questionable whether a 3-year-old should be on a horizontal ladder? Was the 3-year-old developmentally able to grip the bars of the ladders? What about the lack of maintenance, which resulted in inappropriate surfacing under and around the equipment? It is evident that all four elements contributed to the injury.

These four elements will be completely explained in the succeeding chapters. Chapters 2 and 3 examine the importance of supervision; chapters 4 and 5 discuss how an understanding of children's developmental needs translates into designing developmentally appropriate play areas; chapters 6 and 7 investigate the latest information about surfacing materials; and chapters 8 and 9 describe maintenance factors that contribute to safe play areas.

Returning to figure 1.5, we can also see that the four elements depicted in the S.A.F.E. model can also be called risk factors. For instance, if a doctor says that you are at risk for a heart attack, she probably is basing her assessment on the fact that you have certain risk factors such as high blood pressure, too much body fat, high cholesterol, and so on. The more risk factors present, the higher the probability that you will have a heart attack. The same thing can be said about the four elements of the S.A.F.E. model: The absence of proper supervision, developmentally appropriate equipment, adequate surfacing, or proper maintenance raises the probability of injury.

How Playground Injuries Occur

Being aware of risk factors in the environment is only the first step in coming to a complete understanding of how children are injured. These risk factors provide us with a broad understanding of what can contribute to injuries but does not provide us with specific reasons why a child is injured. To further understand playground injuries, we must turn to another model, shown in figure 1.6, for a more detailed explanation of the causes and effects of injuries in the play environment. The components of this injury model are triggers, unsafe actions and conditions, prevention, and consequences.

Triggers

Risk factors are the triggers that initiate the possibility of injury. For every risk factor, there are unsafe conditions, unsafe actions, or a combination of the two that, unless prevented, will lead to injury. For instance, in the area of supervision, an unsafe condition would be the presence of an industrial trash container on or adjacent to a playground where children play on a daily basis. In a real-life legal case, the lid of such a container blew over as children were lining up at the end of recess. The lid landed on top of a child, causing a severe brain injury. Was the cause of the incident improper supervision by the adult who allowed the children near the container, or

How Injuries Occur

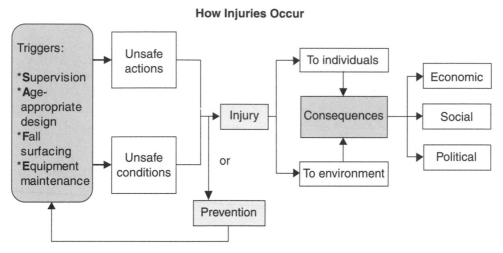

Figure 1.6   The injury prevention model.

was it the existence of an inappropriate condition (trash container on the perimeter of the playground)? In this case, both the supervision and location proved to be the deciding factors in the settlement of the case for the plaintiff.

Unsafe Actions and Conditions

For each of the elements in the model, unsafe actions and conditions might exist. For instance, in the area of supervision, an unsafe behavior would be children playing on equipment without adult supervision. An unsafe condition would be a piece of equipment that lacks viewing holes to show whether a child is present (as in the cautionary tale at the beginning of the chapter).

In the area of age-appropriate design, an unsafe action would be older children inappropriately using equipment meant for younger children. This can lead to two problems. First, the older children might get hurt through unsafe play behavior, and second, younger children may model the inappropriate behavior of older children. An unsafe condition would be a lack of separate play areas for children aged 2 to 5 years and children aged 5 to 12 years.

An unsafe action in the area of surfacing would be when children leave toys and other equipment under and around elevated playground equipment, which generally occurs at child care centers. When children fall off the equipment, they fall on the toy as well as the surface. An unsafe condition would be a lack of sufficient loose fill material to absorb a fall.

Finally, an unsafe action in equipment maintenance would be a lack of inspections of the play area. If no one routinely checks the equipment, an unsafe condition, such as loose bolts on a swing set, may occur. As a result, the swing hanger may come loose when a child is midflight on a swing.

Injury Prevention

If no preventative measures are taken, unsafe conditions and actions can lead to injuries. While we have been discussing injuries to children, injuries can also occur to the environment. For instance, lack of routine surfacing maintenance (i.e., replenishment of loose fill materials under swings) can lead to the development of holes (see figure 1.7). The hole is not only an unsafe condition that can lead to injuries such as a broken leg, but it also deteriorates the overall integrity of the ground, leading to further erosion and drainage problems.

Prevention comes from awareness of the elements of the S.A.F.E. model. That is why understanding the information in this book is so important. It is through awareness, education, and training that action can be taken to avoid the risks associated with each of the S.A.F.E. elements.

Consequences of Injuries

As shown in the injury prevention model (figure 1.6), no injury, whether it is to an individual or the environment, is without consequences. These consequences can be categorized as economic, social, and political.

Economic Consequences

According to the U.S. Office of Technology, the estimated annual cost of playground injuries is $1.2 billion (Office of Technology Assessment, 1995). Included in these costs are medical bills, litigation, and loss of productivity (parents missing work)

Figure 1.7 The surfacing beneath this swing has been poorly maintained.

as a result of an injury to a child. Based on the authors' experiences of 12 years of legal cases, the average cost of litigation for a broken arm runs between $50,000 and $70,000. It is estimated by the NPPS (National Program for Playground Safety, 2006) that lawsuits against public schools over playground injuries have a potential price tag of at least $421,200,000 per year in total costs. By any calculation, that is money that is better spent enhancing children's lives, preventing rather than paying for debilitating or life-threatening injuries.

Social Consequences

When a child is injured, the injury has a ripple effect throughout the entire family. When there are multiple children in the family, the injured child receives more of the parents' attention than the other children. If the injury involves a long rehabilitation period, this attention disrupts the normal ebb and flow of socialization that occurs in any family setting. Because children tend to be the most uninsured individuals in society, an injury may also strain social services (i.e., federal and state assistance programs). When both parents must work, they have to figure out how to take care of a child who is confined to a bed at home. The strain on the family may lead to other social problems such as divorce, alcoholism, and drug usage. In addition, the injured child is unable to play or be with friends during rehabilitation and thus suffers a lack of socialization. Because the early years (3 to 5 years old) are crucial to the healthy development of children, this inability to socialize may have long-lasting effects on the child.

Political Consequences

Finally, injuries can have political consequences that affect what services and programs social institutions can offer. For instance, one response to playground injuries is simply not to provide playground equipment. This was observed in a 2004 national survey conducted by the NPPS in several big cities in the eastern United States, where schools and parks tend to have asphalt game areas rather than any playground equipment (Hudson, Olsen, and Thompson, 2004).

The reasoning goes, if there is no equipment, then an agency can't be held accountable if a child is injured. However, this approach is the antithesis of the holistic philosophy of play as a means by which children are able to develop physically, emotionally, socially, and intellectually. Such an absence of play equipment also devalues children and the importance of play in their lives.

Evolution of Playground Safety

Before we explore the four components of the S.A.F.E. models in the following chapters, we'll examine the history of playgrounds and look at some organizations that help provide safe and appropriate play environments. As we will see, the development of playground safety has been evolutionary in nature, not revolutionary.

Origins of Playgrounds

Organized play environments for children in the United States were first created in the early 19th century in part as a response to the Industrial Revolution. Up until the late 1880s, there were sporadic attempts across the country to develop play environments for children, but there was no great movement. For instance, the first outdoor playground and gymnasium with supervision and instruction were constructed at Round Hill School in Northampton, Massachusetts, in 1825. The first park playground was built in 1876 at Washington Park in Chicago (Mero, 1908). However, the Boston sandgartens, or sand gardens, developed in 1885, are generally cited as the first time a public play area was set aside for young children (see figure 1.8). They are considered to be the beginning of the playground movement.

The first sand garden was, literally, a pile of sand placed in the yard of the Parmenter Street Chapel in the North End of Boston. During the summer of 1885, "children came there, dug in the sand with their little wooden shovels and made countless sand-pies, which were remade the next day with undismayed alacrity" (Miller and Robinson, 1963, p. 90–91). Over the years, the playground area was enlarged, with paid matrons replacing the volunteer staff. By 1893, a general superintendent was hired to oversee 10 summer playgrounds in Boston (Knapp and Hartsoe, 1979).

All that exists of that first play space today is a sign on a wall in the North End to commemorate the site. The importance of sandboxes as a place where children can use their imagination can still be seen today in public play areas and private homes.

From these humble beginnings, setting aside play areas for children became a national movement. In the 1890s, play areas with equipment started to appear. One of the first modern playgrounds was built at Hull House in Chicago in 1894 (Mero, 1908). The term *modern* refers to the fact that there was a designated area with upper-body equipment where children (primarily boys) could run, jump, and test their muscles on steel equipment pieces. No attention was given to safety in these areas. Rather, adults considered children to be safe because they weren't playing in the streets, where their play spaces conflicted with the growing traffic from automobiles and trolleys.

Photo courtesy of NRPA.

Figure 1.8 The Boston sand gardens represented the beginning of the playground movement.

Play Areas in the 20th Century

In the first half of the 20th century, individuals and professional organizations that valued the importance of play in children's lives built the foundation for organized play areas. Early leaders in education and recreation such as John Dewey and Henry Curtis were strong advocates of play for children. Dewey emphasized that playgrounds promoted social, physical, and intellectual development in children (Dewey, 1899), while Curtis sought to incorporate playgrounds into every school in New York City (Dickerson, 1985).

In 1904, the Department of Public Recreation of the American Civic was formed, the first organized national effort promoting the benefits of playgrounds. This was followed in 1906 by the formation of the first professional organization that dealt with playgrounds, the Playground Association of America (PAA), which became the Playground and Recreation Association of America (PRAA) in 1911, and then the National Recreation Association (NRA) in 1929, and finally the National Recreation and Park Association (NRPA) in 1965, as it is known today. The PAA held its first organizational meeting in 1906 at the White House at the invitation of President Theodore Roosevelt. The purpose of the PAA, according to its constitution, was to

> collect and distribute knowledge of and promote interest in playgrounds throughout the country. It shall also seek to further the establishment of playgrounds and athletic fields in all communities, and directed play in connection with the schools. It shall aim . . . to establish . . . a national Playground Museum and Library, which shall have models of every form of playground construction and apparatus, a library of all published books and articles relating to play. . . . (National Recreation Association, 1907, pp. 13-15)

Clearly, play for children was on the national agenda.

In 1907, the first outdoor play festival was held in Chicago on the closing day of the first PAA convention. In 1908, the Department of Physical Education at the University of Missouri spread playgrounds and physical training to all towns and cities in Missouri. In 1911, the PAA changed its name to the Playground and Recreation Association of America (PRAA). By the late 1920s, the PRAA began recommending specific equipment:

- Preschools should have a sandbox, small slide, low climber, and six-chair swings.
- Elementary schools should have a slide 8 feet (2.4 meters) high, a giant stride, a balance beam, a horizontal ladder, six swings on a frame 12 feet (3.7 meters) high.
- Optional equipment included seesaws, traveling rings, and low climbing devices (Butler, 1938).

Fortunately, by this time companies had begun to produce playground equipment so those needs could be met. The two first commercially manufactured pieces were a slide in 1920 by BCI Burke and a whirl (merry-go-round) by Miracle in 1927. These early equipment pieces were rather rudimentary by today's standards. In addition, most pieces would be discarded today as being unsafe both in height and bulk.

Early on, safety was a concern of playground advocates. The PRAA evolved into the National Recreation Association (NRA), which published the first standards for playground apparatus in 1931. They indicated the necessity of caring for the surfacing under the equipment, and they advocated equipment designed particularly for younger children. In addition, they proposed that heights for slides should be no more than 8 feet (2.4 meters) and the maximum height for swings for young children should be no more than 6 feet (1.8 meters) (National Recreation Association [NRA], 1931).

The NRA also indicated that giant strides should be eliminated from playgrounds as a result of injuries from falls from such equipment. (See figure 1.9 for other equipment that has been recalled since 1931.)

The influence of the NRA's stand on these pieces of equipment was probably minimal. At the time, no organizations collected injury data, so it is difficult to ascertain the NRA's sway on the manufacture and use of the equipment. In addition, no organizations trained inspectors to check whether the equipment was present on playgrounds. However, it was at least a start in trying to develop safe play areas for children.

Thus, during the first half of the 20th century manufacturers were busy creating equipment made of steel with little concern for the developmental needs of children. Many pieces of equipment were very high and some had heavy moving parts as well as shearing motions. Although modified to meet today's safety standards,

CPSC Consumer Alerts

Swings not recommended for public use:

- Animal swings
- Multioccupancy swings
- Rope swings
- Swinging dual exercise rings
- Trapeze bars

Consumer alert issued in 1981: Remove all monkey bars (also called jungle gyms).

Consumer alert issued in 1995: Remove all animal swings.

The CPSC advises adults to check hot metal surfaces before allowing children to play on them.

The CPSC recommends that caregivers completely remove the hood and neck strings from all children's outerwear, including jackets and sweatshirts.

Lead paint alert: Public playground equipment might have lead paint that is a potential hazard.

Arsenic safety alert: Chromated copper arsenate (CCA) is acceptable for use as a treatment of playground equipment in wood if the dislodgable arsenic on the surface of the wood is minimized.

Figure 1.9 Playground equipment recalled since 1931.

many of the equipment pieces on today's playgrounds had their origins during this era, including:

- Traditional swings
- Slides
- Merry-go-rounds
- Jungle gyms (monkey bars)
- Giant strides
- Seesaws
- Horizontal ladders

These early pieces were made to last. In many small towns across the United States, they have done just that.

The years from 1950 to 1970 have been categorized as the novelty era of playground design (Frost, 1992). In contrast to the traditional equipment of the previous era, this period saw the creation of sculptures made of cement or wood. Commercial playground companies began producing fantasy play pieces in the shape of rockets, ponies, turtles, and so on. This era also saw the creation of nursery play yards and amusement parks.

By the 1970s, another evolution in design had begun. Decks were introduced with play pieces attached to them, and two other materials were introduced: wood and plastic. More designs were created—many large and permanent—though little attention was paid to the developmental needs of children. During this period, research by the University of Illinois found that children spent more time going between play components than on them (Wade, 1971). As a result, composite structures were created (see figure 1.10).

© NPPS

Figure 1.10 Composite play structures were introduced in the 1970s.

In contrast to large manufactured structures, another kind of playground originated in Europe and made its way to the United States in the early 1970s—adventure playgrounds. At adventure playgrounds, children could build structures and create objects rather than play in preformed environments (Frost, 1992, pp. 137-139). The structures were temporary, sometimes made of cardboard, with no intention of lasting for a long period of time. There were no standards or guidelines for these playgrounds, which were difficult to supervise and looked rather chaotic; many people viewed them as junkyards. As a result, adventure playgrounds had few advocates in the United States, and the movement eventually died out.

The Safety Era

Toward the end of the 20th century, as more and more play areas were being developed, concern about the safety of children's play spaces began to emerge. Injury statistics were collected and the profile was alarming. It seemed that with the proliferation of play areas, children began to suffer major injuries. Taking the lead in this area was the U.S. Consumer Product Safety Commission (CPSC).

Consumer Product Safety Commission

The CPSC was created in 1972 with the passage of the Consumer Product Safety Act. According to this act, the CPSC is charged with the following (Kitzes, 2001):

1. Protecting the public against unreasonable risk of injury and death from consumer products
2. Assisting the public in evaluating the comparative safety of products
3. Developing uniform safety standards for consumer products
4. Promoting research and investigation into the causes of product-related deaths, illnesses, and injuries

To aid the CPSC in its work, the National Electronic Injury Surveillance System (NEISS) was created that same year. The NEISS uses approximately 100 representative hospital emergency rooms to help determine the place and nature of injuries and to project rates. In addition, the CPSC provides safety alerts about dangerous equipment (see figure 1.9 on page 14).

In 1972, a report by the U.S. Bureau of Product Safety indicated that playground equipment ranked eighth among product hazards in the United States. As a result, the CPSC asked the University of Iowa to analyze the accident data collected by the NEISS. In addition, they asked the University of Michigan to prepare anthropomorphic data (data based on children's physical developmental size, such as height, weight, grip, grasp, and so on), and they hired the Franklin Institute, a well-known research lab, to conduct impact attenuation tests on various kinds of surfacing used under playground equipment.

However, the real impetus for developing playground safety guidelines came in 1974, when two women petitioned the CPSC to issue a consumer product safety standard for playground equipment. Elaine Butwinick, an elementary school teacher and member of NRPA's national task force on park and recreation playground equipment safety standards, based her petition on an evaluation of 1,100 equipment accidents at 30 public school and recreation playgrounds. Of those incidents, 85 percent involved falls from climbing equipment and 63 percent involved falls from slides. That same year, Theodora Sweeney, a parent of a child who was severely injured on a playground, a PTA chairperson, and later a playground safety consultant, also petitioned the CPSC to create a playground standard. In her petition, she included information compiled by the Bureau of Product Safety, studies by the University of Iowa, and her own research.

As a result of these studies and petitions, the CPSC commissioned the NRPA to develop a safety standard for playground equipment. In 1976, the NRPA produced the first formal playground guidelines, called the *Proposed Safety Standard for Public Playground Equipment.*

Using these guidelines, in 1981 the CPSC produced its first series of guidelines in two volumes, called *A Handbook for Public Playground Safety, Volume I: General Guidelines for New and Existing Playgrounds* (Consumer Product Safety Commission [CPSC], 1981a) and *Volume II: Technical Guidelines for Equipment and Surfacing* (CPSC, 1981b). The first volume contained guidelines written for the consumer public while the second volume was directed toward the playground industry.

Individuals at the CPSC who were instrumental in promoting playground safety include Ann Brown, former chair of the CPSC; John Preston, an engineer who wrote the guidelines and pursued accurate technical information; and Deborah Tinsworth and Joyce McDonald, epidemiologists for the CPSC who authored a special study about playground safety in 2001.

American Society for Testing and Materials

In the late 1980s, the American Society for Testing and Materials (ASTM), an organization with a long history of setting manufacturing standards, approached the CPSC to develop technical specifications for playgrounds in lieu of volume II of the CPSC guidelines. This was initiated by playground manufacturers who turned to the ASTM to try to standardize the equipment manufacturing process in order to enhance the safety of children. The CPSC agreed because it wanted to remain open in its approach to communicating with the public and because the ASTM was more accustomed to writing technical documents. Since that time, the ASTM has developed various standards in relation to playground surfacing and equipment (see table 1.1).

Like the CPSC, the ASTM has made an enormous commitment to playground safety. There are 534 members involved in six committees that make 13 playground equipment and surfacing standards. The standards committees have included representatives from manufacturers, users, and interested parties. The public-use playground equipment committee is one of the largest in the ASTM, boasting a membership of 170. Since the standards must be revised every five years, the most recent edition reflects updated information.

The ASTM's first playground standard was the home playground standard (F1148), published in 1988. Its purpose was to provide standards for manufacturers of home playground equipment.

It is important to test the depth of surfacing materials under and around playground equipment, so the ASTM standard F1292 was developed. This standard outlines the testing protocol for checking the shock-absorbing properties of surfacing materials in order to try to prevent concussions. The initial standard was developed in 1991 and was revised in 1995, 2001, and 2004. These revisions were made to ensure that

Table 1.1

ASTM Standards

Number	Common name	Purpose
F1148	Home playgrounds	To provide a standard for manufacturers of playground equipment for use at home
F1292	Surfacing	To provide a standard for checking the impact attenuation of surfacing materials
F355	Surfacing	To provide a standard procedure for testing the impact attenuation of surfacing materials
F1487	Public-use playground	To provide a standard for manufacturers of playground equipment to be used at child care centers, schools, and parks, ages 2-5 and 5-12
F1816	Drawstrings on children's clothing	To limit the use of drawstrings to prevent strangulation by upper outerwear
F1918	Soft contained play equipment	To provide a standard for playground equipment used in restaurants
F1951	Testing for ADA compliance for surfacing and equipment	To check whether surfacing allows wheeled components and children with crutches or canes to get to playgrounds
F2049	Fencing	To provide a standard for fencing around playgrounds
F2088	Infant swings	To provide a standard for manufacturers of swings for home use
F2075	Wood fiber	To provide a standard procedure for testing the impact attenuation of wood fibers used as surfacing
F2223	Standard for surfacing	To explain surfacing standards to the public
F2373	Under 2	To provide a standard for manufacturers of equipment for children 6 to 23 months of age
In the process of being written	Aquatic playgrounds	To provide a standard for manufacturers of playground equipment used with water
In the process of being written	Foam playground equipment	To provide a standard for manufacturers of foam playground equipment

the testing measured the impact of the hit on the material, the speed with which the object hit, and the consistency of the mats that were used during testing.

Standard F355-01 describes the procedures to use in impact attenuation testing and increased the accuracy of F1292 in relation to testing the shock-absorbing properties of play surfaces. Because of the technical jargon in F1292, standard F2223-04 was created to provide a readable interpretation of F1292. In addition, in order to provide a specific means of evaluating engineered wood fiber in relation to particle size, consistency, purity, and drainage ability, standard ASTM F2075 was created in 2001.

1885	First public play space created in Boston, Massachusetts
1906	Playground Association of America (PAA) formed
1917	First manufacturer of playground equipment formed (BCI Burke)
1931	First playground safety guidelines formed (NRA)
1974	Elaine Butwinick and Theodora Sweeney petition the CPSC for guidelines
1981	First CPSC handbooks published*
1988	First edition of the ASTM home playground standard F1148 published*
1988	First national survey of elementary school playgrounds published (AALR)
1989	First national survey of community park playgrounds published (AALR)
1990	First national survey of public child care playgrounds published (AALR)
1991	Second edition of the CPSC handbook published
1991	First edition of surfacing standard ASTM F1292 published
1992	National Playground Safety Institute (NPSI) formed
1993	First edition of public-use playground standard ASTM F1487 published*
1994	First edition of surfacing standard ASTM F355 published
1994	Third edition of the CPSC handbook published
1995	National Program for Playground Safety (NPPS) formed at the University of Northern Iowa
1997	Fourth edition of the CPSC handbook published
1997	First edition of drawstring standard ASTM F1816 published
1998	First edition of soft contained standard ASTM F1918 published
1999	First edition of ADA compliance of surfacing standard ASTM F1951 published
1999	International Playground Equipment Manufacturers Association (IPEMA) formed
2000	First edition of fencing standard ASTM F2049 published
2000	International Playground Contractors Association (IPCA) formed
2005	First edition of the CPSC home playground handbook published
2005	First edition of the under two standard, ASTM F2373 published

Figure 1.11   A time line of play area safety. *Other editions may be noted in the text or references.

Since the CPSC's intent is to remain consumer friendly, the ASTM developed a technical standard for the manufacturers to use when developing public-use playground equipment. Standard F1487 was first published in 1993 and has been revised in 1995, 1998, 2001, and 2005.

In response to a mother's plea to Ann Brown, the chair of the CPSC, the CPSC asked the ASTM to look at strings used on young children's clothing. The mother's child had died when strings on the child's jacket became entangled in spaces in playground equipment. The result was ASTM F1816, which prevents strings from being used in children's clothing in sizes 2T to 12, in 1997.

The soft contained play standard, ASTM F1918, was created in 1998 in order to protect children who play on equipment in enclosed play areas found primarily at fast food restaurants and other commercial venues. A specific standard for these play areas was necessary since the materials used to create such areas are much different than those found in public-use playgrounds.

With the passage of the Americans with Disabilities Act (ADA), it was necessary to provide a standard to test whether surfaces of pathways to play equipment are firm, stable, and slip resistant. In 1999, the ASTM published standard F1951. Then anxiety was expressed about fencing for public, commercial, and multifamily residential use in outdoor play areas. In response, ASTM F2049 was created in 2000.

An infant swing standard (ASTM F2088) was produced in 2001 as a result of incidents identified by the CPSC. This brought about a concern for play equipment for children under the age of 2 years. ASTM F2373 was created to meet that need in 2005. Currently, two new standards are being developed, one for aquatic playground equipment and another for soft foam equipment. They will be produced in the future.

As you can see, the ASTM has been very responsive in creating standards to help manufacturers produce equipment and surfacing that are safe for children.

Professional Play Organizations of the 20th Century

In addition to the work of the CPSC and ASTM, other professional organizations began to deal with playground safety. During the late 1980s, the American Association for Leisure and Recreation (AALR), now part of the American Association for Physical Activity and Recreation (AAPAR), conducted three major surveys of public-use playgrounds and published their findings in four books:

- *Where Our Children Play: Elementary School Equipment* (Bruya and Langendorfer, 1988)
- *Play Spaces for Children: A New Beginning* (Bruya, 1998a)
- *Where Our Children Play: Community Park Playground Equipment* (Thompson and Bowers, 1989)
- *Playgrounds for Young Children: National Survey and Perspectives* (Wortham and Frost, 1990)

These studies were the first attempt to take a comprehensive look at the state of public playgrounds at child care centers, schools, and parks. In addition to determining safety factors, the authors in the four books provided insight into developing play areas that match the needs of children.

Two more organizations that deal with playground safety emerged in the 1990s. The first is the National Playground Safety Institute (NPSI), sponsored by the NRPA. Its purpose is to provide safety inspectors who inspect public playgrounds to determine whether or not they are safe. The NPSI held its first training institute in 1993.

The second organization, located at the University of Northern Iowa, is the NPPS, a national nonprofit organization created in 1995 by funds from the CDC. The purpose of the NPPS is to raise awareness of playground safety and injury prevention. Since 1995, the NPPS has been the leading advocate of and information clearinghouse on playground safety and injury prevention in the United States. Through workshops, seminars, research, and writing, the NPPS has provided the public with cutting-edge knowledge to help create safe play environments for children.

Clearly, play area design and safety awareness have come a long way since the Boston sand gardens. Early advocates of play areas faced a lack of information, but today many organizations have contributed to modern play spaces, and the public can turn to them for information and assistance. Appendix A includes a list of these organizations. While their missions may be different, in the end they all have one common goal—to ensure safe play environments for children.

The reason behind their goal is simple: Children deserve to be safe. Since play is children's work, they deserve to have a safe environment in which to play, grow, and develop. That includes safe equipment and surfacing and adults who care enough to provide appropriate supervision of the children and adequate maintenance of the environment.

Summary

It should be apparent that creating safe play spaces is not a haphazard process; rather, it should be based on principles gathered from the growing literature and research on child development, play, and design. It should also be apparent that the development of safe play areas has experienced a positive evolution. It is up to you to keep that positive momentum going by understanding and carrying on the messages about creating, maintaining, and renovating play areas that follow the S.A.F.E. model.

It shouldn't take the death of a child to make people aware of the need for safe play areas. Chapters 2 through 9 examine the theory and practice behind the four components of the S.A.F.E. model. By understanding the theory and putting the techniques to work, we can all help to prevent the conditions and actions that led to Jacob's death (see page 2). If children are our most important resource as a nation, then we owe them safe play areas.

Supervision

The greatest need of American life today is some common meeting ground . . . where business might be forgotten, friendships formed and cooperations established. The playground seems to have great possibilities in this direction.

Henry S. Curtis

© NPPS

Josh was an energetic 6-year-old whose favorite time during school was recess. On a sunny April day, Josh and 149 other children in the kindergarten, prefirst, and first grades raced outside to the afternoon recess. A 20-year veteran teacher followed them outside and then lined up eight students along a wall as a time-out for misbehaving in the classroom. A part-time aide took her four students with special needs to the far end of the play environment.

Josh didn't notice any of this activity because he was intent on playing with his rubber playground ball, which kept getting away from him. Because his eye–hand coordination was not well developed, every time he bent over to retrieve the ball, he ended up kicking it. As is the case with rubber balls on asphalt, the ball then rolled away, with Josh in hot pursuit. The ball rolled past the orange cones that marked the roadway entrance to the school playground. It kept rolling, rolling, and rolling until it rolled out onto the four-lane county highway. It was there that Josh, the ball, and an 18-wheeler going 45 miles (72 kilometers) an hour in a school zone all met in one tragic moment (Bruya et al., 2002, p. ii).

In this chapter, we'll present a framework for supervision practices on the playground and explore the following questions:

1. What is supervision?
2. Why does supervision matter?
3. How does the supervision model encourage safety?
4. Why anticipate dangers and problems?
5. Why does behavior matter?
6. Why does the context or environment matter?
7. Why have a supervision action plan?

This chapter presents research to explain the *why* of playground supervision. Chapter 3 explains *how* by addressing the application of these ideas.

What Is Supervision?

Supervision in outdoor play areas requires adult supervisors who are alert, are aware, know safe playground rules, and intervene when inappropriate behaviors occur. To supervise is to oversee or manage someone or something. Supervision is the active yet unobtrusive monitoring of the play environment.

As implied in the definition, playground supervision is more than just watching children. Supervision is crucial because it helps ensure safety. Supervisors need to focus on inappropriate behaviors and pay attention to hazardous situations. For example, as we all know, playground equipment tends to break or wear. If you are supervising at an elementary school, on a field trip, or at a child care center, you need to move throughout the play environment anticipating potential problems, looking for broken or worn equipment. If you notice broken or damaged equipment, you should not allow children to play on that piece of equipment. Thus, supervision includes overseeing the environment to make sure that dangerous situations are not present.

Playground supervisors are individuals who have been hired or appointed on a paid or volunteer basis and have been trained by the operator to oversee use of the playground, report hazards and injuries, and administer first aid in the case of an emergency (California Playground Regulations, 2000). However, parents, grandparents, aunts, uncles, teachers, teacher associates, principals, and other adults all play a role in playground supervision.

Why Does Supervision Matter?

Supervision matters because we have a responsibility to keep children safe. Children can't grow and learn if they are not in a safe play environment. We have identified four specific benefits of supervising children on the playground:

1. Saving lives
2. Preventing injuries
3. Avoiding litigation
4. Complying with guidelines and standards

Saving Lives

Playgrounds can be dangerous for children, especially those young enough to accept a challenge without knowing the risks involved; thus, supervising children at the playground can save lives. A heartbreaking situation occurred in Arkansas in 2004 when an 8-year-old boy was playing by himself on old and broken equipment in a housing project and he slipped off the top of the equipment. The hood of his sweatshirt caught on a swing hook and he choked to death as he dangled a few inches off the ground. No adults were around to lift him up so he could extricate himself. Situations like this are devastating and often can easily be prevented by adult supervision.

Preventing Injuries

Nearly 30 years ago, it was suggested that adequate supervision on playgrounds could help reduce the number of injuries to children (Bruya and Wood, 1998); in other words, "there is probably a higher correlation in injury reduction between the quality of supervision and the number of children being supervised (teacher-student ratio)" (Brown, 1978, p. 15). Increased knowledge about the cause of playground injuries has increased the concern for providing proper supervision. Parents, teachers, child care providers, and other adults can take an active role in supervision to help keep children safe in the play environment. Elementary schools, child care centers, and other youth-serving organizations need to be aware of proper supervision policies and understand supervision practices in order to help keep children safe.

Avoiding Litigation

The majority of legal cases involving playground incidents cite three major factors (Wallach, 1997b):

1. Supervision
2. Environment (play equipment and playground site)
3. Activities taking place on the playground at the time of the accident that relate to the accident

While public agencies cannot guarantee that a child will not get hurt while on the playground, they can be held liable if they expose children to unreasonable risk (Edginton, Hudson, and Lankford, 2000). An unreasonable risk occurs when the potential for injury can be foreseen and prevented (see figure 2.1). Ignoring foreseeable harm is known as negligence. For instance, an open, jagged sewer pipe in close proximity to a play area is a foreseeable harm.

There may come a time when your agency will be involved in a lawsuit that charges negligence on your playground. The legal definition of negligence is the failure to do something that a reasonable person guided by ordinary considerations would do, or doing something that a reasonable person would not do. If an organization requires children to participate in playground activities, then that organization has a duty to provide a safe environment and adequate supervision for children when they are in the playground environment.

Most states have recesses or outdoor periods at schools and child care centers. These agencies have the same responsibility for children outside of the classroom that they do inside: to provide a safe environment.

In 1989, the National Association of Elementary School Principals (NAESP) conducted a survey on recess practices in the United States. The survey found that 90 percent of the school districts had some form of recess, and 96 percent of the recess periods occurred once or twice per day. Recess lasted 15 to 20 minutes in 75 percent of the cases (Pellegrini, 1995).

© NPPS

Figure 2.1 A hard wooden swing seat poses an unreasonable risk to children.

In 2000, another study was conducted to investigate school health policies and programs in the United States. It was found that only 4 percent of states require recess, and 22 percent recommend recess. Approximately 90 percent of elementary schools offer recess nearly every day for an average of 30.4 minutes a day (Burgeson et al., 2001). In states not requiring recess, it is left to the individual school districts to decide whether or not to provide recess.

One way to help ensure a safe environment is to provide competent and trained supervisors. Not only will the provision of supervisors help in the event of any legal action, it also meets state guidelines and regulations.

Complying With Guidelines and Standards

A number of national and state guidelines and standards deal with the subject of supervision. Agencies must be aware of any state guidelines and standards that they should follow concerning the provision of safe playgrounds. The CPSC, the National Association for the Education of Young Children (NAEYC), some state regulations, and the NPPS all have guidelines for playground supervision. These guidelines are described in the following sections.

Guidelines of the Consumer Product Safety Commission

As mentioned in chapter 1, the CPSC's *Handbook for Public Playground Safety* (1997) includes technical safety guidelines for designing, constructing, operating, and maintaining public playgrounds. In the first edition of the handbook in 1981, it states that because children will use playground equipment in ways for which the equipment is not intended, close supervision of children as they play and intensive classroom and home instruction about safe behavior on playground equipment are an important contribution to playground safety (CPSC, 1981a).

However, it was not until the most recent edition, published in 1997, that a strong emphasis was placed on the importance of supervision. Section 6.4 states the following:

> Playgrounds that are designed, installed, and maintained in accordance with safety guidelines and standards can still present hazards to children in the absence of adequate supervision.
>
> Depending on the location and nature of the playground, the supervisors may be paid professionals (full-time park or school/child care facility staff), paid seasonal workers (college or high school students), volunteers (PTA members), or the parents of the children playing in the playground. The quality of the supervision depends on the quality of the supervisor's knowledge of safe play behavior. Therefore, supervisors should understand the basics of playground safety.
>
> Playground supervisors should be aware that not all playground equipment is appropriate for all children who may use the playground. Supervisors should look for posted signs indicating the appropriate age of the users and direct children to equipment appropriate for their age. Supervisors may also use the information in Section 6.3 of this handbook to determine the suitability of the equipment for the children they are supervising.
>
> CPSC indicates that it is important to recognize that preschool-age children require more attentive supervision on playgrounds than older children. (p. 9)

From *CPSC handbook for playground safety 1997*.

Because the CPSC has recommended safety guidelines for public playgrounds, this means that schools, child care centers, and other youth-serving organizations can be held liable if an unforeseeable risk occurs through the lack of proper supervision. Any agencies that do not meet CPSC standards could be found negligent in the duty to care.

Guidelines of the National Association for the Education of Young Children

The NAEYC has published national guidelines for supervision at licensed child care centers in the United States (NAEYC, 2005). Table 2.1 shows staff-to-child ratios for proper supervision as recommended by the NAEYC.

Table 2.1

Teacher[a]–Child Ratios Within Group Size

AGE GROUP	GROUP SIZE									
	6	8	10	12	14	16	18	20	22	24
Infants										
Birth to 15 months[b]	1:3	1:4								
Toddlers/twos (12-36 months)[b]										
12 to 28 months	1:3	1:4	1:4[c]	1:4						
21 to 36 months		1:4	1:5	1:6						
Preschool[b]										
2.5-year-olds to 3-year-olds (30-48 months)				1:6	1:7	1:8	1:9			
4-year-olds						1:8	1:9	1:10		
5-year-olds						1:8	1:9	1:10		
Kindergarten								1:10	1:11	1:12

Notes: In a mixed-age preschool class of 2.5-year-olds to 5-year-olds, no more than two children between the ages of 30 months and 36 months may be enrolled. The ratios within group size for the predominant age group apply. If infants or toddlers are in a mixed-age group, the ratio for the youngest child applies.

Ratios are to be lowered when one or more children in the group need additional adult assistance to fully participate in the program (a) because of ability, language fluency, developmental age or stage, or other factors or (b) to meet other requirements of NAEYC Accreditation.

A group or classroom refers to the number of children who are assigned for most of the day to a teacher or a team of teaching staff and who occupy an individual classroom or well-defined space that prevents intermingling of children from different groups within a larger room or area.

Group sizes as stated are ceilings, regardless of the number of staff.

Ratios and group sizes are always assessed during on-site visits for NAEYC Accreditation. They are not a required criterion. However, experience suggests that programs that exceed the recommended number of children for each teaching staff member and total group sizes will find it more difficult to meet each standard and achieve NAEYC Accreditation. The more these numbers are exceeded, the more difficult it will be to meet each standard.

[a]Includes teachers, assistant teachers–teacher aides.

[b]These age ranges purposefully overlap. Programs may identify the age group to be used for on-site assessment purposes for groups of children whose ages are included in multiple age groups.

[c]Group sizes of 10 for this age group would require an additional adult.

From NAEYC's 2005 Early Childhood Program Standards and Accreditation Criteria (visit www.naeyc.org for more information on NAEYC Accreditation for early childhood programs). Reprinted with permission from the National Association for the Education of Young Children. All rights reserved.

These guidelines require the proper adult-to-child ratio when children are outside. In addition, the outdoor play area must be arranged so that staff can supervise children by sight and sound (NAEYC, 2005).

State Regulations

Many states have passed regulations concerning supervision practices in schools, child care settings, and other youth-serving organizations. These regulations vary greatly among states. For instance, Louisiana allows grass to be used under and around playground equipment at child care facilities, whereas a neighboring state, Texas, does not. Texas adopted the CPSC guidelines for child care facilities. However, the surrounding states of Oklahoma and Arkansas have not passed any regulations.

How Does the Supervision Model Encourage Safety?

Playgrounds are great places for children and adults. However, playgrounds can also cause adults to worry because it is impossible to predict every move children will make. Adults must be prepared to supervise children at the playground. Every day, principals, child care directors, teachers, teacher associates, and others struggle to manage the day-to-day school and agency operations. Countless hours are spent cleaning house, running errands, organizing classrooms, developing curricula, and grading papers. Unfortunately, in this struggle, many personnel at schools and child care centers do not take an active role in the prevention of playground injuries.

The outdoor environment is largely overlooked. Outdoor time for children is usually treated as time off for staff and parents. When children are outside, the majority of the staff (especially at schools) and some parents stay inside. The results in the school environment are large adult–student ratios, sometimes as high as 1 to 150 (Bauer, 2001), and children are left primarily on their own. It is little wonder that the most dangerous place at school is the playground.

Training staff in playground supervision can help reduce injury statistics. Research has shown that approximately 50 percent of playground injuries can be reduced with just four hours of supervision training (Bruya, 1998b).

It is the responsibility of parents, schools, and child care centers to provide a safe outdoor environment so that children will be in the safest environment possible and will receive the best education. The supervision model is the framework for understanding the ABCs of supervision: anticipation, behavior, and context (see figure 2.2).

Why Anticipate Dangers and Problems?

It was 8:15 in the morning, just before school started in the middle of a town of 1,000 people. A first-year male teacher was assigned early-morning recess duty every Wednesday morning. During his second Wednesday recess duty, a kindergartner ran up to him and said, "Mr. Teacher, what is this?" The teacher was shocked and a little

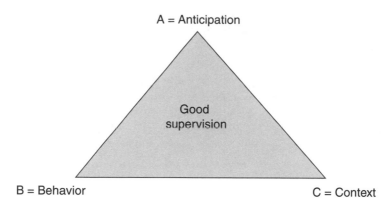

Figure 2.2 The supervision model focuses on the ABCs of supervision.

Reprinted, by permission, from L. Bruya et al., 2002, *S.A.F.E. playground supervision manual* (Cedar Falls, IA: National Program for Playground Safety).

embarrassed as he looked at the used syringe in the girl's hand. He knew what it was but was concerned about how to explain it to a 5-year-old. He simply told her that it was a needle and asked where she found it. The girl said she found it underneath the slide. The teacher thanked her and directed her back to her friends. After recess, he turned the syringe into the principal's office, and the school reported it to the police.

Unfortunately, there have been numerous stories of supervisors finding inappropriate materials around children's play areas. It is not uncommon for adults and teenagers to leave trash in these areas, so supervisors should look for miscellaneous debris and vandalism before the children arrive. They need to make certain that the play area is free from hazardous conditions. In addition, teachers who are assigned to supervise the playground are not expected to be in all places at all times, but they must circulate among the students in order to determine whether or not any hazardous activities are being pursued.

Supervisors can anticipate the potential dangers of a play area by considering the location of the environment, making sure children use only age-appropriate equipment, and learning to identify different types of hazards.

Location of the Play Environment

First, supervisors must pay attention to the general playground environment. The tragic cautionary tale of Josh on page 24 proves that we need to pay attention to the location of play areas (see figure 2.3). Roads and parking lots are all too common near children's play areas. If a road runs next to a play area, an adult needs to be responsible for supervising the area in such a manner that will prevent children from running into the street.

In Josh's story, unsafe conditions included the location of the supervisors and the asphalt area that led to the four-lane highway. A total of 150 children were playing under the supervision of only two adults. The adult–child ratio was inappropriate. In addition, the supervisors weren't fulfilling their duties to the group; one was watching eight children at the school wall, while the other was focused on four children with special needs. Therefore, 138 children were not being supervised. In addition,

Figure 2.3   The location of a play environment can impact its overall safety.

the school should have installed a fence to protect the children from the four-lane highway.

Equipment location is imperative in preventing conflicts and accidents. For example, swings and other moving equipment should be located away from other structures. Swings are second only to climbers in the percent of injuries children receive on playground equipment, and swings are associated with 19 percent of injuries on public playgrounds. In addition, swings are associated with over 66 percent of all injuries related to home playground equipment (Tinsworth and McDonald, 2001). Many of these injuries may be prevented if the swing structure is located away from other activities so that children do not run into the children who are swinging.

Age-Appropriate Settings

Second, supervisors must pay attention to the ages and grade levels of children who use the different play environments. The CPSC guidelines indicate that playground equipment should be separated for children aged 2 to 5 years and for children aged 5 to 12 years. Parents should be aware when they take their children to the community playground that their children should play on equipment that is appropriate. Child care and school agencies should consider going one step further in the separation of play environments because of the differences in developmental abilities among 2-, 5-, and 12-year-olds. Outdoor play environments at child care centers may be divided into equipment that is appropriate for children aged 6 to 23 months, 2 to 3 years, and 4 to 5 years. Schools may want to separate their play areas for children in preschool, kindergarten through second grade, third and fourth grades, and fifth and sixth grades (NPPS, 2004a).

The one-size-fits-all approach to playground equipment can contribute to serious injuries on the playground. For example, an 8-foot (2.4-meter) overhead ladder may be appropriate for a fourth-grader, but it may be too challenging for a kindergartener. If an agency serves preschoolers as well as older elementary school children, then it should make sure that the play area accommodates all the different ability levels in separate areas.

A father of a kindergarten student in Louisiana brought action against a school board after his 5-1/2-year-old son broke his arm while climbing on the playground climbing tower. The elementary school had two separate playgrounds, designated as the upper and the lower playgrounds. The kindergarten, first, second, and third grades were assigned to the lower playgrounds, while the fourth and fifth grades were assigned to the upper playground. With permission from the principal, the teacher took her kindergarten class to the upper playground because the lower playground was wet. Even though the court did not find the teacher negligent in her supervision of the children, the principal breached his duty to inform the teacher of the rules and restrictions on the playground equipment. That breach of duty was a substantial factor in causing the child's injury (Hunter v. Caddo Parish School Board, 1993).

Hazards

Third, supervisors must be able to identify different types of equipment and surfacing hazards. The administrators of schools, child care centers, and other youth-serving organizations should first create maintenance policies for playground equipment and surfacing. Then administrators must train the supervisors on different types of hazards and common problems. This will enable agencies to provide proof that maintenance procedures did occur in the event that legal action is taken against them.

Parents also can take an active role in eliminating hazards in play areas. Use gloves or bags to pick up trash. If you notice unsafe conditions, report them immediately to the owner or operator of the playground.

In a 2002 South Carolina case, a child fell from playground equipment and was injured. A negligence action was brought against the school district because there was evidence that the industry standards for playground equipment were not met. The school had purchased new playground equipment; however, they did not modify or maintain the existing equipment. The child fell from the older equipment and testimony revealed that the school knew about the standards because they had just purchased new equipment (Elledge v. Richland/Lexington School Dist. Five, 2002).

Why Does Behavior Matter?

Children's behavior in the outdoor play environment has been a well-known and challenging topic in the educational setting during the last decade. Many school-wide reforms have taken an active approach to improving the safety of children in the school environment. School districts have implemented programs on issues from conflict management to preventing bullying behaviors in order to increase safety and to help foster effective life skills and build self-esteem.

In this section, we will refer to the behaviors of both children and supervisors on the playground. First, we'll examine why it is important for supervisors to pay attention to children's behaviors. Second, we'll explain why it is important for supervisors to demonstrate safe behaviors.

Children's Play Behaviors

The playground is one of the main environments in which children congregate together and their social behavior is largely unconstrained by adult influences (Boulton, 1999). An overwhelming amount of research supports and demonstrates the relationship between play and learning (Clements and Fiorentino, 2004).

However, outdoor play areas at any elementary school, child care center, or community park are places where conflicts break out, children are injured, and bullying begins. Children demonstrating unsafe play behaviors are either not playing appropriately with others (calling names, fighting, or disrupting other children) or are misusing the playground equipment (Bruya et al., 2002). It is important for supervisors to recognize unsafe play behaviors and unsafe equipment use.

Unsafe Play Behaviors

An unsafe play behavior occurs when children, whether playing by themselves or with others, initiate something harmful to themselves or others. For example, it was reported by a school in Iowa that during noon recess two sixth-grade boys were caught urinating on all the balls that were for use during recess. At child care centers, young children are often caught throwing sand. In a neighborhood park, children might play with matches. These are all unsafe play behaviors. In one elementary school study, it was reported that without adequate intervention, unsafe play behaviors led to 46 percent of injuries on the playground. After training adults in playground supervision, those unsafe play behaviors decreased to 16 percent (Bruya, 1998b).

Every day in our schools and communities, children bully each other. Bullying occurs when one or more persons repeatedly say or do hurtful things to others who have problems defending themselves (U.S. Department of Health and Human Services [DHHS], 2003). Verbal taunts and name-calling are the most common forms of bullying for schoolchildren (Olweus, 1995), but bullying can also involve hitting, kicking, or threatening. Peer harassment and victimization occur frequently in elementary schools across the nation; 20 to 30 percent of children in elementary school are bullies, victims, or both (Leff et al., 1999; Nansel et al., 2001). Although many bullying behaviors occur in the outdoor environment, supervisors should not accept them as appropriate or dismiss them as normal childhood behaviors.

Unsafe Equipment Use

Supervisors need to recognize the difference between children accomplishing a difficult task that is within their capabilities and tasks that children do not have the strength, agility, balance, or other developmental characteristics to accomplish. For example, 2-year-olds do not have the developmental characteristics to successfully use a climber with moveable components (e.g., tire climber, chain climber): "Very young children do not have the necessary body strength or coordination necessary to handle a horizontal ladder 84 inches [213.4 centimeters] high and 10 feet [3 meters] long. However, at the age of five they don't develop these skills overnight; they must be developed gradually" (Hendy, 1997, p. 104).

You also want to make sure that older children do not use equipment that is intended for younger children (see figure 2.4). For example, you would not want to put an 8-year-old on a spring rocker. Equipment that is designed for younger children is not challenging for older children. We have often seen older children misusing equipment that was designed for younger children. Younger children then try to copy the older children's behavior, which can lead to injuries.

Child care centers and schools should separate playground sites according to the developmental levels of all the children who use the playground. At community playgrounds, parents should guide their children to age-appropriate equipment. (See chapters 4 and 5 for more details about age-appropriate play environments.)

A recent study found that 70 percent of the schools in the state of Iowa had only one playground. It seems likely that all children at these schools use the same equipment regardless of age and developmental ability. Of the schools that had more than one playground, 67 percent separated the playground sites by different grade levels.

© NPPS

Figure 2.4 Children's abilities should match equipment use.

However, there was no common pattern for separating the play equipment (Bauer, 2001). This suggests that there is very little or no systematic planning within school districts, child care centers, and park departments. The unfortunate reality is that there are only standards for manufacturers to develop playground equipment for children aged 6 to 23 months, 2 to 5 years, and 5 to 12 years (ASTM, 2005). Child care centers and schools need to put some thought into designing outdoor play areas that meet the developmental levels of all children.

Supervisors' Behaviors

The actions and behaviors of supervisors can play a role in children's safety. This behavior includes the supervision practices of movement, observation, and interaction that should take place in order to produce a safe play environment. In Bruckman v. Los Angeles Unified Schools, the supervisors were found to be passive and to be doing their job poorly, which was found to be negligence as a lack of supervision (Bruya and Wood, 1998). Supervisors must understand why it is important to conduct presupervision activities and actively monitor children on the playground.

Presupervision

Most playground injuries occur within the first five minutes of a play period (Bruya, 1998b). Therefore, at least one supervisor should arrive at the play area before the children do. The supervisor who is assigned to arrive before the children can quickly assess the play area to look for broken equipment, trash, and vandalism.

Another way to help reduce injuries and inappropriate play behaviors is to discuss playground rules and expectations with children. Children should be aware of the rules before going to the playground. Owners and operators of playgrounds can help reinforce rules by posting signs at the entrance of the area.

In a 1985 case, a 9-year-old girl broke her legs while trying to get off a moving merry-go-round on her school playground. The child was found to be at fault because she was riding on the inside of the merry-go-round even after she had been instructed on the proper way to use the equipment and after she had been admonished by her teacher for riding the merry-go-round improperly (Rollins v. Concorida Parish School Board, 1985). There must be proof of negligence in failing to provide required supervision and proof of causal connection between the lack of supervision and the cause of accident, and the risk of injury must be reasonably foreseeable.

Active Monitoring

Supervisors must be active when out on the playground. Active monitoring can ensure safety and help prevent injuries. In one Florida school district, playground supervisors must sign an affirmation of their responsibilities as supervisors. It reads, "I, an employee of the Florida School District, have been provided playground guidelines with regards to direct supervision. I understand **direct supervision** is defined as watching and directing children's activities within the designated outdoor play area and responding to each child's needs. I also understand I must situate myself in the outdoor play area so that **all** children can be **observed** and direct supervision provided."

Adapted from a Florida School District.

Studies have shown that active supervision can reduce inappropriate play behaviors (Bruya, 1998b; Colvin et al., 1997; Roderick, Pitchford, and Miller, 1997). Actively supervising children's playground behavior and encouraging children to play cooperatively is related to lower levels of aggressive behaviors (Colvin et al., 1997; Roderick, Pitchford, and Miller, 1997). For example, in one study, playground supervisors were trained to more actively monitor children's playground behaviors by encouraging playground assistants to reinforce children who exhibited positive behaviors with a raffle ticket. This relatively simple strategy resulted in a 75 percent reduction in kicking and a 47 percent reduction in hitting on the playground (Roderick, Pitchford, and Miller, 1997). The presence of an adult who is actively monitoring playground behavior and encouraging cooperative play is a potentially effective method of shaping children's behavior on the playground.

Why Does Context Matter?

The context of the outdoor play environment in the community, school, and child care center plays a vital role in keeping the play environment safe. It presents the details of the who, what, when, and where that are involved in providing a safe environment.

Supervision Personnel

When schools and child care centers offer opportunities for children to play on equipment, they have a duty to provide a safe environment. It is the duty of the school and teachers in charge of playground supervision to make certain that the play areas are safe and free from hazardous conditions. A study done in 2001 found that at Iowa elementary schools, 98 percent of the supervisors were teachers, followed by 89 percent teacher associates (more than one category of supervisors was present) (Bauer, 2001). Teachers or teacher associates who are assigned to supervise the playground are not expected to be in all places at all times. However, they must be reasonable and prudent and should circulate among the students in order to determine whether or not any hazardous activities are being pursued (van der Smissen, 1990). In community and neighborhood parks, there is no duty to provide personnel to supervise the play area. However, it is important to post signs indicating that adult supervision is necessary.

Ratio of Supervisors to Children

No specific child-to-adult ratio is mandated in the elementary school environment; however, elementary schools should consistently have the same ratio (Bruya and Wood, 1998). Courts have found that some ratios of 1 to 90 and 1 to 40 are legally acceptable (Bruya and Bruya, 2000). However, it is not uncommon to find ratios of 1 to 150 on some playgrounds (Bauer, 2001; van der Smissen, 1990). While it may not be practical for supervisors to maintain the one-to-one watchfulness that many parents would, a certain minimum ratio should be maintained. A ratio of not greater than 1 to 30 is suggested as appropriate for supervision of elementary school children on the playground (NPPS, 2004a). As mentioned previously, there are national and state regulations for supervisor-to-child ratios in the child care environment. It is important for agencies to follow state regulations.

Emergency Kit

A portable kit of various safety supplies is a valuable resource for supervisors on duty (figure 2.5). In the state of Iowa, 20 percent of all schools require that supervisors have first aid training, and 71 percent of supervisors carry an emergency kit while supervising on the playground (Bauer, 2001). First aid supplies (70 percent), a whistle (43 percent), behavioral cards (28 percent), and communication devices (23 percent) were the most common supplies found in safety kits (Bauer, 2001).

Supervision Training

Supervision training is becoming a necessary function for keeping the outdoor play environment safe. Trained supervisors become more confident in their responsibility and understand the importance of supervision. Supervisors must have an understanding of the playground environment, students' behaviors, and styles of play in order to meet the unique needs of each student and to provide a safe outdoor environment. Good supervision training also breaks down communication barriers among supervisors.

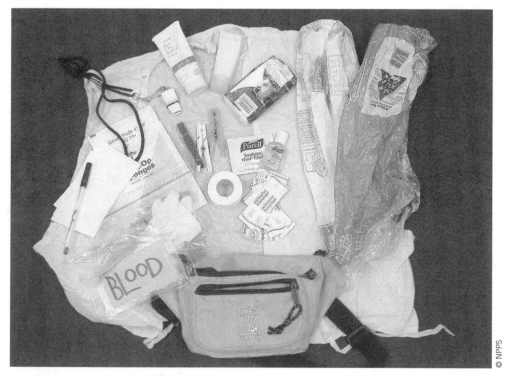

© NPPS

Figure 2.5 An emergency kit typically contains numerous safety supplies.

Because each play environment is different, it is imperative for each school to develop a supervision plan that fits their environment. A 2001 study reported that only 19 percent of elementary schools in Iowa required supervisors to have playground safety training (Bauer, 2001). The study reported that the majority of school districts seem to think that teachers trained to manage indoor classrooms will know how to supervise children on the playground. Unfortunately, this assumption can lead to serious liability for schools. In 1998, for example, a $100,000 lawsuit was filed in the Midwest after a child was injured on the playground at school, and the district lost the lawsuit. Lack of proper supervision was cited as a major factor, largely because the school's principal said the teachers were not trained to watch over students on the playground (Olsen, Hudson, and Thompson, 2002).

Training supervisors regarding playground responsibilities, rules, behaviors, injury reports, and equipment hazards will give them confidence to provide quality supervision. As mentioned, a study conducted in the state of Washington showed that with four hours of supervision training, there was a reduction in the number of playground injuries and types of playground injures. The training program focused on playground inspections, appropriate ratios, and being aware of the environment during supervision (Bruya, 1998b).

Training also helps build trust among supervisors. It is the supervisors' goal to provide a safe environment for children. Therefore, supervisors have to trust one another that they are all fulfilling their responsibility. This trust can be developed by using a variety of communication techniques.

Communication barriers that cause misunderstanding can be brought out during training. Many teachers have reported more frustration during recess than during classroom time because their school does not have a systematic plan for communication on the playground. Administrators would be surprised at how many teachers want to have a better understanding of supervisors' responsibilities, more communication, and support for the supervisors in the outdoor environment.

Why Have a Supervision Action Plan?

To decrease potential accidents, schools, child care centers, and youth-serving organizations need to do more than just comply with the CPSC and ASTM guidelines. It is essential that agencies implement the necessary preventative measures regarding supervision. A supervision plan should concentrate on the specific details of supervision in order to provide a safe playground experience. The duty to supervise has evolved because of three reasons (van der Smissen, 1990):

1. A duty inherent in the situation
2. A voluntary assumption of duty
3. A duty mandated by law

Supervisors are to provide a reasonable degree and quality of supervision in order to cover all of their responsibilities. The condition of the environment or activity determines whether general or specific supervision is necessary. General supervision is required in situations where students are involved in activities that are not considered dangerous, such as recess. Specific supervision is required when activities are usually dangerous or when students are not familiar with an activity being explained by the teacher (Shoop and Dunklee, 1992).

For example, imagine that you're in charge of 50 children during a summer day camp. Every Friday, you take them to the local park to have lunch and play on the playground equipment. During this time, you and your staff spread out to provide general supervision. In addition, a goal of your summer program is to increase the fitness of the children, which includes moving across a horizontal ladder forward, backward, and then alternating bars to improve their upper-body strength. When you are running fitness tests, you would want to give specific supervision, because there may be many children who have never gone backward or alternated bars across a horizontal ladder. You should be close by to explain the activity to them. More examples of these techniques will be given in chapter 4.

When children are hurt on the playground, the ramifications extend beyond the injured child. Playground accidents take time, energy, money, and follow-up work on the part of the playground supervisors, nurses, secretaries, and administrators. It was found that one elementary school with 350 students averaged 540 minor playground injuries each school year (Bruya, 1998b). Dealing with those injuries required about 135 hours of staff time. If the number of injuries can be reduced, the savings are substantial.

Combining a safety training program for school children with a program for supervisors can reduce injury rates for a school of this size to as low as 44 per year, requiring about 11 hours of staff time (Bruya, 1998b). At an estimate of $25 per hour, the reduced injury rate represents a savings of $3,100 over a single school year. If more severe injuries are prevented, the savings increase exponentially (Olsen, Hudson, and Thompson, 2002).

 ## Success Story

One playground manufacturer is going beyond the nuts and bolts to provide added safety value to their product. The BCI Burke Company recognizes the importance of teaching teachers, parents, child care directors, and other youth-serving teachers about the importance of supervision, and in a commitment to ensure safer play for all children, they are providing NPPS supervision safety kits free to every customer who orders one of their play systems. "It is our commitment to creating the safest play experiences possible which motivates us to contribute a free NPPS Supervision Safety Kit with every order of a Burke modular play structure," says Tim Ahern, BCI Burke president and chief executive officer. "In addition to providing high quality and safe play equipment, we also want to provide our customers with the best tools for a safe play environment" (T. Ahern, BCI Burke president, personal communication, March, 2003).

Summary

Supervision plays a key role in the prevention of playground injuries. One of the most valuable lessons learned from this chapter is to make sure an adult is always present and actively supervising when children are playing in the outdoors. We have a responsibility to provide adequate supervision and keep the area free from hazards. Child care centers, elementary schools, youth-serving organizations, community parks and neighborhoods, and parents can be instrumental in preventing playground injuries by understanding the importance of supervision. As we continue to encourage children to be healthy and active in the outdoors, we must play a role in keeping those play areas safe. Chapter 3 gives practical ideas on how to develop, plan, and implement supervision.

A New Way of Looking at Things

If pleasures are greatest in anticipation,
just remember that this is also true of trouble.

Elbert Hubbard

© NPPS

Cautionary Tale

Eight-year-old LaToya was out on the playground minding her own business when she heard a scream. She looked over to see Kevin, the playground bully, socking her best friend, Marissa, in the stomach. Upset over this unprovoked attack, she shouted at Kevin to stop. He looked right at LaToya and said, "You're next!" Kevin came over to her and grabbed her arm. As LaToya struggled to get away, he bent her arm behind her to the point that she screamed as something snapped.

Kevin let go, and LaToya sought out the two playground supervisors who were standing together by the building talking to each other. Neither one paid much attention as LaToya approached them, rubbing her hurt arm. She tried to explain what had occurred, but one simply remarked, "Don't be a tattletale," while the other said, "Get in line; it's time to go in." Reluctantly, LaToya got in line to go back into the classroom. Once she was back inside, she told her teacher that she hurt her arm on the playground, leaving out the cause of the injury since she didn't want to be a tattletale. The teacher responded by saying, "After the rest of the students start their work, I'll try to get you some ice." The ice never appeared.

At 3:30 in the afternoon, two hours after the playground incident, LaToya's mom picked her up at school and saw tears in her eyes. The girl took off her sweater to show her elbow, which had swollen to the size of a small grapefruit. Her mom immediately took her to the emergency room, where X rays confirmed a broken growth plate in the elbow. The orthopedic surgeon who set the arm gave LaToya only a 50 percent chance that she would ever regain full use of the limb.

LaToya's story should make it clear that supervision is more than just being present on the playground. Playground supervision is an active yet unobtrusive monitoring of the play environment (Bruya et al., 2002). It includes paying attention to hazardous situations in the environment and responding to emergencies on the playground (NPPS, 2004a).

To become a good supervisor, you must understand the ABCs of supervision (Bruya et al., 2002).

- *A* stands for *anticipation* of dangers and problems so you can intervene before an injury occurs.
- *B* stands for knowing which *behaviors* are appropriate for children and supervisors.
- *C* stands for assessing the *context* or environment in which supervision takes place.

In this chapter, we'll address these ABCs in depth. Chapter 2 explained why supervision is important, and now we'll explore practical guidelines and appropriate behaviors for active supervision in the face of common dangers and problems. In addition, we'll discuss how to design, implement, and evaluate a curriculum for training playground supervisors.

Supervision Model

The supervision model is the framework for training staff on the ABCs of supervision: anticipation, behavior, and context. All supervisors need to understand what it means to supervise children in the outdoor play environment. Thus, all supervisors must be trained how and when to take disciplinary actions, emergency measures, and precautions.

Anticipation

Anticipating dangers and problems associated with the play area will help ensure that children are safe. Supervisors should be acquainted with the layout of the playground and should be able to identify different types of hazards.

Playground Layout

The layout of the playground can directly affect the supervisors' responsibilities. For example, soccer goals are found in many play environments. When the goals are located in the middle of the playground, children often like to climb and hang on them, and soccer goals have been known to tip over and injure a child. But the same soccer goal placed in the corner of the play area away from the traffic pattern of children would not pose the same problem. Creating a hazard in the playground design and then expecting the supervisor to overcome the hazard by talking to young students isn't very practical, but if attention isn't paid to the layout, this becomes the standard procedure rather than the exception.

Supervisors must examine four location elements (see figure 3.1):

1. General playground environment
2. Age-appropriate settings
3. Open sight lines
4. Zones for play

General Playground Environment

The first element that supervisors need to pay attention to is the general playground environment. For example, if electrical units (e.g., air conditioners, heaters, electrical outlets) are found in the play environment, then they must be protected by a barrier. It is common to find electrical units around child care centers and schools, and these must be blocked off with a fence, locked box, or some other barrier.

Supervisors at schools, child care centers, communities, and park departments need to pay close attention to the surroundings of a play environment, including parking lots, sidewalks, open field areas, streams, and utility lines. These items can be attractive nuisances and present hazardous situations.

Anticipating the potential dangers of the play environment can save lives. Fencing is one solution to keep children away from streets, parking lots, utility lines, and so

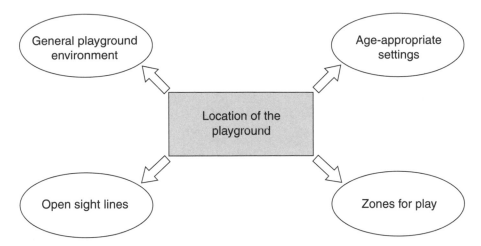

Figure 3.1 Supervisors must pay attention to four location elements.

on. Fencing around the playground helps keep children in the play area and prevents unwanted animals and individuals from entering the environment. It also helps the supervisors by defining the boundaries of the play area. Fences are versatile and serve numerous functions; they help ensure the safety of children, separate play areas, stop intrusions, control security of the play environment, and enhance the protection of the user (Mittelstaedt, 2004, p. 73). Fencing is necessary anywhere kids play with balls, as it will keep children from chasing balls into the street.

Age-Appropriate Design

The second element that supervisors need to take notice of is the ages of children who use the different play environments. The playground should be suitable for the children using the equipment and should meet their different developmental needs. Agencies need to select age-appropriate equipment and develop separate play areas for different age groups.

Open Sight Lines

The third element that supervisors should pay attention to is sight lines. Open sight lines refer to several angles of visual access for the supervisors, who need to be able to see places where children play from several different viewpoints (figure 3.2).

Supervisors must have clear sight lines through equipment and natural vegetation (see figure 3.3a). Even closed structures and playhouses used for quiet play should provide unobstructed visibility. If supervisors are unable to see the entire play area, they may not see a potential injury developing. Enclosed tubes, concrete barriers, and other blind spots require supervisors to move around and through the area continually to see the children on all sides (see figure 3.3b).

It is also important for supervisors to be able to get to the interior as well as the exterior of all structures in order to aid an injured child. Geodesic domes are one example of equipment that is difficult to get into in order to attend to an injured child. If a child falls inside a geodesic dome, it may be difficult for an adult to get inside to rescue the child (see figure 3.4).

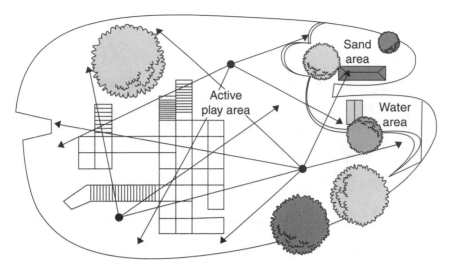

Figure 3.2 Supervisors must stand in locations that offer clear sight lines.

Play Zones

The fourth element that supervisors need to pay attention to is zones for play. Play zones are defined by the type of behavior children might engage in given the space and equipment that is present. Zones should be divided into different activity types to prevent children from running into one another. They could include an area for playground equipment; an area for gross motor activities such as soccer, basketball, kickball, and so on; a blacktop area for activities such as four square and jump rope; a garden or nature area; and an area for socialization.

Another common user conflict in the play environment involves moving equipment such as swings, merry-go-rounds, and seesaws. These pieces of equipment should be located away from other play structures. Swings are second to climbers in the number of injuries children receive on playground equipment.

Surfacing and Equipment Hazards

Supervisors should be able to identify different types of surfacing and playground equipment hazards because such conditions cause many playground injuries (Wallach, 1997b). A hazard involves exposure to danger. Limiting hazards as much as possible will significantly reduce the occurrence of playground injuries (Vogelsong and Christiansen, 1996).

Typically, the maintenance personnel of the school, child care center, or park department are responsible for conducting routine equipment and surfacing inspection. However, all supervisors can assist with the general upkeep of the playground environment if they are trained to watch for common hazards. The supervisors' assistance will help keep the equipment in good repair and the surface at the appropriate depth.

Supervisors should know that three types of hazards are present in any play environment: material and trash hazards, surfacing hazards, and equipment hazards.

a

b

Figure 3.3 *(a)* In play environments with no blind spots, supervisors can see children throughout the area. *(b)* Blind spots, such as an enclosed tube connecting two platforms, make it more difficult to supervise children.

Figure 3.4 A geodesic dome can hinder efforts to help an injured child who falls inside.

Material and Trash Hazards

Material and trash hazards can typically be found after weekends and in the early mornings. Supervisors should look for miscellaneous debris, broken glass, alcohol containers, sharp objects, and pop cans. Animal excrement is also a problem on some playgrounds and should be removed before children play in the area. At one school, a student teacher had early Monday morning recess duty. He did not see the dog excrement at the end of the slide and a first-grader rushed down the slide. The student teacher not only had to clean up the dog mess, he had to help clean up the first-grader.

Surfacing Hazards

Supervisors also need to check surfacing materials for hazards. Surfacing materials should be at the appropriate depth so that they cushion a child's fall. Supervisors thus should examine loose fill material so that it is at the right depth, paying particular attention to popular equipment, such as swings and slides, where loose fill materials may get kicked out or compacted. In addition, supervisors should check for debris on sidewalks, paved surfaces, steps, and platforms because debris can cause children to slip and fall. Chapters 6 and 7 provide more detailed information about surfacing.

Equipment Hazards

Supervisors need to also be aware of equipment hazards. If maintenance problems are not fixed immediately, they are likely to increase. Supervisors should keep an eye out for broken equipment, missing parts, or loose bolts. They should also check for kinked, twisted, or broken chains. Supervisors who find these problems should report them to the maintenance department. In addition, supervisors should prevent children from using the equipment until repairs have been made. Chapters 8 and 9 provide more detailed information about equipment.

Behavior

Playground behavior includes the actions of both children and supervisors. Supervisors must have an understanding of unsafe play behavior and unsafe equipment use as well as what type of supervision behavior is necessary. For example, supervisors must make sure that children use slides safely (figure 3.5).

This section will look first at children's play behaviors and then at those behaviors that supervisors should exhibit.

Children's Play Behaviors

Many early educators, such as Piaget, Freud, Gulick, Pestalozzi, Locke, and Comenius, believed that play was essential for children to learn and to enhance developmental skills. Play is an activity that allows children freedom and is linked to exploratory work (Frost and Klein, 1979). But not all play behaviors are suitable for the playground.

Figure 3.5 Staying seated while using a slide is an example of safe equipment use.

Unsafe Play Behaviors

Many play environments have limitations regarding appropriate behavior, because certain behaviors are more likely to cause injury. Supervisors need to recognize behaviors that have the potential to cause an injury. For example, if children are allowed to use jump ropes during recess, you may need to develop rules for using the ropes (e.g., the ropes should be used for jumping, they should not be used as a weapon, and so on). Supervisors should communicate with one another about the potential for unsafe play behaviors. Often, it is the same children who repeat unsafe behaviors. If supervisors are aware of the children who carry out these behaviors, they can redirect the behaviors before they start. When unsafe play behaviors occur, supervisors should intervene to ensure that these actions are channeled into positive play behaviors.

Unsafe play can be placed in two categories: individual unsafe behaviors and inter-active unsafe behaviors (Bruya and Wood, 1998). Individual unsafe play behaviors refer to when children choose to play by themselves and initiate an unsafe behavior. For example, playing alone in prohibited areas would be considered an individual unsafe play behavior. Interactive unsafe play behavior, on the other hand, occurs when groups of children interact during play and initiate an unsafe play behavior that affects their own safety or the safety of others. Common interactive unsafe play behaviors are pushing, shoving, tackling, dog piling, or throwing objects.

Children's safety should be the number one concern of schools, child care centers, and other youth-serving organizations. However, supervisors face other concerns on the playground such as arguing, fighting, and bullying. These behaviors also come under the supervisors' umbrella of responsibilities.

Recess at any elementary school is a place where conflicts break out, children are injured, and bullying begins. The playground is one of the main contexts within a school in which children's social behavior is largely unconstrained by adult influences (Boulton, 1999). Unsafe behaviors need to be corrected immediately in order to maintain a safe environment. Supervisors should have an understanding of what behaviors are acceptable; thus, they should be trained on how and when to take disciplinary actions to maintain consistency in the supervision process.

Just as there are rules in the classroom, there should be rules for the outdoors. These rules should be developed from discussions among supervisors, teachers, children, and staff. In addition, parents or caretakers should determine rules before they take their children to the playground. There can only be a few rules if children are to learn and use them. For preschool children, the list of rules should be limited to three (Bruya et al., 2002). For elementary school children, it is recommended that you limit the number of rules to five. Keep the rules simple, as in the following examples:

- Be respectful.
- Take turns.
- Respect property.

It may be appropriate to use the same rules as those used in the indoor classroom.

Unsafe Equipment Use

Supervisors must have an understanding of unsafe equipment use, which will vary among play environments. It is important for supervisors to be consistent when it comes to unsafe equipment use. It is not fair to the children or the supervisors if one supervisor allows children to do twirls on the chinning bars and another supervisor does not.

Supervisors must be on the same page as to what constitutes unsafe equipment use. There are two categories of unsafe equipment use: unsafe use of stand-alone structures and unsafe use of composite structures (Bruya et al., 2002). Schools and child care centers should establish what behaviors are considered unsafe use for both types of structures. Having a set of rules for the equipment can provide a framework for the supervisor's intervention when these unsafe play behaviors occur.

After rules are established, students need to learn and understand those rules. Classroom teachers or physical education teachers may want to take their classrooms out to the play environment while they discuss the rules with the children. Table 3.1 lists some unsafe uses of stand-alone equipment and composite equipment (Bruya et al., 2002).

Stand-alone structures are not connected to any other play component. Examples of stand-alone structures include geodesic domes, spring rockers, swings, and horizontal ladders that are not connected to another structure.

A composite structure has at least two play components that are attached, such as a slide and a climbing wall that are connected. Another example of a composite structure may include a slide, a horizontal ladder, a spiral climber, and a climbing wall. All of these pieces would be connected together.

Table 3.1

Examples of Unsafe Uses of Play Equipment

Single-use stand-alone structures	Composite or linked structures
1. Selecting equipment that is too large despite directions otherwise from the supervisor	1. Climbing outside of the bed of tube slides
2. Standing on top of parallel bars or horizontal ladders	2. Standing on top of the slide hood
3. Jumping competitively for distance from the top of the equipment	3. Playing tag on equipment
4. Going up single wide slides while others are coming down	4. Pushing and shoving in king-of-the-mountain activities on platforms
5. Jumping out of swings for distance	5. Dropping off the track ride halfway along and giving a departing shove to make the track mechanism go to the other end with a bang

Reprinted, by permission, from L. Bruya et al., 2002, Behavior. In *S.A.F.E. playground supervision manual* (Cedar Falls, IA: National Program for Playground Safety), 24.

Supervisors' Behaviors

Like children's behaviors, supervisors' behaviors can either help or hinder the safety of the play environment. The supervisor's behavior refers to the practices of movement, observation, and interaction that should take place in order to create a safe play environment. Supervision is more than just being present—it is the active monitoring of the play environment to help ensure safety and prevent injuries. Supervision activities in the play environment can be classified into two distinct types: presupervision and active monitoring (Bruya and Wood, 1998).

Presupervision

Because most incidents occur within the first five minutes of a play period, at least one supervisor needs to arrive at the playground before the children in order to make sure the area is safe. It is crucial that a child care center's or school's supervision plan designate a person or persons who are responsible for getting to the play area before the children arrive. Once the children enter the playground area, their behaviors can become rather chaotic because they are full of energy. Arriving before the children is especially important for early morning play periods and after weekends and holidays when preplay inspections are crucial to ensure a safe play environment. Early arrival to the play environment gives supervisors enough time to make sure all the equipment and surfacing materials are in good condition.

When supervisors arrive with the children, they are a part of the frenzy at the beginning of a recess period and can spot potential conflicts from the classroom. In the initial minutes of the play period, good supervisors are ready to work with the children to divert them to other areas of the playground or activities away from sources of conflict.

Active Monitoring

Supervisors must be active when in the play environment. This includes moving throughout the area in random patterns and scanning the play area. Good supervisors are constantly aware of the playground environment. The job of the playground supervisor can be likened to that of a lifeguard. The lifeguard is there for safety purposes, not to give swimming lessons. Likewise, playground supervisors are there to ensure a safe environment, not to facilitate play. However, both jobs involve active monitoring of the environment through

- proper positioning,
- scanning, and
- interaction with other people (Bruya and Wood, 1998).

Proper Positioning Proper positioning includes being able to see the children from different angles. Untrained supervisors tend to stand in one place the entire recess period; however, supervisors should not remain in the same location on the playground. When supervisors frequently change locations, they are able to see children playing from different angles.

Proper positioning also means that supervisors should be constantly moving throughout the area of responsibility. Movement patterns should be unpredictable because safety problems increase when children are able to predict supervisors' locations (Bruya and Wood, 1998). Random location change maintains the supervisors' availability to monitor conflict. It may be necessary to walk in and around the playground equipment. It is also a good idea to change elevation when viewing the children.

Scanning   Just as supervisors' bodies move, so should their eyes. Scanning allows supervisors to see more actions and behaviors. Supervisors need to look up and down, right and left, and over and under in order to actively view all areas of the environment. Good scanning also enables the supervisor to give children "the eye" to prevent conflict and potential injuries. Many times children will watch to see if the supervisor is paying attention before they engage in behaviors that they know they shouldn't. By maintaining good eye contact with children, supervisors can intervene nonverbally into potential injury-producing situations.

Interaction With Others   The major responsibilities of supervisors are to observe and monitor children's activities on the playground. Interactions with other adults must be brief and to the point. This is not the time for supervisors to catch up on social events. When supervisors stop to talk with another person, they stop moving and scanning their area of responsibility.

Supervisors need to take their job seriously. They should be confident in telling other adults or children that they are not interested in carrying on a conversation at that time. They should say, "I have a job to do. I have to keep an eye on the children to make sure they are safe!" If another adult does require the supervisor's attention, then the supervisor should do one of the following (Bruya et al., 2002, p. 32):

1. Continue scanning the area and maintain physical contact (e.g., holding arm, hand on shoulder) with the other adult. Keeping physical contact will help show that you are not ignoring the person.
2. Immediately have someone else assume the supervision duties during the conversation.
3. Ignore the other adult and carry on with supervision duties.

Interactions with children need to be just as concise as those with adults. Supervisors can spend a lot of time redirecting play patterns, stopping dangerous play, and reminding children of safety rules. When supervisors need to stop and help a child, they should still continue scanning the area.

While interactions should be kept to a minimum, no supervisor should be isolated when out on the playground. Therefore, it is important to have a communication link among supervisors and between the supervisors and the main office at all times. At least four methods of communication can be employed on the playground (Bruya and Wood, 1998):

- Electronic devices, such as walkie-talkies or cell phones (see figure 3.6)
- Whistles
- Hand signals
- Student messengers

Figure 3.6 Supervisors must have a way to communicate with others without leaving their posts.

These communication methods may be used when supervisors need help, injuries happen, natural disasters occur, or an unknown adult enters the playground.

Playground Context

Every child care center and school is unique. Therefore, each playground environment will have specific supervision needs and challenges. It is imperative that child care centers and schools establish a supervision plan. The planning process should be ongoing; the plan may need to be changed due to new knowledge that staff have developed while supervising.

The supervision plan should detail the who, what, when, and where involved in providing a safe environment. The plan should answer the following questions:

- Who has the duty to supervise?
- What should be the ratio of supervisors to children?
- What are the responsibilities of the supervisors?

Duty to Supervise

Schools, child care centers, and youth-serving organizations have a duty to supervise when children are required to participate in playground activities. As discussed in chapter 2, many states have mandatory recess periods. When children enter the school property for educational purposes, as required by the state's compulsory school attendance and truancy laws, it becomes required that children take part in recess periods (School District of Stanley-Boyd vs. Auman, 2001).

Playground supervisors come from various sources including teachers, teacher associates, volunteers, part-time staff members, and parents and other caregivers. The principal or director and all staff should have a schedule of when the children in different grades will be on the playground. In addition, the schedule should indicate who is responsible for supervising those periods.

Typically, schools do not have a duty to supervise playgrounds during nonschool hours (Edmondson v. Brooks County Board of Education, 1992). However, if schools give permission for children to use outdoor facilities (e.g., baseball fields, track fields, playground) and parents are told that children will be properly supervised, the school can be held liable if a child gets injured (Augustus v. Joseph A. Craig Elementary School, 1984).

Ratio of Supervisors to Children

Student-to-staff ratios as high as 1 to 150 in the school environment are not uncommon. In the child care environment, the NAEYC, the American Public Health Association (APHA), and the American Academy of Pediatrics (AAP) have indicated that the child-to-staff ratio affects the quality of care the child care provider can give to each child.

The ratio of staff to children will vary depending on age of the children, the type of program, the inclusion of children with special needs, the time of day, and the size of the play environment. Chapter 2 outlined the NAEYC's recommended staff–child ratios. Practical implications, state regulations, and legal precedents all determine the appropriate ratios. To learn about your state's required staff-to-child ratio, contact your state's child care licensing department or department of education.

In the child care and preschool environments, the staff needs to discuss the difference between supervision and play facilitation. Often teachers are present on the playground, but they are engaged in the children's activities. If a teacher is outside and needs to be fully engaged into the children's activities, then another teacher must be supervising the children. For instance, let's say two classroom teachers take a group of 12 toddlers out in the play environment. One teacher takes four children to the sand-and-water table to make mud pies while the other teacher supervises the rest of the area. In this case, the teacher who is at the sand-and-water table is a play facilitator and would not be considered an appropriate supervisor even though there is a child–staff ratio of 2 to 12. Since one teacher is fully engaged at the sand-and-water table, it is best to have another adult supervising the children. Then, two supervisors and one play facilitator would be present.

Supervisor Responsibilities

After the agency has determined who the supervisors are and how many are needed, the next step is to outline the responsibilities for each supervisor. It may be necessary to designate one person as the lead supervisor. This person's job is to help coordinate responsibilities with the other supervisors and to communicate with the principal or director and maintenance personnel.

Other Considerations

Other considerations related to supervisors' responsibilities include uniforms, supervisor kits, emergency planning, and injury reporting.

Uniforms

Supervisor uniforms work! Supervisors are visible on the playground when they are wearing an identifiable piece of clothing in a fluorescent color. When an emergency occurs, it is thus easy for children and other adults to locate the supervisor quickly. The least expensive and most efficient supervision uniform is a fluorescent traffic vest. The uniform must fit over clothing in cold weather and not be too heavy in hot weather. The vest should be light and easy to put on and take off.

Supervisor Safety Kits

A portable kit filled with first aid and other supplies is necessary for each supervisor. Supervisors should carry the kit at all times when they are on duty. Supplies may be chosen by the school nurse or the supervisors, and might include the following:

- Bandages
- Bandage compresses
- Biohazard bags
- Cold compress
- Color-coded messenger cards
- Face shields
- Hall passes
- Injury report forms
- Maintenance forms
- Nonlatex gloves
- Notepad
- Pencil

- Plastic bags or plastic bread sacks for trash removal
- Pocket masks
- Scissors
- Self-adhering gauze
- Sunscreen for supervisor
- Tape
- Whistle

The kit should be large enough to hold the appropriate contents, and the contents should be arranged so that materials can be found quickly without unpacking the entire contents. Individual materials inside the kit should be wrapped so that unused portions do not become dirty through handling. It is important that all supervisors know where the kits are located before the play period begins so that they do not have to take a lot of time to pick up the kit before heading to recess duty. In addition, a schedule should be developed for checking and restocking kit supplies.

Emergency Planning

Unfortunately, even under the best circumstances injuries do occur. Child care centers, schools, and other youth-serving organizations must be prepared to respond to emergency situations, including injuries, natural disasters, violent incidents, and unknown adults on the playground. All supervisors must know the procedures to follow in case of an emergency.

It is necessary for organizations to develop plans for potential emergency situations (see figure 3.7). A valuable resource during the planning process is local emergency medical technicians (EMTs). They can help map out emergency routes for moving an injured child from the playground to medical facilities. The school or community nurse is also another key person to include on the planning team. The nurse can provide valuable training to school personnel in terms of handling a first aid crisis.

The emergency plan should include how supervisors should alert school personnel to an urgent situation. Possible methods of communicating are walkie-talkies, cell phones, or student messengers. The plan should also outline how supervisors should manage other children during the crisis, which staff members are first aid providers, and how emergency personnel will be contacted and directed to the site.

Any good emergency process is one that is practiced with the supervisory staff. Just like a fire, tornado, or hurricane drill, supervisors, administrators, teachers, and children need to know what to do when an emergency occurs in the outdoor environment. Finally, to be effective, the supervision plan must be reassessed and revised on a regular basis.

Injury Reporting

No supervision plan is complete without an injury report form. Injury reporting can help administrators pinpoint potential hazards and injury patterns. For example, are children being injured from falls, from bumping into equipment, or from unintentional (or intended) contact with others? Knowing the location and circumstances of all injuries that have occurred can help the organization in reviewing safety procedures. See the sample Injury Report Form in appendix B.

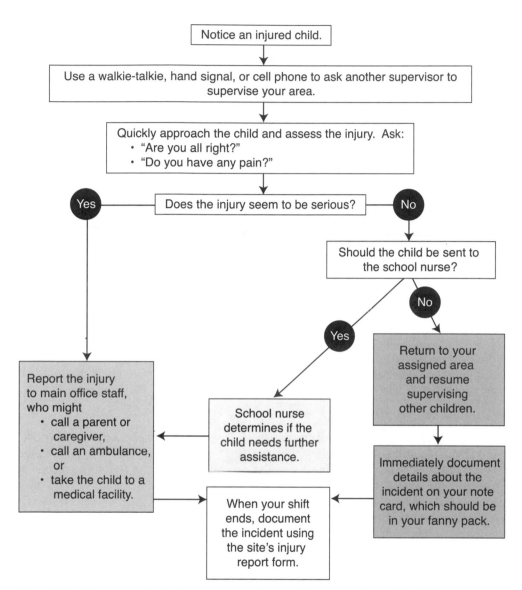

Notice an injured child.

Use a walkie-talkie, hand signal, or cell phone to ask another supervisor to supervise your area.

Quickly approach the child and assess the injury. Ask:
- "Are you all right?"
- "Do you have any pain?"

Yes — Does the injury seem to be serious? — **No**

Should the child be sent to the school nurse?

No

Yes

Return to your assigned area and resume supervising other children.

School nurse determines if the child needs further assistance.

Report the injury to main office staff, who might
- call a parent or caregiver,
- call an ambulance, or
- take the child to a medical facility.

Immediately document details about the incident on your note card, which should be in your fanny pack.

When your shift ends, document the incident using the site's injury report form.

Figure 3.7 This process is just one example of responding to an injured child. Child care centers, schools, and other youth-serving organizations should follow their policy.

Developing a Supervision Action Plan

Child care centers and schools face numerous challenges. Reform is occurring in many elementary schools in order to sustain school improvement and improve high-stake testing scores. These changes are coming too quickly for many child care centers and schools to easily assimilate. As a result, they may be seen as resisting change. We all want our children to learn, to have a safe play area, and to have fun. Can children learn if they are not safe? Safety must be a priority in any organization that serves children. Spending thousands of dollars on educational materials does no good if we are not willing to change or think about our behaviors as supervisors.

Child care centers, schools, and youth-serving organizations need to take a closer look at the number of injuries that occur during a year. They also need to develop their supervision policies and then routinely examine them. Developing a supervision policy will get a plan in place so that every staff member will know the rules of the play environment and what preventative measures to take in case of an injury. Changing from an agency that does not value the outdoor play area to one that believes the outdoor play area is part of children's total learning environment means teachers, teacher associates, principals, directors, counselors, and students must alter their beliefs and actions. This section will take a look at how child care centers, schools, and other youth-serving organizations can develop an action plan for designing, implementing, and evaluating staff training for playground supervision.

Staff Training for Playground Supervision

Planning is the process by which any child care center, school, or other youth-serving organization determines how they are going to develop staff training for playground supervision. The planning process must begin with people. As Robert Evans, an expert in strategic planning, writes, "Most people treat reform as a product and, focusing on its structural frame, often overlook its human face. But change must be accomplished by people . . . To do this, we must broaden our perspective on change and rethink the essentials of leadership" (1993, p. 19).

Designing Staff Training

Committed teachers and teacher associates who are concerned about the responsibilities of the playground supervisors need to band together to develop an initiative for supervision training. The planning process can begin when the stakeholders come together to form a leadership team that will spearhead the reform. The stakeholders for the supervision training include the parents, teacher associates, teachers, school nurse or child care licensing consultant, maintenance staff, principal or director, and school administrator.

Parents   Parents are an invaluable resource because they are invested in their children's safety and education. Parents will work hard to provide the safest outdoor play environment possible. Some parents may bring financial resources that allow supervisors to carry first aid supplies, a whistle, bathroom and drink clips, and a first aid kit they can wear around the waist. Some parents may also volunteer to serve as supervisors. Parents may be willing to spend a few hours on the playground. If parents are willing to volunteer their time, make sure that they are trained and understand the supervision rules and policies.

Teacher Associates and Assistants   Teacher associates and assistants understand what types of activities, behaviors, and events happen on the playground. They are one of the most important stakeholders because they are the ones who actually supervise the children. They probably are going to have several good ideas on how to improve safety. They will also be a great resource for determining what type of staff development would be helpful.

Teachers and Counselors   Teachers and counselors know who the children are in each classroom. They also have a good understanding of which children are friends and which ones don't get along so well. In addition, teachers maintain relationships with their students' parents. When there are problems on the playground, the teacher associates report it to the classroom teachers, who are responsible for talking with the parents about their child's behavior. The teachers are also responsible for supervision duties before and after school. They need to have a clear understanding of the rules and expectations of the playground.

Child Care Licensing Consultant or School Nurse   The child care licensing consultant or school nurse is another important person in the plan. These individuals have a complete understanding of the types of injuries that occur on the playground. They are the ones who usually report and document all playground injuries. For these reasons, they may be the best people to conduct supervision training.

Maintenance Staff   Maintenance staff members are essential on the planning committee because they are the individuals who will make any physical changes to the playground. For example, if playground equipment is broken, the maintenance staff will repair it. They need to have a complete understanding of how to report broken pieces or dangerous parts to their department. Including maintenance staff in the planning process will also help them feel that they are valued.

Principal or Director   The principal or director is another key stakeholder. The principal or director usually is either in charge of the staff training or is supervising the person leading the training. The principal or director oversees the teacher associates and teachers and evaluates and gives suggestions to improve their supervision skills. Principals or directors may also be asked to explain, or even justify, the supervision training and the responsibilities of the supervisors. The more supportive principals and directors are, the more likely the training effort will be successful.

School Administrators   Administrators (board members, superintendent, curriculum coordinator, and risk managers) manage the child care center or school. Their support is critical to the implementation of staff development regarding playground supervision. In addition, they have the ability to allocate funds to initiate or expand the training. Risk managers and school board members have the responsibility to keep the children safe while at school, and they have to answer to any type of liability that occurs.

Implementing Staff Training

Flexibility, practice, accountability, alertness, and attitude are valuable characteristics that supervision training should focus on. Changes in the attitudes and behaviors of both the staff and the children will need to take place; however, change takes time. Playground supervisors need time to practice techniques that they learn. Supervision training is an important component of the overall child care and school safety program. The development of a curriculum for supervision training will give the playground supervisors a better understanding of their duties and will help supervisors keep children safe. The curriculum will give supervisors an understanding of potentially hazardous situations and how to respond to emergencies on the playground.

Six Steps Toward Supervision

To develop a supervision action plan, follow these six steps.

1. Hold a workshop on the S.A.F.E. model for playgrounds.
2. Gather current information.
3. Identify needed changes.
4. Develop a supervision training curriculum.
5. Train staff on new policies.
6. Teach children appropriate behaviors.

Step 1: Hold a Workshop on the S.A.F.E. Model for Playgrounds

It is important that staff understand what good supervision is, the factors that contribute to good playground supervision, the number of playground injuries, the types of playground injuries, the need for safety training, and the techniques of proper supervision. Information from this book can be used to teach staff the importance of playground safety.

When developing supervision training, be sure to involve all the key stakeholders, including the director or the principal, the teachers and teacher associates on playground duty, one lower-grade classroom teacher, one upper-grade classroom teacher, the school nurse, the counselor, and a custodial worker. You can hold a half-day workshop based on the S.A.F.E. model presented in this book.

Step 2: Gather Current Information

The next step is to perform a needs assessment. It is necessary to have an understanding of the current playground supervision policy. This step also includes gathering information on what the other child care centers and elementary schools in the area are doing in relation to playground supervision. It is also important that all staff members have a chance to share their ideas, observations, and concerns. Getting input from each staff member is extremely valuable because you want them all to feel like they are part of the change process.

Step 3: Identify Needed Changes

Conversations when gathering information about the current status of playground supervision will lead supervisors to talk about the changes that need to take place. It will also give them a chance to discuss the types of hazards and behaviors that are not acceptable.

Step 4: Develop a Supervision Training Curriculum

Next, the child care center, school, or youth-serving organization should develop a supervision training curriculum. This curriculum can be used as a guide for discussing challenges and presenting safety information to the staff. To develop the curriculum, do the following:

- Create a site map of the play area. The site map should address natural, manmade, and aesthetic elements that may affect the supervision. It should also allow supervisors to see the area they are responsible for while on duty.

- Formulate rules for the children (see figure 3.8). These rules should be similar to, if not the same as, the classroom rules. Staff members must realize that rule development is an ongoing process. Rules should be reviewed at least twice a year with students.
- Generate a list of behaviors that will not be tolerated (see figure 3.9). Document the discipline procedures that will be used if unsafe behaviors or inappropriate equipment usage occurs.
- Choose an appropriate method of communication while supervisors are on the playground. Also, decide how supervisors should alert the main office in case of an emergency.
- Address any other information that the supervisors and staff need to know.

Once you have gathered the site map, list of rules, list of behaviors, communication methods, and any other information that the supervisors and staff need to know, put the information into a manual. This supervision training manual can be used as a training component each new school year. Consider organizing the manual into three sections:

1. Layout: Map of the playground with graphics indicating the areas for which supervisors will be responsible
2. Actions: Steps for supervisors to take to improve the children's safety
3. Schedule: Times of recess periods, including who is responsible for the different areas of the playground during each period

---

Respect others.

Respect property.

Treat others the way you want to be treated.

Take turns.

Play safely.

Figure 3.8 Establish clear rules for children to follow on the playground.

Don't push, fight, or use bad language.

Don't go down the slide head first.

Don't throw rocks.

Don't jump out of swings.

Don't play tackle football.

Figure 3.9 Specify which unsafe or inappropriate behaviors will not be tolerated from children on the playground.

Step 5: Train Staff on New Policies

The content of the supervision training curriculum should come from ideas that the committee has identified. The training program should focus on anticipating the potential dangers and problems, being aware of appropriate supervisor behavior, and assessing the environment in which supervision takes place. More specifically, the course should focus on playground inspections; adult–child supervision ratios; supervisor responsibility; arrival time; playground hazards; arguments, fighting, and misuse of equipment; positioning on the playground; and injuries. Each person attending the training should receive a copy of the supervision training curriculum.

Step 6: Teach Children Appropriate Behaviors

The staff should decide how to teach children the rules of the playground and appropriate play behaviors. It is important to include the children in formulating the rules. Children will remember what they have planned. It will make the job of the playground supervisors easier, because they can enforce the rules. It will also empower the children to know about dangers on the playground. Long-term commitment to safety is expected as the major outcome of establishing rules for the playground.

Evaluation of Supervision

Evaluation is the process of determining whether programs are appropriate, adequate, effective, and efficient. Educational institutions evaluate curricula in order to improve teaching; to better meet the needs of students; to examine any effects of introducing a new curriculum; to justify school practices to the public; to respond to dissatisfaction with child care and school procedures; and to settle conflicts within the child care center and school about power, roles, or personalities (Marsh and Willis, 2003).

The purpose of evaluating the supervision training curriculum is to determine whether the supervisors are doing a better job keeping the children safe. The evaluation also helps the administrators understand supervisor responsibilities. In addition, evaluation can boost employee morale because supervisors have the pleasure of seeing that their efforts are not wasted. Evaluation is evidence either that the supervisors' work is paying off or that the administrators are taking steps to see that needed improvements are made (Thompson and McClintock, 1998).

First, clearly lay out the evaluation process. The administrator of the child care center, school, or youth-serving organization must determine what type of evaluation needs to be conducted. For example, they may want to examine injury data or behaviors of children. Evaluation should be continuous throughout the year.

Second, decide who should carry out the evaluation. We recommend that one person be designated as the evaluator. This person may be an administrator or a lead supervisor, but it does not have to be. The evaluator can be elected or appointed or may volunteer. The director or principal should work closely with the person who is responsible for the evaluations.

Third, examine what areas should be evaluated. The evaluation should be based on the goals of the supervision training program. The evaluation should cover student–student interaction, supervisor–student interaction, supervisor–supervisor interaction, child care licensing consultant–supervisor interaction, and school nurse–supervisor interaction. How effective was the program? What should be done differently to improve the program?

Fourth, think about how to collect the injury information and monitor students' behavior. The staff should be encouraged to interact with one another to collect and share information. Remember to value the supervisors' time throughout the planning, implementation, and evaluation process; it should not become a headache for them.

Fifth, decide how to report the information. Thought should be given before reporting the evaluation results to the staff and to the public. How should the information be passed on to the staff? Is it necessary to have a meeting, or is it better to pass the information through e-mail? Also, consider whether it is necessary to pass the findings to board members or parents. If you have taken steps to create a supervision plan and it is reducing injuries and behaviors, report the efforts you have made to keep children safe in the outdoor play environment.

Without careful design, implementation, and evaluation, proper supervision practices will not occur. This section has provided a coherent and practical method to engage playground supervisors, teachers, principals and directors, students, and parents in developing and implementing supervision policies to reduce playground injuries.

Success Story

When Mark White was hired as the environmental risk manager for the Lee's Summit School District in Lee's Summit, Missouri, he knew something wasn't right. Too many children were getting hurt on the playgrounds, so he convinced his administrator to send him to Cedar Falls, Iowa, to attend the NPPS Safety School. Afterward, White returned to Lee's Summit with a goal to change the way his school district valued the outdoor play environment.

First, White formed a plan to assess the play areas. The school district developed a maintenance checklist to assess both the equipment and surfacing on a regular basis. When schools were installing new equipment, White also helped them choose age-appropriate equipment. Further, understanding that play was a right for all children, he made sure that the play areas were designed for children of all abilities.

White required that all supervisors receive playground supervision training. Working with other staff, he developed a supervision training program that was used to train all the supervisors in the district's 16 elementary schools. He and his staff talked to the supervisors about appropriate behaviors to exhibit when supervising and taught them which play behaviors are acceptable and unacceptable.

Have White and the Lee's Summit School District made a difference? You be the judge. In the six years since Mark attended the NPPS Safety School, playground injuries in the district have been reduced by 27 percent, and the severity of injuries has been reduced by 35 percent.

Summary

A strong case can be made for the importance of developing, planning, and implementing a supervision plan. Supervision is more just being in the play area; it involves anticipating potential dangers and being active while supervising children. It is all too common to see supervisors standing around in clusters while children are playing. Many teachers use children's outdoor time as a break time, an opportunity to socialize with other adults and to take their minds off the children. Those behaviors are inadequate and ineffective. We must be active supervisors!

This chapter has addressed the ABCs of the supervision model as a guide to help you understand how to *anticipate* problems, what *behaviors* are acceptable, and how to assess the *context* or environment in which supervision takes place. It is imperative that child care centers, youth-serving organizations, and schools have a supervision plan in place. The plan should detail the who, what, when, and where involved in providing a safe environment, and the planning process should be ongoing. By practicing the ABCs of supervision, you can create a safe outdoor environment for all children.

4

Age-Appropriate Design

To deny children the opportunity to reap the many benefits of regular, vigorous physical activity is to deny them the opportunity to experience the joy of efficient movement, the health effects of movement, and a lifetime as confident, competent movers.

David Gallahue

© MarinMedia.org

Julio was a large 2-year-old attending a commercial child care center. Although the center did have tot (bucket) swings for children under the age of 4 years (as recommended in the CPSC guidelines), the caregiver, Donna, was tired of lifting Julio into the bucket. On a sunny spring day, Donna decided to let all the 2-year-olds in her class use the swing set that only had sling seats. After all, she decided, they would have to learn how to use the swings sometime.

There were enough swings to accommodate four children at once. She put Julio in the first seat and gave him a push and then proceeded to work down the line of children. She was at the fourth child when, out of the corner of her eye, she saw Julio do a backflip off the swing and land face down. When Donna got to Julio, he was crying and complaining of pain in his left leg. It turned out that in the course of letting go and flipping backward due to the violent motion of his legs as he tried to pump, Julio sustained a broken femur. His medical bills alone ran over $30,000.

Children should play on equipment that fits their developmental abilities. In this chapter, we'll discuss what children are like at various developmental stages and track changes by age: 6 to 23 months, 2 to 3 years, 4 to 5 years, 5 to 7 years, 8 to 9 years, and 10 to 12 years. The overlap of age 5 in two categories is intentional because some 5-year-olds are in preschool and some are in elementary school.

Note, too, that in most child care centers, children aged 6 to 12 months are considered infants, 1-year-olds are pretoddlers, 2-year-olds are toddlers, and 4- and 5-year-olds are preschoolers. In most school settings, ages 5 to 6 years old correspond with kindergarten and first grade, ages 7 to 8 years old correspond with grades 2 and 3, and ages 9 to 12 years old correspond with grades 4 through 6.

We'll discuss the typical physical, emotional, social, and intellectual abilities of children in each age group. This information will set the stage for the following chapter, which explores the implications of developmental abilities for equipment selection.

What Are Children Like?

Are children of different ages all alike? Of course every child is unique, but in a larger sense children also vary in their characteristics by age. When you look at playground designs, remember that children are different. Before selecting playground equipment, consider the developmental characteristics of children. If all children came in the same size and had the same developmental characteristics, then one piece of equipment would fit all of them. However, that is not the case.

Public playground equipment is built for children aged 6 to 23 months, 2 to 5 years, and 5 to 12 years (CPSC, 1997). The ASTM has provided standards (F1487) for manufacturers of public equipment for the age ranges of 2 to 5 years and 5 to 12 years (ASTM, 1993), and recently they developed a standard (F2373-05) for play equipment for children aged 6 to 23 months (ASTM, 2005). The NPPS takes the position that those age ranges should be divided even further since a 2-year-old is not the same as a 5-year-old and a 5-year-old is not the same as a 12-year-old. Just try to get a 2-year-old to wear shoes meant for a 5-year-old or have a 5-year-old wear the shoes of a 12-year-old! In order to have proper equipment and play areas for children, it is important to look at developmental characteristics of children at each age level (see figure 4.1).

Figure 4.1 Children aged *(a)* 6 months, *(b)* 2 years, *(c)* 5 years, and *(d)* 12 years.

Within the literature on early childhood and elementary education, the developmental characteristics of children are generally categorized as cognitive, psychomotor, and affective. However, a more user-friendly approach is to characterize these developmental domains as intellectual (cognitive), physical (psychomotor), emotional (affective), and social (affective). We've split the affective domain into two categories, emotional and social, because we believe that a child develops these two abilities independently. *Emotional* describes the individual's response to a situation, whereas *social* considers the individual's interaction with others.

Of course, children are whole individuals, but it is easier to consider their needs if we look at these discrete categories. By combining current theoretical knowledge about growth, development, movement, and observation of the ways children act and recognizing that they develop in stages, we can begin to consider the development of play environments that fit their needs.

How Children Develop Physically

Several elements within the category of physical development deserve attention in the creation of age-appropriate play areas. These include the following:

- Physical gross motor actions
- Vision
- Figure–ground perception
- Ground perception
- Movement awareness
- Auditory awareness
- Perceptual motor development
- Vestibular stimulation
- Size differences

Physical Gross Motor Actions

Children learn to roll, sit, crawl, creep, and stand before they walk. Then they walk before they run, jump before they hop, gallop and skip before they slide, and slide before they leap. This physical developmental progression can be seen in figure 4.2. There are progressions within each of these actions as well. For example, children gallop with one foot leading before they learn to gallop with the other foot leading. That leads to skipping, where they alternate the lead foot. In general, children achieve the most advanced coordination patterns in all locomotor skills by the time they are around 7 years old (Whitall, 2003).

Vision

The development of vision is crucial since it gives children the sense of where they are in space as well as where other children and things are. Visually, most children can perceive the spatial orientation of objects, or where objects are located in space, by the time they are 8 years old (Gabbard, 1992). Therefore, it is normal for children younger than 8 years old to run into other children and things. It would make sense to provide more space between objects (play equipment) and limit the number of children in the play environment. These actions give younger children time to perceive where they are in space and figure out how to relate to the people and objects they observe. The younger the children are, the more time they need to figure out where they are in the environment in relation to other children and objects.

Figure–Ground Perception

Similar to visual perception, figure–ground perception is the ability to perceive the difference between an object and its background. This type of visual perception is important in designing areas for younger children since the development of figure–ground perception develops rapidly between the ages of 4 and 8 years (Gabbard, 1992). Thus, it may be useful to provide objects that are near the ground in a contrasting color from those at ground level itself, especially for younger children.

Movement Awareness

Movement awareness, or kinesthetic acuity, is the ability of the body to detect differences or match abilities such as location, distance, weight, force, speed, and acceleration (Gabbard, 1992). This ability reaches adult levels by the age of 8 years. It is a good idea to provide greater distances between nonlocomotor objects (objects that do not move, such as stationary playground equipment) for younger children in order for the children to move safely from one piece to the other. At the same time, young children also do not fully understand the speed of moving objects. Thus, a track ride is not a good idea for 3-year-olds. As a matter of fact, some manufacturers of playground equipment label their track rides as appropriate for children aged 8 years and older in accordance with the development of this characteristic.

Figure 4.2 Developmental progression of physical actions.

Auditory Awareness

Auditory awareness is the ability to discriminate among sounds in the environment. This characteristic provides clues as to the placement of various objects and people in the environment. Auditory awareness improves significantly between the ages of 8 and 10 years and it reaches adult levels by the age of 13 years (Gabbard, 1992). This suggests that younger children need time to respond to the placement of individuals and objects in the environment. It may also suggest that too many people in a small space may be the reason for auditory interference that causes children to respond to individuals or objects either inappropriately or with confusion. The development of this characteristic may have implications for the number of children that should be allowed in a given play environment at any one time.

Perceptual Motor Development

Perceptual motor development, or intersensory integration, is the ability to perceive stimuli with various senses and translate that information into movement. Children need time to listen, process what they hear, and then decide upon an appropriate motor response. Also, they need time to see and observe a situation, determine what it means, and again choose a suitable course of action. Children are dependent on the environmental stimulus and its quality in order to determine ways to respond. Therefore, it is important to provide more time and space among equipment with distinct stimuli for younger children. It is also necessary to use consistent playground rules among teachers and to provide clear visual and auditory stimuli for physical responses.

In terms of visual stimuli, children do not perceive the distance of horizontal ladders from the ground; therefore, they do not understand that they may fall harder from a higher height. For this reason, it is important to provide a lower fall distance until children learn how to fall. We suggest that height for 4-year-olds be no more than 4 feet (1.2 meters), for 5-year-olds no higher than 5 feet (1.5 meters), for 6-year-olds no higher than 6 feet (1.8 meters), and for 7-year-olds and older no higher than 7 feet (2.1 meters).

Vestibular Stimulation

Vestibular stimulation is the ability of the hearing system to provide information to the brain about movements of the head. The ears are extremely important in the development of this element, and they need to be stimulated in infancy in order for children to know whether they are upright, static, involved in a range of movement, accelerating, or decelerating (Gabbard, 1992). Activities that stimulate this system include swinging, sliding, and balancing in various positions. Lack of experience with these actions may cause specific disabilities.

For example, a high school student was having trouble performing a headstand in a physical education class in Seattle, Washington. A trip to the doctor revealed no inner-ear physical disorder. However, the doctor asked how much time the student spent on her head, and the answer was, very little. The lack of stimuli of placing the body upside down earlier in life led to the inability to perform a recognized gymnastics move in high school. The vestibular apparatus was normal but undeveloped. The student would have been able to balance better if she had been given an opportunity to practice headstands earlier in life.

Size Differences

Children of different ages come in different sizes. A description of those sizes is available in *Playgrounds for Public Use: Continuum of Skills and Size Differences* (NRPA, 1992). Age–size charts are based on the majority percentile of the age group. There will always be 3-year-olds who are the size of a normal 6-year-old or 5-year-olds who are the size of a 2-year-old. What is important is not just the size but the developmental ability. In the cautionary tale that opened the chapter, 2-year-old Julio may have been big for his age, but his developmental abilities were consistent with those of other 2-year-olds. It was the caregiver's lack of attention to Julio's developmental abilities that resulted in his injury on an inappropriate piece of playground equipment.

How Children Develop Emotionally

There are emotional motives for play. Nature and nurture contribute to the development of a child's personality. Since we are born with biological inner drives, known as the id, that include hunger, social contact, and sex drive, we must deal with society's limits on the degree to which we may fulfill those drives. For example, adults often limit the amount of time they allow children to play. As children internalize that social limitation, they develop their superego, or conscience, in order to provide an internal representation of society's rules. In other words, we learn when we can fulfill our desires. Last, the interplay of the internal id and the external superego shape us into who we are: our ego (Freud, 1918). Freud claimed that much of this development occurs unconsciously, but some develops at the conscious level.

Parents and teachers can contribute significantly to the development of children's emotions by the way they place limits on activities. An imbalance of social restrictions can result in emotional development that may be unhealthy. For instance, studies have shown that when chimpanzees are denied play as young primates, they tend to become emotional drones or social outcasts as adults. Some studies of child abuse victims show the same pattern (Freud, 1918).

Importance of Emotional Balance

It is easy to see the importance of developing this emotional balance on the playground. For instance, observe how children on the playground deal with challenge and fear. Consider 14-month-old Sabine, who walks outside into the play area only to fall down again and again. However, Sabine's caregiver encourages her to get up and walk again. She does so, and by the time Sabine is 15 months old, she rarely falls down (see figure 4.3).

Figure 4.3 Emotional balance can help a child improve her physical balance.

As another example, consider 3-year-old Renee, who is challenged by the caregiver to climb the ladder to the top of the 6-foot (1.8-meter) slide. She thinks it looks high. However, she decides to take the gamble, walks up the steps, and considers the risk of falling as she sits down at the top and gets ready to slide down. Her ride down is successful so she runs around to the ladder to try again. Repetition breeds success. The risk of falling becomes a challenge to be successful as she develops skills of using her hands and feet as she climbs, and that increases her confidence, makes her happy, and relaxes her so that she increases her ability to climb and slide again. Her supervisor also recognizes her success and encourages her to practice her new skills. Her confidence increases as does her skill level; thus she is less likely to be injured as she performs those actions.

Egocentricity of Children

Children are egocentric until they reach kindergarten—that is, their own emotional needs must be met first. Emotional needs include those in the biological realm (i.e., the need for food and fresh diapers on a regular basis) and those in the emotional realm (i.e., the need for love from adults and to know that they can count on adults to meet their needs). They do not require a great deal of money to meet their needs—just assurance that those basic requirements will be met. They need assurance that they are progressing developmentally in a normal fashion. Children need appropriate stimulation of their senses in order to develop in an orderly manner. They need to feel like they are making progress and that the adults approve of their progress.

Need for Approval

As children progress beyond the egocentric stage, they play by themselves. However, during this stage, children still need approval in order to know that they are doing the right thing. As they progress toward kindergarten, they need the opportunity to repeat actions that they have performed successfully. Repetition increases children's abilities to perform actions and strengthens their confidence that they are good performers; it makes them feel successful.

As children get older, they become enthralled with adults. They want adults' approval of their actions. In addition, they need the praise of adults. However, adults should be careful not to encourage young children to perform actions at adult levels. We need to remember that children develop in various stages and express approval of the stage of development that children have achieved. We need to be patient and show children that we are pleased with their progress.

As children progress, they become less egocentric and more interested in others. They develop individual differences and become aware of their own abilities and those of others. By the time children are at the end of elementary school, they are becoming self-conscious and egocentrism is disappearing.

How Children Develop Socially

Children develop from being egocentric early in their lives to a point where they want to be with other children and eventually begin to share things with others. They consider playing next to others, or parallel play, about the time they are 4 years of age. Some try to engage in parallel play at 3 years old. However, they don't begin to test sharing toys with one another until about the time they enter kindergarten. They like to play alone, but they will consider playing with one or two others. As social skills improve, children increase the number of other children that they interact with at any given time. They also make little distinction between playing with children of the same or opposite sex, although they begin to recognize that children have different skill levels.

This change from playing alone to playing in small groups and then in larger groups is the normal progression of social abilities. Figure 4.4 shows the various stages of social development as described by Parten (1932). In sum, children interact with the environment first by active movement. However, they are not necessarily interested or involved in other children's play. They progress from this stage of development to watching others. From there they play alone with things, but not other children. At about 4 years of age, children play near others with things, but do not share. About the time children enter kindergarten, they learn to play with others but may have different purposes for playing. Finally, children begin to learn how to cooperate with other children. That is the time when small-team games may be appropriate.

Many researchers have confirmed these stages since the publishing of Parten's description. Children may be progressing through these stages at a faster rate than they were over 60 years ago when Parten first developed them, but the description of the stages is still accurate.

For example, assume that 2-year-old Colin is playing with his cars at the bottom of a slide. He is most interested in letting the cars move down the slide from a height

Parten's Description of Social Development

Uninvolved: The child is active and mobile but seemingly aimless; there is no sense of others' play.

Onlooker: The child attends to others' play and may speak with players, but does not participate.

Solitary: The child plays alone, with own toys; typical of 2- to 3-year-olds.

Parallel: The child plays beside or near others, but not with them—no sharing. Includes play goals.

Associative: The child plays with and converses with others, but purposes of play may not be similar.

Cooperative: Goals of play are shared and negotiated. Tasks and roles relate to play's purpose; group sense is marked by turn taking and a common goal, product, or game.

Figure 4.4 Parten's stages of social development.

Adapted from M.B. Parten, 1932, "Social participation among preschool children," *Journal of Abnormal and Social Psychology* 27, 243-262.

that he can reach. On the other hand, Jill and Aleisha, two 4-year-olds, are busy climbing the steps to the top of the slide and want to slide down. The girls are not playing together, but they are playing near each other and doing the same activity. Colin is an example of solitary play, while the girls are an example of parallel play.

An expansion of the cooperative stage finds children becoming more aware of their peers; they start to place more importance on approval from peers than from adults. Friendships become exclusive to the same sex. In addition, children become aware of sexual roles and interests. Eventually, children form definite groups according to age and sex. They seek group approval of their actions and accomplishments.

Finally, children establish values. Adults must contribute to rationales for the selection of those values and thus influence the choices that children make. If children have not been exposed to good values and why those values are appropriate, they will not be able to choose between positive and negative values.

How Children Develop Intellectually

There many ways to describe children from an intellectual point of view. Many child development theorists and psychologists have described children's characteristics and development, but we'll present Piaget's model (see table 4.1). Piaget (1962) suggests four broad periods of development for children: the sensorimotor period, the preoperational period, the concrete operations period, and the formal operations period. Each period has distinct characteristics that manufacturers of playground equipment should note and designers of play areas for children should apply.

From J. Piaget, 1962, *Play, dreams and imitation in childhood* (New York: W.W. Norton Company).

Table 4.1

Piaget's Periods of Intellectual Development

Piaget's period	Approximate age range
Sensorimotor period (six stages)	
1. Exercising the ready-made sensorimotor schema	0-1 month
2. Primary circular reaction	1-4 months
3. Secondary circular reactions	4-8 months
4. Coordination of secondary schemata	8-12 months
5. Tertiary circular reactions	12-18 months
6. Invention of new means through mental combinations	18-24 months
Preoperational period	2-7 years
Concrete operations period	7-11 years
Formal operations period	11-15 years

Adapted from J. Piaget, 1962, *Play, dreams and imitation in childhood* (New York: W.W. Norton Company).

Sensorimotor Period

During the sensorimotor period, children are experiencing the ways that the senses work. This includes the use of sight, hearing, touch, and taste. In addition, children are dealing with their reactions to the stimulation of those senses. Since this stage covers the ages of 6 to 23 months, it is important to include playground equipment that provides sensory stimulation.

There are six stages in the sensorimotor period (Gallahue, 1976).

- During stage 1, children work on reflexes, such as blinking, from both internal and external stimulation. This practice will allow them to develop the reflexes into voluntary movements later on.

- During stage 2, children begin to understand the stimuli behind the reflexes, such as adults blinking at them.

- During stage 3, children try to repeat the actions, such as blinking. The primary sense for stimulating this action is vision.

- During stage 4, children are able to distinguish the means from the end. They try to achieve the results in more than one way, for example, by closing the eye by blinking and by moving the eyelid manually.

- During stage 5, children develop spatial relationships upon discovering objects, and they begin to manipulate the objects.

- During stage 6, children discover that they are separate from the items that they are manipulating. They can control the objects.

Adapted from D.L. Gallahue, 1976, *Motor development and movement experiences for young children* (New York: John Wiley and Sons, Inc.).

Preoperational Period

The preoperational period covers ages 2 to 7 years. During this period of time, children become less egocentric and begin to understand conservation.

At age 2, children are egocentric and cannot see the viewpoint of another person. Their thoughts are their own, and they are the only thoughts possible so they must be correct. However, by the time children are 7 years old, they begin to realize that their thoughts and the thoughts of others may be different and that their peers may be in conflict with their own thoughts. As a result, children begin to accommodate others, and the egocentric tendency starts to give way to social pressure. They begin to consider ideas of others.

During this developmental stage, children also begin to understand the idea of conservation—that more than one combination of items can fit into the same space. For example, one set of swings that is 8 feet (2.4 meters) high with four seats takes the same space as a horizontal ladder that is 8 feet (2.4 meters) long. Similarly, six boys take the same space as six girls, and four boys weigh about the same as four girls.

Concrete Operations Period

The concrete operations period lasts from ages 7 to 11 years. During that period of time, children's reasoning powers start to become logical. They begin to understand that others may come to conclusions that are different from theirs. For example, if Oksana breaks her arm, Daniel may conclude that the injury occurred because she fell. On the other hand, Marissa may believe that Oksana fell because she was pushed, while Sabir may understand that the lack of surfacing contributed to the fall.

In addition, children begin to understand seriation, or the idea that items can be ordered by increasing or decreasing size. Thus, children can be lined up by size to perform actions on the playground. During this period, they also begin to classify items. For instance, children can classify equipment by size, length, color, or type of material.

Children also begin to understand the idea of causality. For example, a slide may be hotter in the sun than the shade. They may also understand that the higher the height that they fall from, the harder they hit the ground.

Last, by the time children are 10 or 11 years old, they begin to understand the relationship between time and velocity. For instance, the faster they go down a slide or cross a horizontal ladder, the less time it takes and the more turns they get.

Formal Operations Period

By the time children are in the fifth or sixth grade, the formal operations period begins, lasting from the ages of 11 to 15 years. In contrast to the concrete operations period, where each problem was considered in isolation, children can begin to consider rationale for causes of situations. For example, if Anathalie falls from the horizontal ladder before she makes it across to the other side, observers might conclude that she wasn't strong enough, that the rungs were slippery, that she was pushed, or that she tried to climb faster than her coordination would allow. They are able to consider several possibilities as the solutions to problems. In addition, children in this stage can solve problems with logic and realize that there may be more than one reason why a conclusion was made.

Children With Special Needs

Along with the so-called normal developmental abilities of children, playground planners should also consider children who have special needs due to some physical, emotional, social, or intellectual disability. It is important to remember that they are more similar to children without special needs than they are different from them. In 1990, the civil rights of Americans with disabilities were recognized with the passage of the Americans with Disabilities Act (ADA). This act prohibits the discrimination of individuals based on disabilities. In relation to children, this act is interpreted to mean that children of all abilities should have the opportunity to play together.

In 2000, the Access Board (a federal agency responsible for the development of design guidelines for accessibility) submitted a plan to the Justice Department that determined how the ADA should be implemented in children's play environments. Basically, the plan states that children must have access to playgrounds and equipment as well as opportunities to play with children who do not have disabilities. However, the act says nothing about providing for the varying needs of children who have disabilities.

In developing a playground based on the developmental needs of children, it is necessary to provide a universal playground that will fit children of varying abilities, including those with disabilities. It is only when we put the equipment first and then try to adapt the children to the equipment that a problem occurs. It is easier to change equipment than change a child.

For a more complete understanding of the ADA guidelines, visit www.access-board. gov.

Matching Developmental Characteristics to Age Categories

Now that we've discussed different developmental characteristics, let's consider how those characteristics change specifically by age. As mentioned, children generally go through different developmental stages by chronological age. Although exceptions exist, four tables of developmental characteristics by age grouping (see tables 4.2 through 4.5) illustrate this progression. The categories of characteristics are physical, emotional, social, and intellectual. The age categories are 6 to 23 months, 2 to 3 years, 4 to 5 years, 5 to 6 years, 7 to 8 years, and 9 to 12 years.

Table 4.2

Physical Characteristics: Gross Motor Skills

Ages	Walking	Implication
6-23 months	Sits, stands, rolls over	Provide opportunities to do these activities.
2-3 years	Walks by hanging onto things	Provide places for stability.
4-5 years	Walks alone	Provide large, level area for walking.
5-6 years	Walks on things	Provide larger bases of support such as balance beams 1 foot (.3 meter) wide.
7-8 years	Walks on things that tip	Change the angle and length of the equipment; increase the length of the beam.
9-12 years	Walks on narrower items	Provide narrow pieces to walk on; increase the speed; have child walk backward or with partners.

Table 4.3

Emotional Characteristics: Egocentricity

Ages	Relates to others	Implication
6-23 months	Meets own needs	Allow child to play alone.
2-3 years	Plays alone but near others	Needs space to play alone but near others; needs repetition.
4-5 years	Plays alone but near others	Needs space to play alone but near others; needs repetition.
5-6 years	Plays near others but needs praise	Provide equipment on which child may have success.
7-8 years	Needs quality approval	Provide feedback when successful.
9-12 years	Becomes self-conscious	Provide for individual differences.

Table 4.4

Social Characteristics: Relationship With Others

Ages	Relates to others	Implications
6-23 months	Uninvolved, onlooker	Provide activities children can do by themselves.
2-3 years	Solitary—plays alone	Let children play with toys and play on equipment by themselves.
4-5 years	Parallel—plays near others but does not share	Let the children play alone near each other. Do not force them to share.
5-6 years	Associative—plays with others; begins to share. Play may not be similar. Plays in small groups	Let children play in small groups (two to four) to share objects and toys.
7-8 years	Associative—Plays in larger groups	Encourage children to play in groups of four to six.
9-12 years	Cooperative—Goals of play are shared and negotiated. Takes turns; shares common goals with others	Encourage team play.

Table 4.5

Intellectual Characteristics: Concrete to Abstract

Ages	Ability to make decisions	Implications
6-23 months	Dependent on adults	Observe child and make decisions.
2-3 years	Understands instructions in simple terms	Give one-word commands.
4-5 years	Understands implications of following instructions	Provide safety instructions.
5-6 years	Understands the amount of space it takes for a certain number of children to play together	For example, provide space for four children to play together.
7-8 years	Can decide the number of people needed to play in a larger space	Provide varying spaces for children to use for activities.
9-12 years	Considers rationale for decisions	Prevent children from playing on wet or broken equipment.

Ages 6 to 23 Months

Physical characteristics for children in this age group include the fact that they have just begun to turn over and move themselves. That was the major reason why the ASTM chose the 6-month level instead of birth for developing play equipment. By the time children are 2 years old, they have begun to roll, sit, crawl, creep, and stand.

Ages 2 to 3 Years

Children in this category are becoming more physically active as they have become upright. The ability to climb becomes evident, although once at a height, children may freeze at the idea of coming down. As mentioned, children at this age are egocentric, which means they want things for themselves and generally are unwilling to share with others. The result is that they will play with toys and equipment alone. They are also learning how to process things intellectually, but they tend to have short attention spans, so they need to be given small amounts of information and few directions at a time.

Ages 4 to 5 Years

Physically, children in this age group are developing the ability to perform locomotor actions. It is easier for them to control gross motor skills than fine motor skills. They can manipulate objects and descend a ladder with alternate feet. Emotionally, they are very egocentric and impatient. They need praise and approval. They enjoy repetition. Socially, they are learning to share. They are transitioning between individual and group play. Intellectually, they are eager to learn. In general, they lack fear. They are sorting out differences between what is real and make-believe.

Ages 5 to 6 Years

Physically, children in this age range experience rapid growth in the figure–ground concept. They also experience rapid growth in spatial relationships. Legs are short in relation to the trunk, which means their center of balance is still high. Emotionally, children this age are in awe of adults. Generally they will follow directions and they like the nearness of adults. However, they are also easily discouraged. Socially, they are still transitioning between individual and group play. There is little differentiation between friends of the same or opposite sex. They recognize that some children are more skilled than others. Intellectually, they have the power of some reasoning. Their memory is improving. Concepts of space, force, and time are developing.

Ages 7 to 8 Years

Physically, height and weight gains are strong and steady. The upper body is in good proportion to the lower body so balance is excellent. Emotionally, children in this age group are overactive, hurried, and careless. Even so, they desire approval and want to do things well. Socially, awareness of peers is increasing. Friendship is exclusive to the same sex. Intellectually, their memory sharpens. Their thought processes are like those of adults.

Ages 9 to 12 Years

Physically, individual differences become obvious. Strength develops rapidly. Girls tend to be taller and heavier than boys. Flexibility may decrease. Emotionally, self-consciousness appears and egocentricity decreases. Group and peer pressure increase.

Socially, definite groups form according to age and sex. Children this age seek peer approval. They are establishing values. Intellectually, they enjoy solving problems.

 Success Story

Manufacturers originally produced playground equipment for children aged 2 to 5 years and 5 to 12 years according to ASTM standards. But as professionals observed children under the age of 2, they realized that the safety concern needed to be extended to children of those ages. As a result, an ASTM subcommittee of child care providers; experts in child development; designers; physical educators; professional child care associations; and manufacturers of playground equipment, play equipment, and surfacing met for 10 years. The group considered characteristics of young children, statistics about injuries that occur in child care and home settings, and current child care settings.

As a result of those careful deliberations, a draft of the ASTM F2373 standard was produced in June 2005. The subcommittee then visited child care centers to observe the practicality of the standard and fine-tuned the document. It was finally published in December 2005 as ASTM F2373, *Standard Consumer Safety Performance Specification for Public Use Play Equipment for Children 6 Months Through 23 Months*. It provides manufacturers with standards to produce play equipment for places of public assembly, including early care and education facilities, parks, and playgrounds. In addition, such equipment is not classified as toys.

Products that fall under this standard are now being manufactured. However, if a slide is produced for this age range, the slide will be narrower than current slides to fit the narrow hips of a 6- to 23-month-old child so that children of this age will not be able to turn as they try to slide down the slide bed.

We look forward to the development of more age-appropriate equipment that fits the needs of children. This is an example of ways the industry and the public are responding to the needs of children by looking at current research to make playgrounds safer.

Summary

In this chapter, we described the physical, emotional, social, and intellectual characteristics of children. We encourage you to consider these characteristics when choosing the design, equipment, and surfacing of a play area. No single layout, piece of equipment, or type of fall surfacing will serve children of all different ages. We'll offer practical suggestions in chapter 5 to help you match equipment to children's needs.

In addition, think about ways to divide the settings even further. After all, a 6-month-old child is different from a 23-month-old child, a 2-year-old is different from a 5-year-old, and a 5-year-old is different from a 12-year-old. Your job is to meet their needs in the best manner possible rather than simply putting equipment outside and allowing them to figure out ways to use it that are beyond their abilities. How can you provide the best outdoor learning environment based on your knowledge of children's developmental abilities? That is your challenge.

Developmentally Appropriate Play Areas

Don't limit a child to your own learning,
for he was born in another time.

Rabbinical saying

⚠ Cautionary Tale

Three-year-old Artesia was excited that she was going to be attending a preschool located at her neighborhood elementary school. She liked the fact that she would be going to the same place as the older kids in the neighborhood. However, while the school district had remodeled the building to house the new preschool, they did nothing to renovate the outside play environment. After all, five years ago they had just spent $75,000 putting in a large composite play structure.

Finally, the first day of preschool arrived and Artesia was the first child into the classroom. At 10 o'clock in the morning, she and her new friends headed outside to play in the school yard. It wasn't long before they started climbing the large composite play structure. It was at that point that Artesia's first day at preschool abruptly came to an end as she fell off a high deck, breaking her arm.

During the course of the investigation that occurred when her parents sued the school district, it was found that the company that sold the large composite structure had designed the equipment for children aged 5 to 12 years. In fact, the playground had no equipment appropriate for children aged 2 to 5 years. Further, there was no signage to indicate who the equipment was intended for, so the preschool teacher allowed the children to play on the equipment. Inappropriate design, lack of signage, and lack of supervisor training resulted in an injury that could have been avoided.

When it comes to equipment, one size does not fit the needs of all children. Rather, equipment should match the developmental skills and abilities of children. In this chapter, we'll consider the design of play areas for children aged 6 to 23 months, 2 to 5 years, and 5 to 12 years, both in the school setting and in the park setting. Finally, we'll discuss how universal design relates to planning for children of all abilities.

Ages 6 to 23 Months

Children aged 6 to 23 months are just beginning to gain mobility. In addition, they are starting to learn about their environment but have little understanding of cause and effect. Thus, they may know that a surface is hot, but they may not understand that putting their bare feet on a hot surface will cause a burn. As a result of all of the physical, emotional, social, and intellectual development that occurs in children at this age, it is important to provide a setting that is safe for children to creep, crawl, walk, and fall on.

To help develop the physical abilities of creeping, crawling, and walking, we suggest that soft surfacing (such as rubber tiles or poured-in-place materials) be provided for pathways from the door of the building to other surfaces in the play setting. It seems inappropriate for children who are learning to walk to use cement or asphalt to get to their play areas when they are so prone to falling. The extra expense of soft surfacing will decrease the severity of an injury when a child falls and will also decrease the required surfacing maintenance. Since the use of the play settings for children of that age is usually controlled, the surfacing will last for many years and offset the original cost.

It would be wise to have a separate play area for children in this developmental category. It is no more appropriate for children aged 6 to 23 months to play on equipment designed for children aged 2 to 5 years than it is for children aged 2 to 5 years to play on equipment designed for children aged 5 to 12 years. Children at the lower end of the age range of each of those categories are the same size as children at the lower end of the next category. For example, a 6-month-old does not have the foot size to fit into the shoes of a 2-year-old. A 2-year-old does not have the grip strength of a 5-year-old. Thus, even though the children may want to use equipment designed for older kids, it is not appropriate. Adults who supervise children need to heed signs and labels provided by manufacturers, child care centers, schools, and parks that inform the public about the age ranges appropriate for the equipment.

Children in this age category need a play area large enough to meet the guidelines of the NAEYC. The area should have at least 75 square feet (22.9 square meters) for each child playing outside at any one time. There should be opportunities for children to creep, crawl, and walk. In addition, the play area should have space for children to manipulate objects, a separate space for ball activities, and a separate space for manipulating objects such as cars and trucks (those kinds of objects should be used away from playground equipment where children may fall).

Choose equipment for this age range based on the physical, emotional, social, and intellectual abilities of the children. Children aged 6 to 23 months are just beginning to move. They are able to turn over by themselves, crawl, and creep, and they are beginning to stand and walk.

Shade: A Universal Need

Children of all ages and abilities need shade, so it must be provided on playgrounds at child care centers, schools, and parks. Shade prevents the children, the equipment, and the surfacing from getting too hot.

The NAEYC recommends that one-third of the area be shaded. To protect children in this age category, we encourage you to acquire trees or structures for shade. Consider asking board members or community organizations to donate trees that are already several years old, because saplings take too long to grow tall enough to provide suitable shade.

Shade is especially important for children under 2 years of age, who have more sensitive skin, wear less clothing, and often have bare feet. If the play area has any dark rubber surfacing, be sure to keep it cool by providing shade. Children in this age group spend most of their time on the ground and might suffer burns from contact with hot surfacing.

In terms of social skills, children at this age generally play alone, responding to simple suggestions by adults. Because this is a time of curiosity, it is important to provide sensory stimulation. It may be appropriate to provide a sand-and-water table or a sand box. You may want a place to put up or take down a wading pool. You may also want a swing for children to increase their vestibular stimulation. In addition, consider a slide.

It is more appropriate for children in this age category to have space to move in and objects to manipulate than it is to have what we traditionally think of as playground equipment. The ASTM standard F2373, which should be used to select play equipment for this age category, even refers to *play* equipment rather than *playground* equipment.

The arrangement of the space may be more crucial than the kind of equipment provided. It may not be necessary to provide much equipment at all—just space to move in and perhaps toys to manipulate.

Ages 2 to 5 Years

The ASTM standard and CPSC guidelines category of ages 2 to 5 years can be further broken into two groups: ages 2 to 3 and ages 4 to 5. The developmental differences between ages are so great during these years that it makes sense to separate them into categories that emphasize the developmental changes. A 2-year-old is very different from a 5-year-old.

First, we'll look at some suggestions for 2- and 3-year-old children.

- Children this age are crawling and developing opposition of hands and legs, so consider offering several different crawl tubes in different places around the play area.
- They're learning to jump down, so include low elements for jumping.
- They have not yet learned to share equipment with others, so offer some stand-alone equipment that you can explain using short, simple instructions. For example, you might tell them to walk up the steps one at a time, or go down the slide one person at a time.
- They still like to play with equipment, but not alone (i.e., parallel play). Offer equipment such as a sandbox and sand toys, which allow children to be in the sandbox together playing with their own toys.

Children aged 4 to 5 years are developing other locomotor abilities. They need repetition to reinforce physical skills. They can jump up and are beginning to hop, so they need space to develop those abilities. Even though they are eager to learn, they lack fear. Therefore, it is not a good idea to provide areas to jump from that are too high. Consider including the following equipment:

- A balance beam helps children develop a sense of balance. A portable beam with more than one section could be arranged so that children can increase the distance they balance using different fundamental motor actions on the beam.

- Short ladders reinforce children's abilities to descend a ladder with alternate feet.

- A sandbox allows children to begin to share objects with one another as they transition from individual to group play (see figure 5.1).

- A large structure such as a house or boat allows children to explore the difference between real and make-believe. However, some themed equipment (such as a re-creation of Noah's ark) can actually inhibit the imagination. At this age, children might want to be sailors one day but firefighters the next, and providing only a boat inhibits the ability to "fight fires." Instead, a cloth draped over a clothesline can serve as an office, a house, a barn, a hiding place, or whatever else children think of.

It may also be useful to have tables for painting, reading, or game playing. The areas may be designated for a period of time and then periodically changed. However, you want to avoid succotash syndrome—simply dumping materials in the play area does not provide an organized approach to using the space. This approach would probably not be used in the indoor learning environment and therefore should not be used outside, either. Think of an outdoor play area as a learning environment. What children learn depends on the available materials, people, organization, and ways they are treated. They'll benefit from consistent application of learning principles.

A play area for this age group also needs a place for storing loose items such as manipulative materials and tricycles. If a trike path is available, it should be located away from the playground equipment. Paths can have curves, changes of pitch, and

© Jim West

Figure 5.1 A sandbox lets children learn to share as they play together.

Figure 5.2 A play area designed for chldren ages 2 to 5 should offer challenges for everyone.

smooth and rough areas. Children should be taught to use bicycle helmets, to take them off when using playground equipment, and put those items away when they are finished using them.

Children in this age group need opportunities to develop their climbing abilities. Try to have equipment for children with different levels of ability (see figure 5.2). In addition, consider providing swings, because they develop vestibular stimulation of the ears. However, remember that swings take up a lot of space and require much supervision for two children per bay. (A bay is the area between two uprights of a swing. There should be only two swings in this area.)

Child Care Centers

Most states recommend that 75 feet (22.9 meters) of space be allocated per child in play areas at child care facilities. Thus, the size of the space depends on the number of children who will use the area. Not all of the children in the center will use the space at the same time. In addition, the size of the materials is important—for example, is the space better served by swings or climbing equipment? Because swings require a large use zone and take up more space, perhaps teachers could take the children on a field trip to use swings in a nearby park instead.

Of course, the child care center will provide separate spaces for children who are aged 6 to 23 months and 2 to 5 years. Hopefully there will also be an opportunity to provide separate spaces for children aged 2 to 3 years and children aged 4 to 5 years.

For children aged 6 to 23 months old, see the recommendations in the previous section on children in this age group.

For 4- to 5-year-olds, offer space for performing locomotor actions, places for climbing, and space for manipulating objects. In this manner, the facilities fulfill the idea that the outdoor environment follows the principles of the indoor environment and is indeed a learning environment. In addition, there should be fencing with a gate that only adults can open. This fencing should keep the children in the play area away from vehicles (see figure 5.3).

Elementary Schools

If a child care center is located at an elementary school, the children should not be allowed to play on the elementary school equipment, which is designed for children aged 5 to 12 years. A separate area should be designated for preschool children following the principles noted earlier. In addition, signage should be provided to inform adults about the two different playground settings, including age designations and a notification of the importance of adult supervision.

Figure 5.3 A fence can protect children from vehicles nearby.

Ages 5 to 12 Years

Play areas for children in elementary school should be developmentally different from those for younger children. Children in this age group are bigger and more skillful in the ways they use their bodies. They used to enjoy books full of pictures, but now they are beginning to like books with words. By the same token, kindergartners may enjoy sliding down a 6-foot (1.8-meter) slide, but once they reach sixth grade, they prefer the challenge of a 12-foot (3.6-meter) horizontal ladder that has different angles, curves, and distances between handholds. Thus, in designing playgrounds for children of these ages, we should increase difficulty in the skills to be used by choosing equipment to meet those needs.

Within the elementary school setting, it is reasonable to provide several different areas for play equipment because, as we've stated before, one size does not fit all. One option is to divide the areas by grade. Some schools have chosen kindergarten through grade 2, grades 3 through 4, and grades 5 through 6 as categories. Others have selected kindergarten through grade 1, grades 2 through 3, and grades 4 through 6.

- For children in kindergarten, consider providing areas to continue to develop locomotor actions, climbing, and arm strength. Opportunities to descend a ladder with alternate feet and changes of direction are helpful.

- For grades 1 and 2, continue to develop upper-body strength by making horizontal ladders a little longer and higher. Opportunities to develop understanding of level, range, direction, pathway, time, and force should be included in the design.

- For grades 3 and 4, the upper body is developing well in relation to the lower body, and balance is a good thing to continue to develop. Areas that encourage socialization with peers will be welcomed, as will opportunities to make decisions.

- For grades 5 and 6, strength develops rapidly, and children enjoy solving problems; thus equipment that allows them to practice those activities would be a good idea. In addition, some playgrounds have added a fitness area.

The elementary school staff must decide how to divide the play areas based on rationale that they can defend. They should be based on the developmental needs of children. For example, school officials might choose to have a fitness area to support the physical education area. This area might include playground equipment that focuses on the development of gross motor skills.

Once the decisions have been made, the elementary school staff must create policies and signage to inform the public about those decisions. For example, it may be wise to indicate that composite structures or horizontal ladders should be used in one direction only. Consider placing arrows of contrasting colors on the equipment. Signs are particularly important so that those who use the equipment when school is not in session are aware of the age appropriateness of the play areas. Also, division of space makes it easier to supervise the children. Signs indicate the ages or grades of children who will use the equipment. During school, signs divide the supervision responsibilities among individuals. After school, they tell adults where various age groups should play.

In addition, someone needs to teach the children how to use the equipment. Just as equipment will not supervise the children, it won't demonstrate appropriate use or inform them of the expectations adults have for its use. Just because adults know how to use the equipment does not mean that children do. If adults do not know how to use the equipment, they should refer to the manufacturer's instructions.

Staff should teach proper equipment use at the beginning of every school year, and it's a good idea to review the information in the spring. In addition, consider installing new equipment in the fall rather than later in the year in order to teach the children how to use it along with the rest of the equipment.

Another thing schools should consider is connecting playground equipment with the curriculum. In the indoor learning environment, a curriculum is determined for various subjects such as math, spelling, art, music, and physical education. Then playground items may be chosen for the children to manipulate in order to learn the concepts.

For example, let's say children are going to learn about the Piagetian principle of conservation in relation to the kinds of objects that can fit into a space 12 inches (30.5 centimeters) in length. The children are given six 2-inch (5-centimeter) yellow pieces, four 3-inch (7.6-centimeter) orange pieces, three 4-inch (10-centimeter) red pieces, and two 6-inch (15-centimeter) blue pieces. By manipulating those pieces they learn that different combinations of the pieces all fit into a 12-inch (30.5-centimeter) space. By the same token, children may learn about concepts of different shapes in art; concepts of more, less, the same, and counting in math; ideas about gravity in science; and various locomotor actions in physical education. Equipment can be chosen to help children learn those concepts.

In addition, you may want to consider installing the equipment so that it is spaced out around the play area in order to teach younger children how to use the equipment one piece at a time. Then, if you have a good relationship with the park district, perhaps they would consider putting the same equipment together in some kind of composite structure at a park. That would give the children a different experience in each place and they would have learned how to use the equipment at school before using it at the park. This kind of separation may not be as important for older children as it is for younger children, but it may also prevent injuries since it spreads children around the playground rather than grouping so many on composite structures.

Kindergarten Through Grade 2 (Ages 5 to 7)

Areas for these grades should include opportunities for children to climb, balance, and share. These children have just graduated from parallel play and are learning to share with their peers, so equipment should enhance their opportunities to play with each other. Overhead ladders should be short and close to the ground, not much higher than 7-year-olds can reach.

Also, make sure you purchase items that students will actually use. For example, a recent study indicated that young school-aged children don't use tic-tac-toe boards in play areas (Bowers, 2003). In addition, who uses steering wheels, and how often are they used? Be sure that they are not placed next to equipment that 12-year-olds may use if the area is designed for children aged 5 to 12 years. Steering wheels must be closed rather than open so children cannot break their arms when the wheels are twisted (see figure 5.4).

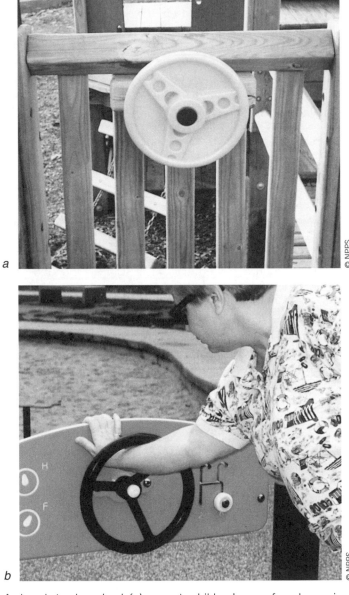

Figure 5.4 A closed steering wheel *(a)* prevents children's arms from becoming trapped within. An open wheel *(b)* is more dangerous.

Grades 3 and 4 (Ages 8 to 9)

Areas for these grades should include opportunities for more climbing; opportunities for increased balance; and increased lengths of horizontal ladders and changes of distances between bars, changes of angles, and changes of shapes that are less predictable than straight horizontal bars. However, do not change two factors at once—change either the shape or the distance so as not to increase the challenge too drastically.

Grades 5 and 6 (Ages 10 to 12)

These areas should include opportunities to develop upper-arm strength, balance, and overall physical fitness. Also include opportunities for interaction among children. These children need increased challenges. Consider longer horizontal ladders, parallel bars, and opportunities to climb and balance (see figure 5.5). Very little equipment is designed to provide challenges for this age group, and more needs to be developed.

Figure 5.5 A horizontal ladder helps children develop upper-arm strength.

Park Play Areas

Parks should provide play areas for children in three separate areas: for children aged 6 to 23 months, for children aged 2 to 5 years, and for children aged 5 to 12 years. If they do not have the space or finances to provide areas for three groups, at the very least they should consider providing equipment for two age groups: ages 6 to 23 months and ages 2 to 5 years. Younger children tend to use equipment more frequently than older children and they tend to be supervised more carefully by adults.

Many of the concepts discussed about ways to choose equipment for child care or school sections should be applied to park settings. For instance, the design should reflect thoughtful consideration of the types of developmental abilities and skills of children that officials want to promote. Therefore, the selection process is based on developmental needs rather than predetermined designs of the manufacturers.

As at elementary schools, the areas should have signage to indicate age levels and the importance of adult supervision. Also, the areas should be physically separated. Then, it is the responsibility of the adults to take children to the appropriate settings. When adults are supervising children in more than one age category, they will have to decide who gets to play first and have children take turns playing—only in the appropriate areas, of course.

Ages 6 to 23 Months

Areas for children this age should include grass, a smooth area for walking (perhaps tiled), a place to use toys, and a space for sand play or manipulation of objects. It doesn't have to be large, but it should be fenced and separate from the area for children aged 2 to 5 years. Currently, swings for this age group are not available, but the recent ASTM standard F2373 (published in December 2005) provides manufacturers with the information needed to produce play equipment for very young children. When such swings become available, consider offering them.

Ages 2 to 5 Years

Children these ages need a large amount of space, but the area needs to be fenced. It might include a place to balance, a sand area, some sliding activities, climbing equipment, and tot swings. Parks have space that schools do not have, and thus swings may be more appropriate here than at schools. In addition, the ratio of supervisors to children is likely to be better at a park, where parents typically supervise their own children, than at school. The same is true for slides.

Ages 5 to 12 Years

Areas for children these ages might include pieces that are similar to those at schools but are arranged differently. Maybe some of the equipment that is separated at schools might be joined together in the park setting. If children learn to do the activity at school, then the actions become a new challenge when the equipment is placed together in a new configuration or is arranged so that children may make choices of access or egress. The area should also be fenced in from parking lots.

Play Areas for Children of All Abilities

As we apply current information about children with special needs to the playground environment, it is critical that we provide an opportunity for those children to

- get from the edge of the playground to the equipment;
- be able to play with other children; and
- get from the equipment to the edge of the playground and into a parking lot or building.

If possible, provide equipment that adapts the playground for children with special needs in that specific neighborhood. Think about the kind of disabilities that children in the neighborhood might have and ways to accommodate that particular disability. Remember, in elementary school, the child will be a resident for six or seven years. If a child is wheelchair bound, then some ramping may be necessary. See the ADA Access Board Web site (www.access-board.gov), where the specifics of this application are provided in the *ADA Accessibility Guidelines for Play Areas*.

Ideally, play areas would go beyond those guidelines and accommodate specific children for a period of time. For example, it might be appropriate to provide auditory cues among the equipment such as chimes, bells, and pipes; visual cues such as braille; foot cues where changes of direction or changes of height are necessary; railings; or gardens with plants that provide various scents. As the children grow older, the play area may need to be adjusted for younger children with other disabilities. The Area Education Agencies in the state of Iowa survey communities in order to determine

 Success Story

When planning their playground, the personnel at Cedar Heights Elementary School in Cedar Falls, Iowa, paid attention to the developmental needs of the children at the school. They knew that one playground wouldn't fit everyone, so they developed different areas for children in the kindergarten and first grade, second and third grades, and fourth through sixth grades.

In addition, they created a general fitness area based on concepts in the school curriculum, including art, mathematics, physical education, and science. For example, in physical education, students in kindergarten and grade 1 enhance their body control and balance; students in grades 2 and 3 work on their balance, agility, and flexibility; and students in grades 4 through 6 increase their strength and flexibility. The division of spaces has also meant that the supervisors are separated.

As a result of this careful attention to children's needs, there have been no serious injuries since the playground was installed. The children love the choice and separation of equipment, which meets their needs and challenges their abilities.

whether children with disabilities will be attending school. They also indicate what disabilities will need accommodation.

If a town is large enough to have several schools or parks, it may be possible to provide specific accommodations for children with visual problems in one area and accommodations for children with auditory problems in another (figure 5.6). Each area should allow children to get to the play area in order to play with children who do not have disabilities.

Summary

We must develop playgrounds to match the ages and developmental abilities of the children who will use them. Most play environments should group children into three main categories (6 to 23 months, 2 to 5 years, and 5 to 12 years), but it's possible to divide ages even further. In addition, playground designs might be influenced by school curricula or geographic environments.

Designs must meet the needs of all children, which means there's a lot to consider. When planning for children aged 6 to 23 months, what objects can we provide to help them creep, crawl, stand, walk, and balance? For children aged 2 to 5 years, what opportunities can we provide for them to jump and hop? For older children, how can we help them develop dynamic balance and upper-arm strength, not to mention the ability to cooperate and compete with others? In park settings, how do we extend the challenges offered in school play areas? And how do we accommodate children with various disabilities?

These and other considerations must factor into the design of playgrounds. It's a complex challenge, but we must be willing to provide the best possible outdoor learning environments for our children.

Fall Surfacing

*It's a matter of physics. The higher the fall
and harder the surface, the worse the injury.*

E. Henzy

Andrew was a happy 5-year-old looking forward to his first day of kindergarten. However, his exciting first day at school was not to be. The weekend before starting school, his family took him to the park to enjoy one last day of unstructured play. At the park, he ran to the old monkey bars that had been at the park forever (see figure 6.1). As he climbed up the 9-foot (2.7-meter) piece of equipment, he lost his grip and fell down through the bars.

The interlocking bars were one reason that the CPSC had put out an alert in the 1980s to warn consumers of the dangers of this type of equipment. However, it wasn't hitting the bars that produced Andrew's major injury, although they did contribute to more than 200 bruises all over his body. Rather, it was the bolt sticking up in the ground, unprotected by adequate surfacing, that did the major damage. The impact of the bolt and the hard surface drove Andrew's jaw back into his head. Luckily, he survived this trip to the playground, and 18 surgeries later he is a handsome young man and a national playground safety advocate.

More than 70 percent of all injuries that occur on the playground involve falls, and the majority of those injuries involve falls to unsafe surfaces. That is why it is crucial to understand the role that adequate and appropriate surfacing materials play in the prevention of injuries. Of equal importance, however, is an understanding of the role that equipment height plays not only in injury prevention but in providing challenging stimulation at minimal risk of injury.

In this chapter, we'll explore research involving the height of playground equipment and its relationship with both injury and play value. We'll also investigate the relationship between height and surfacing materials under and around play equipment. We'll explain how surfacing materials are tested, and we'll examine the role of surfacing under and around play equipment.

Height and Playground Equipment

Height has always been associated with playground structures. A quick review of slides, swings, and climbing equipment from the early 1900s reveals that many ranged from 12 feet (3.7 meters) to 20 feet (6.1 meters) off the ground (see figure 6.2). As Rivkin points out, "The great metal structures of playgrounds from previous eras, the tall slides, the high climbers, the 20-foot [6.1-meter] swings, create unreasonable hazards for young children. Falls from these structures are long falls in which the child's speed increases, such that the resulting sudden stop on the ground is very forceful" (1995, p. 49).

Since the NEISS (see chapter 1 for more on this organization) first began collecting statistics on playground injuries, falls have been cited as the major contributing factor to injuries. Yet, despite the growing body of research that connects equipment height and surfacing materials to injury, many playgrounds in the United States still contain playground equipment over the height of 8 feet (2.4 meters) and inappropriate surfac-

© NPPS

Figure 6.1 Climbing equipment with interlocking bars can be dangerous.

ing materials underneath. To learn why these conditions exist in the United States, it would be beneficial to look at two aspects of equipment height. The first aspect involves what we know about equipment height in relation to injuries. The second aspect involves the relationship between equipment height and play value.

Height and Injury Patterns

Early playground designers rarely considered the relationship between height and injury or play value. Rather, in many cases, they tried to imitate what had been lost in the natural environment (e.g., the ability to climb trees, barn lofts, and so on) by re-creating it in the artificial environment of the playground.

However, even during the early years, a concern about injuries caused by falls from high equipment became a concern. As playgrounds expanded, falls and injuries became common. Hard surfacing, such as asphalt or grass, was beginning to replace dirt as a ground cover and serious injuries were resulting (Frost et al., 2004, p. 59).

The first recorded lawsuit involving playground equipment and surfacing was in 1915, when parents of a child sued the school board of Tacoma, Washington, over an injury that their child sustained from a fall from a swing (Frost et al., 2004). Things apparently went from bad to worse, since in 1917, Henry Curtis, one of the first nationally recognized experts in recreation facilities design, declared that U.S. playgrounds were in a "miserable state" (p. 121). He mentioned that the "surfaces were covered with pieces of bricks, piles of ashes, and gullied by rain" (p. 59).

Rather than concentrating on the surfacing materials as a culprit in the rising injury rate, concerned professionals decided that perhaps the height of the equipment was

© Susan Hudson

Figure 6.2 Playground equipment of the early 1900s often created unreasonable hazards for children.

the major factor. As a result, in 1928, the PRAA published one of the first height guidelines in their book, *Play Areas: Their Design and Equipment*. Specifically, the PRAA advocated that the height of play equipment be limited, although no height specification was given.

As discussed in chapter 1, the first playground standard of any kind was published in 1931 by the NRA (formerly the PRAA). Within this standard, the NRA suggested that slides be limited to a height of 8 feet (2.4 meters) and that swings for younger children be limited to a height of 6 feet (1.8 meters). However, this standard was neither well known nor well publicized. Equipment heights were left to the creative ideas of designers and the public, who seemed to think the higher, the better.

It wasn't until 1974 that the first definitive study linked equipment height to injury. Elayne Butwinick, a member of the NRPA's national task force on playground equipment safety standards, evaluated 30 public school and recreation playgrounds. Analyzing 1,100 equipment accidents that occurred at these sites, she found that almost all accidents (86 percent) on climbing equipment involved falls from the equipment. In a few cases, where these falls occurred on asphalt or pavement, the result was death. Falls were also a major contributor in 63 percent of slide injuries (Butwinick, 1974).

Theodora Sweeney further endorsed the need for limiting the height of equipment in her petition to the CPSC in 1974. In her petition, Sweeney noted that the playground industry had no height restrictions. In a rebuke to the industry, she stated that it appeared that profit rather than safety was the major concern of the industry, because "the bigger and higher the equipment, the more costs, and the greater the profit" (Sweeney, 1974, p. 4).

In 1976, the CPSC asked the NRPA to develop a safety standard for playground equipment. Instead of limiting height, the NRPA standard called only for protective barriers 38 inches (1 meter) high to be placed on equipment between the heights of 8 and 12 feet (2.4 and 3.7 meters).

Today, there are still no limits on the height of the equipment, although falls from height still remain the most cited factor in all playground injuries (Tinsworth and McDonald, 2001). Further, all the hospitalized injuries in a study by Tinsworth and McDonald resulted from falls (2001).

Several research studies in the 1990s and early 2000s also point to the increased probability of injury with increased heights. A 1996 study in New Zealand evaluated the effectiveness of the height and surfacing requirements of the New Zealand standard for playgrounds and playground equipment (Chalmers et al., 1996). The data for this study came from 300 children, aged 14 years or younger, who had been injured by falls to the surface from playground equipment. Over one-third of these children (110) received medical attention for their injuries. The greatest number of falls occurred to children between the ages of 5 and 9 years (220 cases), followed by children between the ages of 10 and 12 years (42 cases) and children up to 4 years old (38 cases). Data were also collected concerning the gender, age, height, weight, and body part to hit first of the injured children, as well as the date, time, place of occurrence, type of equipment, height of fall, type of surface, particle size, depth, and retention of loose fill materials.

The findings indicated that the probability of injury increased with the height of the equipment. Specifically, a marked increase in injury occurred when children fell 1.5 to 2 meters (5 to 6.5 feet). This increase was similar for both impact-absorbing and non-impact-absorbing surfaces. However, the most startling finding was that falls from heights in excess of 1.5 meters (5 feet) increased the risk of injury four times that of falls from 1.5 meters or less. Not surprising, it was concluded that a 45 percent reduction of injuries requiring emergency room treatment could be achieved by reducing fall height from the current maximum height standard of 2.5 meters (8 feet) to 1.5 meters (5 feet).

A similar investigation occurred in the United Kingdom in 1997 (Mott et al., 1997). In this study, researchers looked at the correlation between different types of playground surfaces and various heights of equipment found in Cardiff, Wales. They analyzed 330 children's hospital records at the emergency department of the Cardiff Royal Infirmary for the summers of 1992 and 1993. The conclusions were that "the height of the equipment correlated significantly with the number of fractures ($p <$ 0.005) from falls. . . . Further, it was stated that the data suggest that the proposed raising of the maximum fall height from 2.5 m [8.2 feet] to 3.0 m [9.84 feet] in Europe is worrying" (p. 1876).

Yet another similar conclusion concerning height and injury was found in a case-control study conducted at the Hospital for Sick Children in Toronto (Macarthur et al., 2000). The researchers reviewed the cases of 126 children injured in falls from playground equipment from 1995 to 1996. Injuries were classified either as severe (predominately fractures) or minor (primarily facial lacerations). The median fall height for severe injuries was 199 centimeters (6.5 feet) and 160 centimeters (5.2 feet) for minor injuries. The findings showed that children falling from heights greater than 150 centimeters (4.9 feet) were twice as likely to receive severe injuries as those falling from a lower height. The conclusion of the study was that height of fall was an important risk factor for severe injuries due to falls from playground equipment.

A fourth study, conducted in Montreal, provides even more data supporting the linkage between height and injury. In this study, the heights of equipment at 102 randomly selected public playgrounds were recorded. In addition, injuries at two children's hospitals in Montreal were also reviewed and analyzed. The study found that equipment over 2.4 meters (8 feet) tall had close to three times the injury rate of equipment under that height. This finding led them to conclude that the height for equipment should not exceed 2 meters (6.5 feet) (Laforest et al., 2001, p. 9).

Recent studies also point to the severity of injuries resulting from falls off equipment. A 2005 study by Fiissel, Pattison, and Howard examined major and minor fractures received on the playground. Fractures were classified as major if they required reduction and minor if they did not. The study revealed that fractures from equipment falls were 391 times more likely to require reduction than were fractures from standing-height falls. The authors' conclusions were that "major fractures were strongly associated with falls from playground equipment, whereas minor fractures come from both play equipment and standing height falls" (p. 337). The authors recommended that efforts to prevent major fractures should target playground equipment and the impact-absorbing surface beneath it.

Finally, a study in Australia by Clapperton and Cassell (2005) found that nearly 90 percent of playground injuries were caused by falls. Further, these injuries accounted for more than 50 percent of hospital-treated injuries over the study period. Citing other studies in Victoria and elsewhere, the authors stated that there are "strong associations between playground fall injury (and arm fractures) and equipment-related risk factors (height of the equipment, the height of the fall. . .) and surface-related risk factors (surface impact attenuation, the use of inappropriate surface material; surfacing not meeting recommended standards; and inappropriate undersurfacing substrate material)" (p. 2). Based on their findings, the authors recommended that consumers seriously consider the research evidence that shows that the critical free-fall height for arm fractures from playground equipment is 1.5 meters (4.9 feet).

It is becoming clear from these and other studies around the world that height and surfacing play a major role in contributing to playground injuries. However, there has been great reluctance on the part of government and regulatory officials in the United States to limit the height of play equipment. Perhaps the reason lies in yet another question: Does height increase the play value of equipment?

Height and Play Value

Children love to climb. However, for many children, especially those under 5 years old, it is not climbing up that is the problem; it is coming down. While small children learn the locomotion that is involved in climbing up, their other developmental abilities of balance and fear may not have progressed at the same rate (see chapter 5). The result is that many young children aged 2 to 4 years climb to the top of equipment meant for children aged 5 to 12 years, only to stand on the platform and cry. In a recent study that explored the relation of height to play value, the researchers observed that toddlers and preschool children became frightened when they reached the top of high platforms. Their play behavior became frozen, and in one case, "a child began crying and stamping his feet until a parent came and helped him down from the equipment" (Frost et al., 2004, p. 78). The researchers noted that such behavior was not observed with equipment at lower heights.

Fear in most young children occurs in a predictable sequence, depending upon the interaction of nature (genes) and nurture (learned responses) within a given environment (Marks, 1987). Children around the world begin to experience fear at about 6 months of age (Frost et al., 2004). These fears include those of heights as children become more active in the environment. Walking also enhances fear of heights (Bertenthal, Campos, and Caplovitz, 1983). Further studies (Campos, Bertenthal, and Kermonian, 1992; Gottlieb 1983, 1991) showed that locomotor experience was at the root of a wariness of heights. The researchers concluded that this movement experience was a better predictor than age of wariness of heights.

As children begin to walk upright, they become more likely to fall. This natural occurrence has both positive and negative effects depending on the child's ability to successfully navigate across the room and the adults' responses to the falls that occur. The more powerful the emotions emitted by the adults in relation to falls, the greater the likelihood that children may internalize fear of heights (Campos, Bertenthal, and Kermonian, 1992). As researchers have stated (Frost, 2001; Frost, Wortham, and Reifel, 2001), the logical implication from this observation is that "children must be allowed to assume reasonable risks in order to develop cognitive and locomotor skills, yet be protected from extreme hazards due to their immaturity" (Frost, Wortham, and Reifel, 2001, p. 58). Thus, for small children, the absence of heights is not a solution. However, the heights should be reasonable. That is why the NPPS has advocated that the height of the equipment for preschool children be set at 6 feet (1.8 meters) or under.

But should there be a height restriction for older children? To answer this question, we need to examine the relationship between height and play value for older children. In a study published in 2004, Frost et al. found three reasons why children climb on play equipment.

First, they climb to explore. The researchers found that younger children climb with little purpose in mind; they simply climb in order to reach the highest point possible. In contrast, when experiencing a piece of equipment for the first time, older children generally climb up and down and then attempt to find more challenging ways to climb on the equipment.

Second, they climb for a purpose. In other words, children climb to reach a play event like a slide. In these instances, climbing is merely a means to an end, not part of the play experience.

Third, they climb as part of the play experience. For instance, "one child spoke of climbing 'to outer space' while climbing a rocket slide, and then said, 'I'm going to outer space and driving'" (p. 75). This is an example of incorporating various elements—the climb up, the play equipment (rocket slide), and imagination—into a specific play experience.

Clearly, climbing to heights can be part of the play experience. But does height enhance the play experience? Referring back to chapter 1 and the discussion about the difference between risk and challenge, it was stated that challenge or the play value of the play experience is derived from increased task complexity demanded of the child. Climbing an 8-foot (2.4-meter) ladder versus a 6-foot (1.8-meter) ladder does not significantly increase the complexity of the task. Likewise, sliding down a 10-foot (3-meter) slide versus an 8-foot (2.4-meter) slide does not increase the complexity of the task. However, as shown in the previous section, additional height does significantly increase the risk of injury. As a result, we contend that simply making play equipment taller instead of making it more innovative and challenging does not add play value. It simply increases the probability of injury because in order to increase the challenge, children will misuse the equipment.

Misuse of Equipment

Children often use equipment in ways other than those intended by the manufacturers, climbing up the outside of tube slides, bailing out of swings, and racing up and down on equipment chasing one another (see figure 6.3). As a result, it is easy to predict or even expect a serious injury to occur from a fall off equipment over the height of 6 feet (1.8 meters). This is especially true in settings where adult supervision is inadequate.

Role of Adult Supervision

From general observation, it may be surmised that younger children (under the age of 4 years old) are more closely supervised than older children. Of course, this supervision can also be questionable at times (see chapters 2 and 3 for more details). Many adults have little understanding of the inherent risks involved in placing small children on equipment that is too large for their abilities. While adults may be present with

Figure 6.3   Children don't always use equipment as intended.

older children, the typical supervision is generally indirect observation. That is, adults may be engaged in conversations with other adults, reading newspapers, or occupied in some other activity, infrequently glancing over at the children.

Lack of adequate supervision is another reason to limit equipment height. If equipment over 6 feet (1.8 meters) tall is present, more active supervision is needed. Simply providing high equipment for general use in public playgrounds without demanding adequate supervision is setting up a situation for a possible death or debilitating injury.

Relationship Between Height and Surfacing

Play equipment height and surfacing are directly correlated with regard to injury. Simply put, the higher children are on equipment, the harder they fall. This relationship led both the CPSC and ASTM to develop guidelines and standards for surfacing under and around playground equipment.

In the development of these guidelines and standards, two elements are measured: acceleration from height and the ability of the surface to absorb the impact, or impact attenuation.

Critical Height

The higher the drop point is located, the greater the speed (acceleration) of an object as it hits the ground. Table 6.1 shows the speed of a fall from the heights of 3 feet (.9 meter), 9 feet (2.7 meters), and 12 feet (3.7 meters). We have all seen crash tests where test dummies, protected by car frames and air bags, crash into brick walls at varying speeds. Now think of a child's head, unprotected, hitting a hard surface at 9.4 miles (15.1 kilometers) per hour, 16.4 miles (26.2 kilometers) per hour, or 18.8 miles (30.3 kilometers) per hour.

Table 6.1

Speed of Fall Heights

Fall height of equipment	Distance traveled per second	Miles per hour
3 ft (.9 m)	13.8 ft (4.2 m) per second	9.4 mph (15.1 km/h)
9 ft (2.7 m)	24 ft (7.3 m) per second	16.4 mph (26.2 km/h)
12 ft (3.7 m)	27.7 ft (8.4 m) per second	18.8 mph (30.3 km/h)

The formula for acceleration from height is as follows:

Final velocity = $\sqrt{\text{initial velocity} + 2 \text{(acceleration)(distance)}}$

Based on this scientific evidence, the CPSC and ASTM worked together to determine how they could reduce the likelihood of head injuries in falls. Gathering information from other sources (such as fall-related information from the U.S. Army paratroop corps), the ASTM devised a testing protocol, called F1292, for surfacing.

Two measurements are taken in this testing procedure. The first measurement involves the impact of the head on the surface. Researchers examine whether the peak deceleration of the head during impact exceeds the threshold of 200 times the acceleration due to gravity. This is recognized as 200 *g*. A life-threatening injury would not be expected to occur under 200 *g*. The second measurement examines not only the deceleration but also the time it takes for the deceleration to occur (for the impact to be absorbed by the surface). This value is called the head injury criteria (HIC). If the HIC is less than 1,000, the impact injury is not believed to be life threatening.

Critical height is simply the term used by the CPSC to describe the fall height that upon impact yields both a peak deceleration of no more than 200 *g* and a HIC of no more than 1,000. In simple terms, critical height refers to the fall height below which a life-threatening head injury would not be expected to occur (CPSC, 1997, p. 4).

Various surfaces have different abilities to absorb an impact or elongate the time that the head comes to a stop. It stands to reason that the longer the deceleration rate, the less impact is felt from the stop. An example is the difference between suddenly slamming on the brakes to come to a stop versus slowing up 100 yards (91.4 meters) before the stop sign. In the first case, you are usually thrown forward in the car; in the second, any motion is minimal.

To test the deceleration characteristics, or impact attenuation, of various surfaces, a metal head form is dropped from various heights to a surface. Measurements are taken regarding the force of impact. This testing protocol recently underwent revision because the NPPS identified a problem with the testing mat used under the instrument (Mack, Thompson, and Hudson, 1997). Thus, all surfacing should now be tested to conform to the ASTM standard F1292-04.

Fall Heights

Since equipment comes in varying heights, where is the critical height of a play structure? The CPSC defines fall height as the height of the highest designated play surface on the equipment. Table 6.2 presents the CPSC fall heights for various pieces of equipment. Note that the actual fall height can be higher than those found in table 6.2. For example, consider a child who is 3 feet (.9 meter) tall standing at the top of a slide that is 12 feet (3.7 meters) tall. The child's head would be 15 feet (4.6 meters) from the surface—the equivalent of a second-story window. No one would think it wise to let a child fall to the ground from two stories up, so why would it make sense to have play equipment at that height, especially without a shock-absorbing surface underneath?

Playground Surfacing Materials

At this point, it should be evident that the height of equipment plays a major role in preventing playground injuries. However, of equal importance are the surfacing

<u>Table 6.2</u>

Fall Heights for Equipment

Equipment	Fall height
Climbers and horizontal ladders	Maximum height of the structure
Elevated platforms, including slide platforms	Height of the platform
Merry-go-rounds	Height above the ground of any part at the perimeter on which a child may sit or stand
Seesaws	Maximum height attainable by any part of the seesaw
Spring rockers	Maximum height above the ground of the seat or designated play surface
Swings	Height of the pivot point where the swing's suspending elements connect to the supporting structure (since children may fall from a swing seat at its maximum attainable angle, assumed to be 90 degrees from the at-rest position)

From *CPSC handbook for public playground safety,* 1997, Publ. No. 325, pg. 4.

materials under and around playground equipment. Not all surfacing materials have the same shock-absorbing characteristics.

The CPSC guidelines state that "hard surfacing materials, such as asphalt or concrete are unsuitable for use under and around playground equipment of any height unless they are required as a base for a shock absorbing unitary material such as a rubber mat" (1997, p. 4). Further, the guidelines note that "earth surfaces such as soils and hard packed dirt are also not recommended because they have poor shock absorbing properties. Similarly, grass and turf are not recommended because wear and environmental conditions can reduce their effectiveness in absorbing shock during a fall" (p. 4).

Two types of materials are available for use under and around playground equipment: loose fill and unitary. Following is a discussion of the characteristics of these two types of surfaces.

Loose Fill Materials

Loose fill materials are made up of multiple particles that are not bonded together with glue or other adhesives. Their cushioning abilities depend on air trapped within and between individual particles at particular depths. Because these materials are easily displaced and migrate with use, they should never be installed over an existing hard surface (e.g., asphalt or concrete). In addition, these materials need a method of containment (e.g., retaining barrier or excavated pit). They also need good drainage underneath the material to prevent pooling and migration problems.

Because loose fill materials are not solid, they may mix with other natural or foreign materials in the environment (i.e., dirt, animal excrement, broken glass). They also may become homes for bugs, spiders, and other pests.

Two types of loose fill materials are generally used under and around playground equipment: organic and inorganic.

Organic Materials

Organic materials will decompose over a period of time. Traditional organic loose fill materials include wood chips, bark mulch, and engineered wood fibers. Because these materials tend to get compacted and pulverized and to decompose over time, they need to be replaced on a regular basis. In addition, because the particles are comprised of organic materials, they may be subject to microbial growth when wet. Signs that decomposition is taking place are the presence of weeds and other plant growth in the surface (see figure 6.4).

Inorganic Materials

Inorganic materials will not decompose over time. Traditional inorganic surfacing materials are sand and pea gravel. Since 2000, shredded tires have also gained in popularity as a loose fill inorganic material to use on playgrounds. Both sand and pea gravel may need to be loosened from time to time because they can become com-

Figure 6.4 Weeds can grow in organic surfacing material.

pacted or, in the case of gravel, they can turn into hardpan. Sand also has a tendency to spread easily outside a containment area and to be tracked out of the play area on shoes and become an abrasive on various types of flooring. In addition, when wet, the small particles of sand bind together, making it a rigid material.

Gravel tends to be hard to walk on and presents problems when displaced onto walkways and other areas. It is not recommended as a surface for preschoolers because they tend to place the small pea stones in various body cavities.

On the other hand, shredded tires are not abrasive, are less likely to compact than other loose fill materials, and do not deteriorate over time. However, unless properly treated, steel wires may be present, and the material may soil clothing. In early 2000, this type of surfacing was still new, and some of the problems just mentioned occurred frequently. However, as the technology for extracting, washing, and shredding improved, shredded tires have become more refined. As a result, this type of material is beginning to be used more frequently with fewer problems. However, because the primary color is black, heat could make the rubber surfaces too hot in some climates.

Unitary Materials

Unlike loose fill materials, unitary materials are those where particles are bonded together either through a heating or cooling process or with the use of a bonding agent or adhesive. Common unitary synthetic materials found under and around playground equipment include rubber tiles or mats, urethane poured in place, and rubber compositions.

Because unitary materials are solid, they require no additional means of containment. Once installed, they generally require minimal maintenance. However, over time they may develop holes or cracks that need repairs.

Most unitary poured-in-place surfaces need to be installed by an expert contractor or by the manufacturer. As such, the cost of materials and labor make it much more expensive initially than a loose fill surface (see chapter 7 for more details about costs). In addition, some unitary surfaces are slippery when wet and can be subject to vandalism.

Shock-Absorption Characteristics

Ultimately, when deciding whether to use a loose fill or unitary material, the important thing to consider is the shock-absorbing characteristics of the material. Not all loose fill materials have the same shock-absorption characteristics. For instance, pea gravel will not provide an adequate cushion for falls over heights of 6 feet (1.8 meters). Sand also has some limitations. In addition, the greater the depth of the loose-fill material, the higher the equipment can be before a life-threatening injury would be expected to occur from a fall. However, again, sand and gravel are two exceptions to this rule.

Figure 6.5 shows the height and depth characteristics for compressed loose fill materials. One readily available sample was selected in each of the following categories: sand, gravel, wood chips, engineered wood fibers, and shredded rubber. The following criteria were used to select the samples for testing:

Compressed Loose Fill and Synthetic Materials Depth Chart

	Pea gravel			Sand			Wood chips			Shredded rubber			Engineered wood fiber			Poured in place			Rubber mats/tiles		
Height of equipment	6 in.	9 in.	12 in.	6 in.	9 in.	12 in.	6 in.	9 in.	12 in.	6 in.	9 in.	12 in.	6 in.	9 in.	12 in.	1 in.	2 in.	3 in.	1 in.	2 in.	3 in.
1 ft	Y	Y	Y	Y	Y	Y	Y	Y	Y	Y	Y	Y	Y	Y	Y	N	Y	Y	Y	Y	Y
2 ft	Y	Y	Y	Y	Y	Y	Y	Y	Y	Y	Y	Y	Y	Y	Y	N	Y	Y	Y	Y	Y
3 ft	Y	Y	Y	Y	Y	Y	Y	Y	Y	Y	Y	Y	Y	Y	Y	N	Y	Y	N	Y	Y
4 ft	Y	Y	Y	Y	Y	Y	Y	Y	Y	Y	Y	Y	Y	Y	Y	N	Y	Y	N	Y	Y
5 ft	N	Y	Y	Y	Y	Y	Y	Y	Y	Y	Y	Y	Y	Y	Y	N	Y	Y	N	Y	Y
6 ft	N	N	Y	Y	Y	Y	Y	Y	Y	Y	Y	Y	Y	Y	Y	N	N	Y	N	N	Y
7 ft	N	N	N	Y	Y	Y	N	Y	Y	Y	Y	Y	Y	Y	Y	N	N	Y	N	N	Y
8 ft	N	N	N	Y	Y	Y	N	Y	Y	Y	Y	Y	N	Y	Y	N	N	N	N	N	Y

Based on depth test results conducted by NPPS or manufacturers' literature.
Note that the loose fill results are based on materials tested in a compressed state.
Y = YES, it did meet CPSC recommendations for this critical height.
N = NO, it did not meet CPSC recommendations for this critical height.

Figure 6.5 Height and depth recommendations for compressed loose fill and synthetic materials.
Reprinted, by permission, from National Program for Playground Safety.

- Sand—ASTM C897 plaster sand
- Gravel—Rounded gravel particles no greater than 3/8 inch (1 centimeter) in diameter or nominal size that are washed and free of dust, clay, dirt, or foreign objects
- Wood chips—Random-sized wood chips, twigs, and leaves collected from a wood chipper being fed tree limbs, branches, and brush
- Engineered wood fibers—Random-sized engineered wood fibers from recognized hardwoods
- Shredded rubber—Rubber particles from recycled materials

The chart is based on research conducted by the NPPS in 1999 and expands on the information found in the CPSC guidelines on page 7 (Mack, Hudson, and Thompson, 1997). In its initial test, the CPSC only ran three uncompressed tests and one compressed test. As a result, they reported height and depth for 6 inches (15 centimeters), 9 inches (23 centimeters), and 12 inches (30.5 centimeters) of uncompressed loose fill materials and 9 inches (23 centimeters) of compressed depth. However, the only time that loose fill materials are uncompressed is when they are first installed. As soon as children begin playing on the equipment and jumping up and down on the surface, it begins to become compressed. Thus, the NPPS believes that a chart showing loose fill materials at various compressed levels is a more accurate picture of the amount of loose fill materials needed to provide a cushion of safety for children.

The chart only covers the typical loose fill surfacing used under and around playgrounds. Occasionally, someone will attempt to use an unusual loose fill material such as corn husks or sawdust as a playground surface. Before doing so, however, the surface material should be tested in an independent laboratory according to the protocol outlined in ASTM F1292. That is the only way to ascertain whether or not the surfacing has the shock-absorbing characteristics needed to protect children when they fall from various heights.

Because a variety of unitary surfacing materials are on the market, no standardized chart can be developed to cover all of them. Thus, the consumer must rely on documents supplied by the manufacturer showing that the surfacing material complies with ASTM F1292, as tested by an independent laboratory. If the manufacturer or distributor cannot provide this type of documentation, then the consumer should not purchase the material.

Indoor Surfacing Concerns

Many times playground equipment can be found indoors. This is especially true in child care centers, where attempts are made to provide a place to develop gross motor skills even when weather conditions prevent children from going outdoors.

This discussion does not include large play structures found in fast food restaurants such as Burger King or McDonald's. Those play structures and surfacing materials are covered under a separate ASTM standard on soft contained play areas. What we are discussing in this section are slides and climbing structures deliberately placed indoors to enhance the daily play experience of children in preschools and child care facilities.

Unfortunately, even though the play equipment is placed indoors, no thought may have been given to providing safe surfacing under and around the equipment. Instead, rest mats, carpets, or other inappropriate surfacing materials are used.

In 2001, the NPPS conducted a study to test the various surfacing materials used under and around equipment in childcare centers (Mack et al., 2001). They contacted child care centers around the country to determine the various types of surfacing materials that were being used. They found that 24 different products—including carpets, rest mats, tumbling mats, interlocking rubber mats, and tiles—were representative of materials used. The NPPS then obtained samples of these products from national suppliers and manufacturers of child care equipment and exercise, tumbling, and gymnastics equipment. None of the products came with any tags or other information indicating that they had been tested for use under and around playground equipment.

The NPPS then had all samples tested by Detroit Laboratories, an independent agent, using the protocol outlined by ASTM F1292. The results should give all child care agencies second thoughts about the safety of children indoors.

Nearly 60 percent of the materials tested had a critical height of 12 inches (30.5 centimeters) or less. Carpets and tiles provided virtually no fall protection. Only a landing mat at 4 inches (10 centimeters) of thickness consistently measured a critical height above 3 feet (.9 meter). It was also found that neither the cost nor type of mat was consistently associated with an acceptable critical height. In addition, there were problems with the stabilization of equipment and the ability to maintain the surfacing under and around the equipment. Based on these findings, the NPPS strongly recommends that only material recommended for playground equipment be used for indoor play areas.

 Success Story

Because of the increased evidence supporting the need for safe surfacing indoors, two manufacturers have recently developed surfacing materials in the form of a carpet that passes the F1292 standard for impact attenuation. This is especially important for child care centers in climates such as those in Arizona, New Mexico, Maine, and Alaska where extreme heat or cold forces children indoors for a substantial part of the year. To allow children to develop their gross motor skills, many of these centers have playground equipment indoors. In the past, these areas rarely had proper impact-attenuating surfaces. But the new carpet provides a way for the centers to keep children safe.

This story demonstrates that once research substantiates a need, companies step up to the plate to meet it. Further, the playground movement is evolutionary in nature—as more information becomes available, changes occur. Thus, as researchers continue to investigate the importance of surfacing, manufacturers will develop new products to help keep children safe in both indoor and outdoor environments.

Summary

The research reviewed in this chapter demonstrates the importance of paying attention to the height of equipment and the surfacing under and around it. There is strong evidence that equipment height has a direct relationship with the occurrence and severity of injuries, but little research supports the common belief that height is important to the overall play experience of children. In addition, a seminal study by the NPPS revealed that many child care centers in the United States are putting children at risk by using the wrong type of surfacing materials under and around indoor play equipment (Mack et al., 2001).

We will never be able to prevent all falls from equipment. The nature of free play means that children will use equipment in ways not necessarily envisioned by manufacturers. However, we can attempt to make sure that the surfacing under and around the equipment is able to absorb the impact of the majority of falls that occur. We can also help limit the severity of falls by ensuring that if they do occur, they are from a reasonable height.

By providing adequate surfacing materials under and around playground equipment, we can help reduce injuries. Consider again the cautionary tale on page 98. If the right decisions had been made before Andrew climbed to the top of the monkey bars, he might have been spared the 18 surgeries needed to repair his face and jaw. In chapter 7, we'll discuss ways to put the research into action so that we can make those right decisions.

7

Creating Safe Surfaces

As a result of the continued need for surfaces to protect children from falls, and an increase in use of new linked structure formats for playgrounds, it is now more important than ever to install surfaces which absorb force under equipment.

Jay Beckwith

Cautionary Tale

Eight-year-old Keyshone and his best friend, Mick, raced outside at recess. Pushing and shoving each other, they headed to the horizontal ladder to prove once and for all who was king of the playground. When they reached the platform connecting the horizontal ladder with the rest of the play structure, they both reached up to grab hold of the bar. However, since the equipment was designed for one person, not two, they couldn't both fit in the space at the same time. Keyshone's one-handed grip on the bar was tenuous at best as he launched the rest of his body into space. Falling to the ground was inevitable.

Unfortunately, the surface material under and around the equipment was not shock absorbing. The school district had bought a large quantity of fine gravel to spread around the base paths at the local high school adjoining the elementary school, and someone in the school administration assumed that if the surface material was soft enough to slide in, it must be soft enough to use around the playground equipment. Keyshone's broken arm attested to the fact that this was a dangerous assumption—one that is made too often throughout the United States.

This chapter is designed to help you select appropriate surfacing to be used under and around playground equipment. Using the research cited in the previous chapter, we'll look at the different decisions that need to be made in order to provide safe surfacing under and around playground equipment. Specific topics that will be discussed include the decision-making process for choosing safe surfacing, maintenance and accessibility concerns, and the financial costs of surfacing.

S.A.F.E. Surfacing Decision Model

At an NPPS Safety School, the following question was asked: "With all the variables involved, how do you prioritize the decision-making process to select the best surfacing for your play environment?" As discussed in chapter 6, the number one priority is to choose a surface material that will absorb the impact of a child during a fall. But, how do you know if you have a shock-absorbing surface? This question led to the creation of the S.A.F.E. surfacing decision model (see figure 7.1).

As shown in the figure, there are four major decisions to make concerning the creation of a safe surface. They involve selecting the appropriate materials, having a reasonable height of equipment, maintaining the proper depth of loose fill materials, and having the surfacing material in the right place (use zones). The yes and no arrows in the decision-making model indicate both the priority of the decisions that need to be made and the fact that if an answer to any one element is no, you will never have safe surfacing. For instance, if you have a suitable surface and correct equipment height but not the appropriate depth of loose fill materials, you will not have a surface that will properly cushion falls.

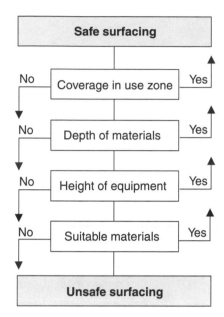

Figure 7.1 The S.A.F.E. surfacing decision model.
Reprinted, by permission, from S. Hudson, D. Thompson, and M. Mack, 1999, *Selecting playground surface materials* (Cedar Falls, IA: National Program for Playground Safety), 4.

Selecting Appropriate Materials

As the yes and no arrows in figure 7.1 indicate, selecting appropriate surfacing materials is the first step in creating a safe surface under and around playground equipment. Chapter 6 outlined appropriate playground surfacing materials, which are listed in figure 7.2. Inappropriate surfacing materials include asphalt, cement, dirt, and concrete. As pointed out in the CPSC guidelines, these materials do not have shock-absorbing properties to protect against falls from equipment (CPSC, 1997).

In a 2004 study by the NPPS, it was found that 87 percent of all playgrounds surveyed used loose fill surfacing under and around playground equipment. The primary loose fill material used was wood chips (32 percent), followed by sand (23.2 percent), wood fiber (20.4 percent), and pea gravel (20.3 percent). Less than 2 percent of the playgrounds used shredded rubber (Hudson, Olsen, and Thompson, 2004). Figure 7.3 lists advantages and disadvantages of each of these loose fill surfaces.

Note that not all wood chips are the same. For instance, many park and recreation departments have chipper machines to render fallen tree branches and other wood materials into chips. Unfortunately, whatever goes into the chipper comes out in varying sizes and lengths. Thus, if chemicals or insecticides have been used on the trees or if the wood has nails or other materials in it, they will still be present in the chips. When these chips are spread on the ground, two things can occur.

First, children will be exposed to whatever chemicals are in the wood. In addition, since wood is an organic material, these chemicals will leach into the soil as the wood

Loose Fill Materials

Organic

- Wood chips—Random-sized wood chips having gone through a wood chipper*
- Double shredded mulch—Landscape mulch**
- Engineered wood fibers—Relatively uniform fibers from recognized hardwood

Inorganic

- Fine sand—White sand purchased in bags marked *play sand*
- Coarse sand—Sand used in landscaping and construction trades
- Fine gravel—Rounded particles less than 3/8 inch (1 centimeter) in diameter
- Medium gravel—River-washed or tumbled 1/2-inch (1.3-centimeter) stones***
- Shredded tires—Shredded tires that meet ASTM F1292 (a guarantee should be obtained from the supplier that the material is free from steel wires or other contaminants)

Unitary Materials

- Rubber mats or tiles held in place by a binder
- Poured-in-place rubber material

Unitary materials are available from a number of manufacturers, many of whom have a range of materials with different shock-absorbing properties.

*Although this material has shock-absorbing attributes, it also raises other safety concerns. Anything that goes into a wood chipper comes out; thus, treated wood or wood that has been exposed to pesticides may be present. In addition, since the pieces are not uniform in size, long and sharp pieces may be found that can cause injuries when thrown.

**Although this material has shock-absorbing attributes, it decomposes quickly.

***Although this material has shock-absorbing attributes, it should not be used with equipment over 5 feet (1.5 meters) tall. Because of the size of the stones, it may also be dangerous when thrown.

Figure 7.2 Appropriate materials are necessary for safe surfacing.
From *CPSC handbook for public playground safety,* 1997, Pub. No. 325.

decomposes. Even if you remove the wood chips and replace them with others, the chemicals will remain at the site.

Second, because the wood chips will come out in varying lengths, the result is potentially hazardous chips with long, sharp points or bulky chips that children throw at each other. In a legal case that involved one of the authors as an expert witness, a sizeable chip thrown by one child during a school recess hit another child in the eye, resulting in permanent blindness.

These problems can be overcome as long as you purchase wood chips or wood fiber from a reputable company that specializes in playground surfacing. The distributor should be able to show that the material meets ASTM standard F1292 and is manufactured for use under and around playground equipment. Be aware that most landscape wood chips have not been tested for playground use and therefore should not be purchased and used as a playground surface.

Organic Loose Fill
(Wood Chips, Bark Mulch, Engineered Wood Fibers)

Advantages

- Low initial costs
- Easy installation
- Good drainage
- Less abrasive than sand
- Attractive appearance
- Less attractive to cats and dogs (compared to sand)
- Readily available

Disadvantages

- Rainy weather, high humidity, freezing temperatures may reduce cushioning potential
- Combines with dirt and other foreign materials over time, which may reduce cushioning potential
- Decomposes, is pulverized, and compacts, requiring replenishment
- Depth may be reduced by displacement due to children's activities or wind
- Can be blown or thrown into children's eyes
- Subject to microbial growth when wet
- Conceals animal excrement and trash (e.g., broken glass, nails, pencils, and other sharp objects that can cause cuts and puncture wounds)
- Spreads easily outside containment area
- Can be flammable
- Subject to theft by neighborhood residents for use as mulch

Inorganic Loose Fill (Sand, Gravel)

Advantages

- Low initial cost
- Easy installation
- Does not pulverize
- Not ideal for microbial growth
- Nonflammable
- Materials readily available
- Not susceptible to vandalism except by contamination
- Gravel: Less attractive to animals than sand

(continued)

Figure 7.3 Advantages and disadvantages of loose fill surfacing materials.

From *CPSC handbook for public playground safety,* 1997, Pub. No. 325.

Disadvantages

- Rainy weather, high humidity, freezing temperatures may reduce cushioning potential
- Depth may be reduced by displacement due to children's activities or wind
- Can be blown or thrown into children's eyes
- Conceals animal excrement and trash (e.g., broken glass, nails, pencils, and other sharp objects that can cause cuts and puncture wounds)
- May be swallowed

Disadvantages Specific to Sand

- Spreads easily outside of containment area
- Small particles bind together and become less cushioning when wet; when thoroughly wet, sand reacts as a rigid material
- May be tracked out of play area on shoes; abrasive to floor surfaces when tracked indoors; abrasive to plastic materials
- Adheres to clothing
- Susceptible to fouling by animals

Disadvantages Specific to Gravel

- Difficult to walk on
- If displaced onto nearby hard-surface pathways, could present a fall hazard
- Hardpan may form under heavily traveled areas

Figure 7.3 *(continued)* Advantages and disadvantages of loose fill surfacing materials.
From *CPSC handbook for public playground safety,* 1997, Pub. No. 325.

The NPPS study found that only 13 percent of playgrounds had unitary surfaces: mats and poured-in-place materials. Of these playgrounds, 35 percent were using rubber mats or tiles and the rest were using a synthetic poured-in-place product. Again, either product is acceptable as long as it has met the ASTM F1292 requirement (Hudson, Olsen, and Thompson, 2004).

Age of Users

Not all loose fill materials are suitable for all ages. For instance, pea gravel is usually not a good choice for preschool playgrounds. Young children tend to put things in their mouths as they explore their environment. They also experiment with putting things in other body cavities. On the other hand, sand is a great surface for this age group because it is easy for preschoolers to manipulate. Many times preschoolers are found playing with the surface rather than the equipment!

For older children, the major concerns may be vandalism and the migration of loose fill materials. Also, as mentioned, large pieces of loose fill material (i.e., large pea gravel, wood chips) can become objects to throw at one another. There have also been instances where vandals have poured gasoline on wood chips and shredded rubber to see how well they would burn. In Waterloo, Iowa, three young teens destroyed a new playground a day after it was opened by pouring gasoline on the wood chips that were present as surfacing material. The resultant fire was so hot that it melted the plastic playground equipment. A similar situation occurred in Anchorage, Alaska, where a 12-year-old poured gasoline on newly installed shredded rubber two days before the opening of school. In this case, the fire department had a difficult time dealing with the fire because rubber smolders rather than burns. Both problems can be overcome with better supervision and control of the play environment.

Climate

Weather is another factor to consider in the selection of appropriate materials. An area like Alaska is not conducive to using sand because it can freeze. In southwestern states, such as New Mexico and Arizona, wood products tend to dry up and blow away. In Maine, the opposite problem occurs—wood products may remain moist, fostering the growth of microbes.

Unitary surfaces are not immune to the weather, either. In hot, dry areas, black tiles or poured-in-place materials may become too hot for children to play on. In other areas that have an abundance of fog or moisture, rubber mats may become slippery.

The point is that there is no one best surface material. Rather, the chosen material should pass the SAC test—standard (whether it meets ASTM F1292), ages (ages of children using the playground), and climate (ability to stand up to the weather in the area).

Equipment Height

Once you think you have selected an appropriate surface, you next must consider the height of the equipment. Height limits the choice of surfacing in two ways. First, some surfaces such as pea gravel provide shock absorbency for falls from heights of only 6 feet (1.8 meters). (Refer to figure 6.5 on page 110.) Second, at this time no surfacing has been tested by an independent testing lab for equipment over the height of 12 feet (3.7 meters). Thus, to date no one can guarantee the shock absorbency of surfacing under equipment over 12 feet (3.7 meters) in height.

A few years ago, a safety officer of a U.S. military base in Asia contacted the NPPS. School administrators wanted to install a structure that was 20 feet (6.1 meters) high on the base. The facilities and safety officer was opposed to the structure, but the civil engineers who worked with the school had assured the administrators that according to their mathematical calculations, no serious injury would occur from children falling off the structure. Of course, none of the civil engineers' children would be using the equipment. As mentioned in the previous chapter, equipment over the height of 6 feet (1.8 meters) doubles the probability of injury. After several e-mails back and forth along with the production of research documents showing the relationship between equipment height and injury, the school backed down in its quest to provide children with a 20-foot (6.1-meter) thrill.

Depth of Loose Fill Materials

Once you have chosen acceptable materials for the height of the equipment, the third decision that needs to be made concerns the thickness (unitary surfaces) or depth (loose fill surfaces) of the surface materials. Generally, rubber mats and poured-in-place materials come in different thicknesses according to equipment height. For instance, for heights up to 5 feet (1.5 meters), you may need 2 inches (5 centimeters) of thickness; for heights of 6 to 8 feet (1.8 to 2.4 meters), the materials may need to be at least 3 inches (7.5 centimeters) thick. However, not all unitary surfaces are the same, so you need to closely review the manufacturer's testing results to verify the thickness requirement for the product relative to the height of the equipment.

All acceptable loose fill materials with the exception of pea gravel will pass the critical height test at 6 inches (15 centimeters) of depth for equipment up to a height of 6 feet (1.8 meters). Pea gravel must be 9 inches (23 centimeters) deep for heights of 5 feet (1.5 meters) and 12 inches (30.5 centimeters) deep for heights of 6 feet (1.8 meters). After 6 feet (1.8 meters) of height, pea gravel will no longer absorb the impact of a fall regardless of the depth. (See figure 7.4.) Wood chips will pass the critical height test at 7 and 8 feet (2.1 and 2.4 meters) if it is 9 inches (23 centimeters) deep. However, both the NPPS and CPSC recommend that 12 inches (30.5 centimeters) of loose fill material be used. Because wood products will decompose, the extra 3 inches (7.5 centimeters) provide a cushion of safety.

Use Zones

The final element in that decision-making model involves the placement of the surfacing under and around playground equipment. The CPSC defines these areas as use zones and outlines their requirements in its *Handbook for Public Playground Safety, 1997* as follows:

- Stationary equipment: 6 feet (1.8 meters) on all sides of the equipment
- Slides: 6 feet (1.8 meters) on all sides; 4 feet (1.2 meters) plus the height of the slide in front of the slide chute

---

9 inches (23 centimeters) of compressed material will provide critical heights up to the following:

Coarse sand	4 feet (1.2 meters)
Fine sand	5 feet (1.5 meters)
Medium gravel	5 feet (1.5 meters)
Fine (pea) gravel	6 feet (1.8 meters)
Engineered wood fibers	6 feet (1.8 meters)
Double shredded bark mulch	7 feet (2.1 meters)
Wood chips	10 feet (3 meters)

Figure 7.4 The relationship between equipment height and surfacing depth.

From *CPSC handbook for public playground safety*, 1997, Pub. No. 325.

- Swings: 6 feet (1.8 meters) on each side; twice the height of the swing beam in front and back of the swing

In addition to the basic use zone of 6 feet (1.8 meters) in all directions from the perimeter of the equipment, the *Handbook* states, "other than the equipment itself, the use zone should be free of obstacles that children could run into or fall on top of and thus be injured" (p. 6). Figure 7.5 shows how these guidelines would apply to a climbing tower.

However, children move off swings and slides in different ways than they move off other equipment. Therefore, swings and slides have expanded use zones (see figures 7.6 and 7.7). For instance, if a swing beam is 8 feet (2.4 meters) high, the use zone extends 16 feet (4.9 meters) in front and 16 feet (4.9 meters) in back of the beam to accommodate children who might jump out of the swing seat while in motion.

Currently, there is a discrepancy between the CPSC guidelines and the ASTM standard F1487 concerning the use zone for slides because the CPSC has not revised its published guidelines recently, whereas the ASTM standard underwent revision in 2001. The current CPSC guidelines for the use zone at the end of slides reads, "The use zone in front of the exit of a slide should extend a minimum distance of H + 4 feet [1.2 meters] where H is the vertical distance from the protective surface at the exit to the highest point of the chute. However, no matter what the value of H is, the use zone should never be less than 6 feet [1.8 meters] but does not need to be greater than 14 feet [4.3 meters]" (1997, p. 7). Under this requirement, a slide that is 6 feet (1.8 meters) high would have a use zone of 10 feet (3 meters). For a slide that is 8 feet (2.4 meters) high, the use zone would be 12 feet (3.7 meters).

The ASTM, on the other hand, has concluded that this spacing is not necessary. According to the latest ASTM F1487-05 standard, "the use zone at the lower exit end of the chute or slide bed shall be a minimum of X where X equals the vertical distance from the protective surfacing at the lower exit to the highest point of the sliding surface. The use zone at the lower exit end of the chute or slide bed shall extend in the direction of the descent a horizontal distance not less than 6 feet (72

Figure 7.5 The CPSC-required use zone for stationary equipment.

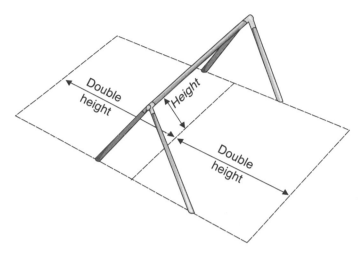

Figure 7.6 The CPSC-required use zone for swings.

Platform height plus 4 ft

Figure 7.7 The CPSC-required use zone for slides.

inches/1830 mm.) but need not be greater than 8 feet (96 in./2440 mm) from the lower exit" (p. 14).

Figure 7.8 presents what this standard means and the difference in measurement between the ASTM standard and the CPSC guidelines. This short excerpt also illustrates the technical language of the ASTM standard compared to the more user-friendly language of the CPSC guidelines.

Do You Have Safe Surfacing?

If the answer is yes to all four elements of the safe surfacing decision-making model (see figure 7.1 on page 117), then you will have a safe, impact-absorbing surface under

ASTM Requirement

The use zone at the exit end of the slide shall be the vertical distance of the slide based on the calculation that the exit region shall be not less than 6 feet (1.8 meters) but not more than 8 feet (2.4 meters). Thus,

- a slide the height of 6 feet (1.8 meters) would have a use zone exit of 6 feet (1.8 meters),
- a slide the height of 8 feet (2.4 meters) would have a use zone exit of 8 feet (2.4 meters), and
- a slide over the height of 8 feet (2.4 meters) would have an exit region of 8 feet (2.4 meters).

CPSC Requirement

The use zone at the exit end of the slide shall be the vertical distance of the slide plus 4 feet (1.2 meters) but need not extend beyond 14 feet (4.3 meters). Thus,

- a slide of 6 feet (1.8 meters) would have a use zone of 10 feet (3 meters),
- a slide of 8 feet (2.4 meters) would have a use zone of 12 feet (3.7 meters), and
- a slide over 8 feet (2.4 meters) would have a use zone not to exceed 14 feet (4.3 meters).

Figure 7.8 The ASTM and the CPSC have different requirements for slide use zones.

and around your playground equipment. However, the surface is unsafe for children if the answer to any one of the items is no.

The recent NPPS study discussed earlier found that the answer was yes for the first two questions of the decision-making model for the majority of the 3,000 playground sites in the study (Hudson, Olsen, and Thompson, 2004). However, only 19 percent of playgrounds surveyed that used loose fill materials maintained this surfacing at the adequate depth. In addition, adequate surfacing was not found for the use zones of slides and swings.

Maintenance Requirements

The maintenance of any playground surface is a critical part of keeping children safe. Without proper maintenance, shock absorbency will decrease. In fact, a poorly maintained surface may be more dangerous than no surface at all. With a poorly maintained surface you are providing an illusion of safety for children, and thus they may be more inclined to engage in risky behavior (Wallach, 1997b).

Maintenance costs and requirements of surface materials vary greatly, with loose fill materials tending to have much higher maintenance needs. In high-use areas, daily raking of loose fill materials may be required to replace materials that have been pushed or kicked away. These materials may also have to be tilled periodically to loosen compaction, and additional materials may need to be added annually. Conversely, unitary materials require relatively low maintenance, needing only occasional repair, cleaning, and sweeping.

Maintenance considerations for surfacing should be part of the initial planning process. If the agency does not have the funds to have someone check the play environment on a regular basis, then putting in a surface that requires high maintenance, such as wood chips, is not a good choice. Simply dumping a load of wood chips around the equipment in autumn and hoping that the surfacing will maintain itself throughout the year does little to protect children from injury or agencies from possible lawsuits.

 Use the S.A.F.E. Model Checklist: Surfacing Materials in appendix C to assess and maintain loose fill surfacing and unitary surfacing. The checklist also appears on the CD-ROM for easy reproduction.

Installation of Unitary Surfacing

Part of the initial decision about surfacing involves the installation of the surface. Unitary surfacing generally requires hiring a contractor who knows the proper mixture of materials needed to pour the surface. The installation of rubber mats and tiles also has particular specifications that may be better left to the professionals. Because of these additional requirements, many people select loose fill materials. However, the installation of loose fill materials should also follow some general guidelines.

Installation of Loose Fill Materials

Proper installation of loose fill surfacing will help in the maintenance of these materials. For instance, if no allowance is made for proper drainage of the playground surface, water may wash away loose fill materials or may pool under the equipment and erode the ground. Slope, drainage, and placement of concrete footers are critical to the proper installation of loose fill surfacing.

Slope of Area

The slope of the playground area will affect the placement of surfacing materials in two ways. First, if the playground is at the bottom of a hill (see figure 7.9), anything on top of that hill will drain directly into the playground area and onto the surface. Second, loose fill material will constantly be washed away as the water runs off the hill into the play space. In a public area such as a park, if a parking lot is above the play area, oils and other substances from cars can wash down the hill into the surface.

On a level area, if there is not a 1 percent slope outward to the perimeter, water will pool in any low spot on the playground. This is especially true if a unitary surface material is used since unitary materials will not absorb water. Instead, the surface will need to be swept dry. A slight elevation is necessary to improve drainage.

Figure 7.9 A playground at the bottom of a slope needs surfacing materials that won't be washed away.

Drainage

Besides elevation, the other way to aid in the drainage of the play area is to provide a system that helps draw off the water. Typically, use 2 to 3 inches (5 to 7.5 centimeters) of gravel as a base, then use a filter cloth to separate the gravel from the loose fill material. Water will drain through the loose fill material into the gravel. This type of system is especially important with wood products since without a proper drainage system, the water will hasten the decomposition of the material.

Concrete Footers

Because playground equipment needs to be stable, it must be put securely in the ground. As a result, large upright posts are sunk into the ground and concrete is then poured into the posthole to hold the post in place (see figure 7.10). The concrete filler must be at least 6 inches (15 centimeters) under the level surface. If you fill the posthole to the top with concrete and then put loose fill over the area, the concrete footer may be exposed as the loose fill material migrates away from the post. In a tragic case that one of the authors worked on, a child fell off a sliding pole in a park and struck her head on an exposed concrete footer. The resulting brain injury was permanently disabling.

© NPPS

Figure 7.10 Make sure a post's concrete footer is not exposed under the surfacing materials.

Accessibility

Another factor to consider when selecting surfacing materials is accessibility. According to the Americans with Disabilities Act (ADA) of 1990 (see chapter 1 for more details), discrimination on the basis of disability is prohibited in public accommodations. In terms of play areas, this law means that accommodations need to be made in order to get all children into the play area and to provide access to equipment. While the entire playground area doesn't have to be accessible, at a minimum there must be an accessible pathway to the equipment (see figure 7.11).

The pathway must be firm, stable, and slip resistant (ASTM F1951). The accessible route begins from outside the play area (e.g., parking lots, walkways, school buildings, child care facilities, recreation centers) to the edge of the playground. The route should be a continuous, unobstructed path connecting all accessible elements and spaces of a building or facility. In addition, the pathway must be wide enough to accommodate a wheelchair.

As long as there is a means to get children to ground-level equipment and onto elevated equipment, the rest of the play area does not have to have an accessible surface. For instance, you might have rubber tile surfacing as a pathway to the equipment, but the surfacing materials under and around the equipment may be a wood product. While testing is still being done to determine what surfaces are accessible, it is obvious that neither sand nor pea gravel has the firm, stable characteristics to make it an accessible surface. Unitary surfaces are primarily used to provide accessible pathways. Some engineered wood-fiber products have also passed the accessibility testing procedures, but this is done on a case-by-case basis. Just because company A's engineered wood fibers meet the ASTM requirements for accessibility doesn't mean that company B's product also meets the requirements.

Cost

A final consideration when choosing surfacing is cost. Cost is usually the first consideration and the major determining factor in the selection of materials. More precisely, the *initial* cost of purchasing and installing the material is often the deciding factor

Figure 7.11   A sidewalk and ramp allow children with disabilities to enter the play area.

for the choice of surface. But while the initial costs are important, there are other factors to consider.

First, the initial cost of the surface should be prorated over the life expectancy of the playground. For instance, a unitary surface can cost 10 times as much as most loose fill materials. However, poured-in-place materials and rubber mats or tiles generally last for at least 10 years, whereas most loose fill materials will need some replacement on a yearly basis. Thus, high maintenance requirements and annual replacement expenses also need to be factored into the overall costs.

Additionally, you must consider the installation costs, including method of containment, trucking costs, and removal of the existing surface. Installation costs can be as high as 30 percent of the overall cost of the surfacing materials.

Thus, while loose fill surfacing initially looks like a bargain compared to many unitary surfaces, the real cost may be very similar to unitary surfaces when all the other expenses associated with installation and maintenance are factored into the equation. Use the following formula to find the true cost of surfacing materials:

Initial cost + installation cost + yearly maintenance cost
(including replacement of loose fill materials) ÷ 10 years = True cost

Table 7.1 provides a guide to help consumers select the proper surfacing for their playgrounds.

Table 7.1

Playground Surface Selection Guide

Kind of material	Wheelchair accessible	Maintenance needed	Flammable*	Initial cost	Estimated 10-year cost**	Professional installation required	Manufacturer warranty product liability
Engineered wood fiber	Yes	Medium	Maybe	$$	$$$	Maybe	Yes
Pea gravel	No	High	No	$$	$$	No	No
Poured in place	Yes	Low	Maybe	$$$	$$$	Yes	Yes
Rubber mats/ tiles	Yes	Low	Maybe	$$$	$$$	Yes	Yes
Sand	No	High	No	$	$$	No	No
Shredded rubber	Maybe	Medium	Maybe	$$	$$$	No	Maybe
Wood chips	No	High	Maybe	$	$$$	No	No

*Some materials are treated to be nonflammable.
**Cost includes purchase price, installation, and maintenance prorated over 10 years.

From *CPSC handbook for public playground safety,* 1997, Publ. No. 325, pg. 4.

 Success Story

In 2003, the Iowa legislature appropriated $500,000 to the NPPS for a special research project involving surfacing. The intent of the research was to see if rubber safety tiles under and around playground equipment helped to reduce injuries. Ten schools from around the state were randomly selected to receive safety training and the rubber tiles. The NPPS collected preinjury data (injuries that had occurred before training and tiles) and postinjury data (injuries that had occurred up to one year after the tiles were in place).

The results were significant. The safety training alone helped to reduce injuries by 50 percent. When combined with the safe surfacing materials, the injury rate dropped by 76 percent (National Program for Playground Safety, 2006). Subsequently, the legislature refunded this project in 2004, 2005, and 2006.

While rubber tiles are not the definitive surfacing to use under and around playground equipment, the advantages of a unitary surface in terms of maintaining consistent shock absorbency and thus helping to keep children safe cannot be overstated. The Iowa Safe Surfacing Initiative (ISSI) is proof that training and good surfacing can help significantly reduce injuries.

Summary

We must take care in selecting the surfacing materials to be used under and around playground equipment. By developing criteria that include considerations of shock absorbency, maintenance requirements, accessibility, and costs, agencies and organizations can help provide safe playground environments for all children.

Since falls to surfaces are cited as a major factor in 70 percent of all injuries, it is critical that agencies and organizations select and maintain safe surfaces under and around playground equipment. The discussion of maintenance will continue in the next two chapters, which look at the importance of maintaining equipment in order to keep children safe in the play environment.

8

Equipment Maintenance

*Rock-a-bye children on the treetop; when the wind blows,
the tire swing will rock. When the bough breaks, the swing will
fall, and down will come children, swing and all.*

Adapted from a traditional nursery rhyme

© Jim West

It was the third day of school, and Heather raced out to the playground with the rest of her classmates. It mattered little to her that the equipment on the playground had been there since the late 1960s. After all, as her parents said, they played on it without any problems so they were sure it was safe for their daughter. A little worn metal wasn't anything to worry about.

Heather headed to the merry-go-round with friends to see who could stay on the platform the longest as others pushed the wheel round and round. As the platform began to spin faster, Heather placed her hands behind her to provide some stability, just like she did when her father took her for rides on his motorcycle. Unfortunately, Heather wasn't riding on a motorcycle. Her hands slipped into the open gearbox in the middle of the platform, which severed three fingers on one hand and two on the other. At the age of 7, Heather had become permanently disabled.

This tragic incident could have been prevented by a comprehensive maintenance plan that outlined the who, what, and when of conducting playground safety assessments at the school.

In this chapter, we'll examine the importance of maintaining equipment and surfaces, as well as the standard of care required for playground safety. In addition, we'll explore whether playgrounds in the United States are measuring up to the standard of care for playground maintenance. Finally, we'll discuss the elements of a maintenance policy.

The Importance of Maintenance

Any new car comes with a maintenance guide. After all, buying a car is a major investment. In order to protect that investment, the car company strongly recommends a schedule of maintenance to ensure that the car will last for many miles on the road. People who ignore these recommendations can void their repair warranty, put themselves in physical danger if a part breaks, and lose their investment.

The same is true with equipment and surfacing in play areas. The lack of a maintenance program in a play area can void a manufacturer's warranty, put children in physical danger, and waste dollars on unusable equipment.

Nearly 60 percent of all injuries that result in litigation list lack of maintenance as the primary cause of injury (Hendy, 2004). A study conducted by King (1995) revealed that one-third of 900 park departments had never conducted a safety inspection on their equipment even though almost half of their equipment was more than 10 years old. Clearly, agencies around the country are putting children at risk and are creating a financial hardship for the organization when a legal issue arises. The number one goal of a comprehensive maintenance program should be the protection of the users—our children.

Maintenance of play areas involves more than simply fixing something that is broken. Rather, a well-designed maintenance program is proactive, responding to needs before crises occur; in other words, "Pay me now or pay me later" (Kutska,

1996). In simple terms, this is what maintenance is all about. By eliminating hazards, keeping equipment operational, and eliminating costly repairs, a comprehensive preventative maintenance program makes good financial sense.

Although this chapter and the next focus on playground equipment, a comprehensive maintenance program is more than just keeping equipment in working order. It also involves everything in the play environment that contributes to the overall well-being and aesthetics of the area, including fields, seating, shelters, sidewalks, and containment barriers.

Maintenance Planning

Maintenance planning should not happen after the area is developed; rather, a comprehensive maintenance plan should begin to be developed during the initial stages of planning the play area. A representative from the maintenance department should be part of any playground planning committee. Without this valuable input, it is easy to create a play area that will soon be in disrepair because it is impossible to maintain. Too often, the maintenance staff is ignored—a critical mistake. These individuals are aware of the durability of various materials, how easy or difficult it is to maintain surface materials, and the amount of vandalism and abuse that is present in a given area. In addition, since they are directly responsible for maintaining a safe play environment, they have a vested interest in what is contained within the area.

Functions of a Maintenance Program

The basic function of maintenance is to ensure the safety of users by keeping the play area and equipment in a safe condition. Good maintenance can also extend the life span of equipment and protect an agency against possible litigation arising from accidents. Last but not least, a well-maintained area is aesthetically pleasing and hygienically clean. All of these functions are important in maintaining a professional standard of care for the play environment.

Standard of Care

Standard of care is a legal term that refers to the duty of a public entity (child care center, school, community park) to protect individuals against unreasonable risk of harm. Unless a public agency has been granted governmental immunity (that is, they cannot legally be sued), they are subject to lawsuits arising from a charge of negligent behavior. Negligent behavior is defined as conduct that is not in accord with the standard of care a prudent professional should give, hence subjecting the participant to unreasonable risk of injury (van der Smissen, 2003, p. 58). For instance, in the cautionary tale at the beginning of this chapter, the court found in favor of the child because the school could not prove that they had any routine preventive maintenance program to check the equipment. Thus, it was found that children were subject to unreasonable risk of injury.

The standard of care may be determined by statute, ordinance, or regulation; by organizations or agencies; or by the profession (van der Smissen, 2003, p. 60). In the case of playgrounds, the CPSC guidelines are widely viewed as the minimum criteria concerning the standard of care at playgrounds. Thus, in most cases related to playground equipment, agency personnel will be held to the standard of care or standards of practice as set forth in the guidelines.

The professional standard of care "does not vary based on the qualifications of the person in charge, whether experienced, older, or certified"; instead, "one's performance is measured against the standard of care of a qualified professional for that situation" (van der Smissen, 2003, p. 60-61). Thus, a child care provider who has a playground on site that does not meet CPSC guidelines may be held liable if a child gets hurt because the provider was not following the acceptable standard of care for the operation of the playground. Ignorance is no defense in the eyes of the law.

In order to protect both children and the organization, any public entity that owns and operates a playground should be well versed in the CPSC guidelines and follow, if not exceed, the recommendations. Since one of the major factors in injuries is inadequate maintenance, these entities should develop a maintenance policy based on the CPSC guidelines.

How well are public playgrounds around the country adhering to the CPSC guidelines for maintenance? To answer this question, let's look at two studies performed by the NPPS in 2000 and 2004.

National Report Card on Playground Maintenance

The NPPS conducted two major assessments of playground sites in the United States (Hudson, Mack, and Thompson, 2000; Hudson, Olsen, and Thompson, 2004). Both of these studies provided snapshots of the maintenance of both equipment and surfacing.

Surfacing Maintenance

Chapters 6 and 7 stressed the importance of maintaining an adequate surface under and around play equipment. Table 8.1 highlights the findings of the two NPPS studies with regard to maintaining safe surfaces. The first column indicates the percentage of

Table 8.1

Surface Maintenance

Surfacing maintenance component	2000	2004	2000 grade	2004 grade
Loose fill materials are at an appropriate depth.	47%	19%	F	F
Materials are in 6-ft (1.8-m) use zone.	67%	71%	D+	C-
Concrete footings are covered.	88%	93%	B+	A-
Surface is free of foreign objects.	84%	80%	B	B-

playgrounds that met the criteria in 2000. The second column indicates the percentage of playgrounds that met the criteria during the revisit in 2004.

It is apparent from table 8.1 that maintaining loose fill materials is a major problem. Since the majority of playgrounds throughout the United States (98 percent) use loose fill materials under and around playground equipment, it.is imperative that the materials be maintained so that they can absorb falls (Hudson, Olsen, and Thompson, 2004). It is clear that children are at risk for potential injury because these surface materials are not being maintained properly.

While table 8.1 shows that progress is being made in maintaining surfaces in 6-feet (1.8-meter) use zones, more can be done in this area. Both surveys also found that use zones around swings and slides were not adequately maintained.

The good news is that the vast majority of playgrounds surveyed (93 percent) have eliminated one potential cause of head injuries by covering concrete footers. In addition, they are doing an above-average job (B-) in removing foreign objects from surfacing, although the 2004 grade was four points less than what was found in the 2000 survey.

Overall, the maintenance of playground surfacing is improving with the exception of the crucial element of maintaining adequate material depth. This exception reinforces the need of having a maintenance policy that stipulates who is responsible for maintaining the surface and how frequently the surfacing must be checked.

Equipment Maintenance

The overall grade for equipment maintenance improved from a C + in 2000 to a B- in 2004 in the NPPS studies. Table 8.2 shows where this improvement occurred. With the exception of one area—noticeable gaps—the scores were maintained or improved in each item on the maintenance list. This is a trend in the right direction.

Without routine inspections and repair, any equipment will deteriorate and pose a hazard to children. It appears that the maintenance of metal and wood equipment

Table 8.2

Equipment Maintenance

Equipment component	2000	2004	2000 grade	2004 grade
Equipment is free of broken parts.	83%	84%	B-	B
Equipment is free of missing parts.	81%	89%	B-	B+
Equipment is free of protruding bolts.	81%	85%	B-	B
Equipment is free of noticeable gaps.	75%	70%	C	C-
Equipment is free of head entrapments.	79%	79%	C+	C+
Equipment is free of rust.	63%	74%	D-	C
Equipment is free of splinters.	61%	65%	D-	D
Equipment is free of cracks and holes.	92%	96%	A-	A

is insufficient in comparison to plastic equipment. Part of this problem lies in the fact that older equipment tends to be made of wood or metal. Proportionately, metal equipment installed before 1991 had more rust present than after that time (see figure 8.1). A similar finding was seen with wooden equipment. More plastic equipment has been installed since 1994 than before that time—older equipment tends to be wood and metal.

Gaps in equipment may be the result of inappropriate installation or aging equipment where joints have separated (see figure 8.2). Again, it appears that the older the equipment, the more gaps are present.

Head entrapments for children ages 2 to 12 years continue to be a problem at 21 percent of playgrounds in the United States. A head entrapment can occur when the spacing between and under guardrails or barriers are greater than 3.5 inches (9 centimeters) but less than 9 inches (23 centimeters) (see figure 8.3). Children cannot get their bodies into an opening smaller than 3.5 inches (9 centimeters) wide, but they can get both head and body through openings greater than 9 inches (23 centimeters).

When young children try to fit through openings, they generally put their body through the opening first, usually the legs followed by the torso and then the head.

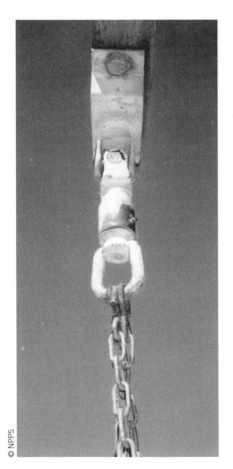

Figure 8.1 Rusted metal equipment.　　**Figure 8.2** A gap in aging equipment.

© NPPS

Figure 8.3 Improper spacing can create a head entrapment.

However, young children's torsos are smaller than their heads. The result is that their body makes it through the opening but not their head. Children then get stuck from the tip of chin to top of forehead. Because they do not have the cognitive ability to realize that if they can turn their head they might get free, children are unable to extract themselves from the opening. Within 30 seconds in this predicament, children can lose consciousness. Within 2 minutes, they stop breathing because of strangulation.

In recent years, the use of bicycle helmets has been an important factor in reducing traumatic head injuries of children, and all children and adults who cycle should wear them. However, helmets should be removed when children use playground equipment. Even a space wider than 9 inches (23 centimeters) is not wide enough to allow a child's helmeted head through the opening. There have been two tragic deaths in Canada and the United States where children died because they were entrapped on playground equipment wearing helmets (CPSC/EPHA, 1999).

Importance of Maintenance Policy

Obviously, it is important for a public agency to develop a maintenance policy for play areas. This policy constitutes the ground rules for what type of inspections will be performed, who will perform the inspections, and how often the inspections will be performed. It also establishes the standard of care for the play area. The following questions can help assist in the development of these policies:

1. Who is responsible for inspection and maintenance of equipment and surfaces?

2. Was training provided in performing inspections and maintenance?
3. How often do inspections and maintenance occur?
4. How is maintenance work reported?
5. How are equipment and surfaces repaired or modified?
6. What records and files document inspections and maintenance?
7. How are annual budget requests for repairs and replacements made?

Assigning Responsibility

An agency should designate a person to maintain the play area. Without such a designation, the routine maintenance necessary to help prevent injuries may never occur. The designated person may delegate responsibilities to others, especially if that person is responsible for more than one site. However, the designated person still acts as a conduit for any maintenance issues that may arise.

At a child care center, the maintenance person may be the center director, an assistant director, or a person hired specifically to maintain the total facility. At a school, this person may be an assistant principal, custodian, head teacher, or playground associate. A community park might designate a park supervisor, staff, or community volunteer to be in charge of maintenance.

Providing Training

Whoever is in charge of maintaining the play area must be trained to look for hazards and problems that can occur in the area. We have seen new playground structures with some serious safety problems because the maintenance personnel were not trained to inspect the equipment (personal safety inspections conducted by authors, 1996-2006). Instead, they simply assumed that since the equipment was new, it was safe.

At a minimum, the maintenance personnel should be familiar with the latest edition of the *Handbook for Public Playground Safety* that contains the CPSC guidelines.

Establishing a Schedule

First, check the information provided by the manufacturer of the equipment. Reputable manufacturers that subscribe to the ASTM standards and CPSC guidelines will have a recommended inspection and maintenance program for the equipment they sell. This information will form the framework for the inspection and maintenance processes. Beyond the manufacturers' recommendations, the frequency of inspections depends on several variables, including size and type of equipment, age of equipment and frequency of repairs, materials used in equipment, playground usage, vandalism, accidents, and types of inspections performed.

Equipment Size and Type

Large pieces of equipment with many nuts and bolts as well as moving parts will need to be inspected on a more frequent schedule than pieces of equipment that are small and have few supporting fasteners. The more connecting parts on equipment, the greater the possibility that a fastener or joint support can work itself loose through normal usage. Unless checked frequently, these areas may create potential entanglement and entrapment hazards.

Equipment Age and Frequency of Repairs

As was shown in both NPPS studies, the older the equipment, the greater the maintenance problems (Hudson, Mack, and Thompson, 2000; Hudson, Olsen, and Thompson, 2004). Equipment will last a long time if it is maintained on a regular basis. But, like anything else, the longer you have equipment, the more care it demands in order to keep it safe and usable.

After awhile, you may find that certain types of equipment break down repeatedly. This might be especially true of moving equipment, such as track rides, that have been on the playground for a long period of time. Over time the bearings wear or children place objects such as rocks in the track. The more frequent the repairs, the more frequent the inspections should be.

Materials Used

Metal rusts, wood splinters, and plastic cracks. There is no such thing as a maintenance-free material. Rust that builds up over time will weaken metal parts. Thus, when rust starts to appear on equipment it should be removed as quickly as possible. Wooden equipment needs to be treated with preservative every 6 to 12 months to ensure that no splinters occur and that dry rot has not set in. Plastic equipment needs to be inspected for cuts, nicks, and cracks that occur as a result of vandalism or heavy use.

Some materials do better in certain locations than others. For instance, metal equipment does not do well in Hawaii because of the corrosive characteristics of salt in the air. Wooden equipment is not recommended for hot climates as it may develop more splinters if not treated properly.

Frequency of Use

How often the equipment is used also determines the frequency of inspections. A school playground that 300 children use every day for nine months will demand more frequent inspections than a city park where 50 or so children use the play structures only on weekends. However, keep in mind one caution: If the equipment is available to children, they will use it. Don't fail to inspect a school playground during the summer just because school's not in session, and don't ignore a park playground in winter just because it's cold outside.

Vandalism

Vandalism can cause problems overnight. In areas where vandalism is a major problem, playgrounds may need more frequent inspections. Unfortunately, sometimes it is hard to predict when vandals may strike. Figure 8.4 shows a new playground in a middle-class neighborhood that had been open for only one day when three teenagers poured gasoline on the wood chips and used a lighter to ignite them. The resulting fire was so hot that it melted the plastic pieces.

At certain times of the year, vandalism may be more problematic. For instance, around Halloween, razor blades and other sharp objects sometimes appear on slides and in loose fill surfacing. The end of summer is another time when some young people show their displeasure about going back to school by destroying property.

Good maintenance practices can also help prevent vandalism. A psychological phenomenon known as *quality of use* affects the actions of many people. For instance, if you go to a well-maintained picnic area in the park where litter is picked up, trash

© NPPS

Figure 8.4 Vandals started a fire that melted the plastic equipment in this playground.

containers are empty, and picnic tables are free of graffiti, you will be more likely to leave the place as you found it. However, if the area is not well kept, with litter strewn all over, trash containers overflowing, and many names carved into the table, people are more inclined to leave the area in as bad if not worse shape than they found it. Human beings respond to visual cues in the environment in terms of our actions and behaviors. While there are always exceptions to the rule, good maintenance contributes to higher respect of the play environment.

Accidents

Certain equipment may be the source of numerous accidents. For instance, figure 8.5 shows a glider that was built for wheelchair users in a public play space. While the concept was good, it was found that nondisabled children were getting behind the glider and shoving it so hard that it was breaking the stopping mechanism on the glider rail. In addition, any child behind the glider was in the direct path of this giant battering ram. The result was that the municipal park and recreation department stopped the gliding motion of the piece to avoid potential lawsuits from injuries.

Accident reports can help track problems. When 90 percent of the reported injuries involve splinters, it's easy to see that there may be a problem with the maintenance of the wooden equipment. When a certain type of equipment shows up time and time again in accident reports, it is time for the agency to decide if that equipment is appropriate for the site.

Types of Inspections

Besides frequency of inspections, it is important to note that two types of inspections take place: routine and periodic. A routine inspection is a cursory look at the play

© NPPS

Figure 8.5 This glider for children in wheelchairs proved too susceptible to accidents.

area to check that it is safe for children. This type of inspection is done frequently (either daily or weekly). A periodic inspection is much more detailed. The maintenance personnel examine every nut and bolt, guardrail and barrier, and equipment piece to ensure that everything is secure and safe. This type of inspection is done less frequently (i.e., monthly, quarterly, or semiannually).

While the maintenance policy should indicate when routine or periodic inspections should take place, it should not indicate specific days. For instance, the policy should state that routine inspections will occur weekly as opposed to every Wednesday. If you miss a Wednesday and do the inspection on Thursday but a child is hurt on the equipment Wednesday night, you may be held liable for not doing the inspection when the policy stated that you would.

Reporting Maintenance Work

What if a problem is found during a routine inspection? Most agencies employ some type of checklist to report and record problems and repairs. In most cases, if the needed repair is minor (e.g., insufficient loose fill surfacing under the swings), it will be done upon its discovery. In these cases both the problem and the solution (raking more loose fill surfacing into the area) should be noted. It is always important to describe the action taken (e.g., fixed, contacted main office, contacted manufacturer) to rectify any maintenance concern. Otherwise, a minor problem, such as a loose bolt, may become a major problem, such as a missing equipment piece, because no one took the initiative to fix the problem. In addition, recognizing that a problem exists but failing to take action puts the agency in jeopardy if someone gets injured.

Making Repairs and Modifications

As important as delineating the procedures for reporting a maintenance problem, any policy should also outline the procedures for repairing broken equipment. In the policy, an agency must provide a complete trail of responsibility and authority from finding a problem to fixing the problem. Thus, the policy becomes the way the agency fulfills its duty or standard of care for keeping children safe on the playground.

Documenting Inspections and Maintenance

It is essential to retain complete documentation of all maintenance inspections and repairs on a playground. This documentation should include the manufacturer's maintenance guidelines as well as any checklists used. With the advent of computerized systems, it is recommended that a spreadsheet be developed for each play site to help store this data.

In addition to maintenance records, a yearly report of any accidents and injuries that occurred at the play site should be collected and retained. Such a report will help identify potential hazards or dangerous design features that might warrant attention.

Any correspondence with the manufacturer representative or others with regard to the play equipment should also be kept. This information could be important in the event of a lawsuit, and it also provides data about the ability to work with a certain company. If an agency has not been able to satisfactorily solve problems with an equipment distributor, they should contact the manufacturer directly. Having this correspondence on file may highlight potential problems when buying new equipment.

All of this information should be kept in a safe but easily retrievable location throughout the life span of the playground and beyond. It can help defend the agency against a lawsuit in the event of an accident. In many states, children have up to two years after they have reached majority age to file a lawsuit. Therefore, it behooves an agency to keep records for many years after the playground is altered or removed. Fortunately, with the advent of electronic data storage this is not an undue hardship.

 The information should be stored in an organized manner so that it can be easily retrieved for purposes such as evaluating the maintenance level for the site each year, locating inspection records, finding warranty information on particular equipment pieces, and contacting the manufacturer for replacement parts. Figure 8.6 is a sample documentation checklist that helps remind people which material to keep on file. The checklist also appears on the CD-ROM for easy reproduction.

Making Annual Budget Requests

Last but not least, information concerning budget requests and monies set aside for maintenance and repair should be included in the overall maintenance policy. A good

Sample Documentation Checklist

For each play area under your jurisdiction, keep these documents on file.

Document	Filed date(s)	Comments
GENERAL INFORMATION		
Planning meeting minutes		
Initial letters for bid		
Acceptance contract		
Invoice		
Equipment warranty		
Site plans/construction details		
Itemized list and quantity of play components		
Parts list		
Initial safety audit		
Inspection history/checklists		
Remedial action history (work orders)		
Incident reports (injury, vandalism)		
Other:		
Other:		
MANUFACTURER'S INFORMATION		
Contact information		
Correspondence with manufacturer		
Manufacturer's compliance letters (certificates for ASTM, CPSC, IPEMA)		
Manufacturer's installation drawings and instructions		
Manufacturer's installation verification		
Other:		
Other:		

Figure 8.6   A sample checklist for documenting inspections and maintenance.

From *S.A.F.E. Play Areas: Creation, Maintenance, and Renovation* by Donna Thompson, Susan D. Hudson, and Heather M. Olsen, 2007, Champaign, IL: Human Kinetics.

rule of thumb is to allocate at least 10 percent of the initial cost of the playground equipment on a yearly basis for repair materials. With good care, the average playground equipment purchased today may last 15 to 20 years. By putting aside money on an annual basis, an agency has a fund to provide for immediate repair of equipment. In addition, any surplus may be able to help defray future replacement costs.

Use the S.A.F.E. Model Checklist: Daily Maintenance Quick Check in appendix C to look for conditions that may change suddenly as a result of use, abuse, or the environment. The checklist also appears on the CD-ROM for easy reproduction.

Evaluation of Maintenance Policy

Having a maintenance policy does not ensure that proper maintenance will be performed; the policy is just the framework for developing a play environment that follows the S.A.F.E. model. In order to be effective, the policy must be known and implemented by staff. Chapter 9 will discuss specific implementation steps.

The maintenance policy should be reviewed periodically to ensure that its procedures are practical. Many times, the written policy may be short-circuited by staff either because they are not aware of the proper procedure or because they know that going through the channels as outlined in the policy doesn't work. To prevent these problems, all administrators and staff should review policy and procedures together once a year. This type of evaluation helps to make the policy a living document, not simply something that gathers dust on a shelf.

Success Story

In a 2004 legal case, a midsized park and recreation department in the Midwest was sued by the parents of an 8-year-old child who had broken an arm while playing on equipment in the park. The parents alleged that the department had not properly maintained the surfacing under and around the equipment. However, the department was able to document that they had a policy for ongoing maintenance and that they performed weekly inspections. In fact, the depth of the loose fill surfacing had been checked the morning of the incident and was found to meet the requirements.

In the depositions taken for the case, it was revealed that the children had been playing a game of tag on the equipment while their parents chatted at a picnic table some distance away. In an effort to avoid being tagged, the child leaped off the 8-foot-high (2.4-meter-high) platform, landing awkwardly on the surface. The injury was the result of the nature of the fall, not because of inadequate surfacing. Subsequently, the lawsuit was dropped.

This story underscores three important points. First, adequate documentation and action can protect an agency from a lawsuit. Second, supervision is always important in controlling inappropriate play behavior. Third, even under the best of circumstances, injuries can occur.

Summary

"If you build it, you must maintain it" should be the motto for all owners and operators of play areas. A proactive maintenance policy must be developed to provide an umbrella of safety for children. In this chapter, we discussed the spokes of that umbrella. But just as important as creating the policy is enforcing it rather than letting it gather dust on a shelf. For example, we participated in a legal case in which an agency had developed a district-wide policy. However, records showed that few if any inspections were done on a regular basis. In this case, having a policy but no documentation actually hurt the agency more than if they'd had no policy at all.

Now that we've set the stage for maintenance, in chapter 9 we'll look at ways to translate policy into action by implementing a maintenance program. Remember, a play area will not maintain itself; only adults who are concerned with the well-being of children can accomplish that goal.

The Nuts and Bolts of Maintenance Policies

Yes, some accidents are caused by poor judgment in risk-taking, but most accidents—and injuries—are caused by the existence of hazards on the playground.

Dr. Fran Wallach

Eight-year-old Terasita could hardly wait until the beginning of school when she and her classmates would be allowed back on the school playground. The only swings in the whole town were located on the playground, which was surrounded by a large fence and an even bigger lock. She didn't understand why grown-ups wanted to keep a perfectly good play area under lock and key during the summer months. But, rules were rules, and unlike some of the other kids that snuck in during the summer, she stayed out.

Determined to get one of the limited swing seats, she raced to the swings during the first recess. As she started to go higher and higher, she felt like she was almost flying. Just as she reached the highest point of her forward arc, a loose bolt at the top of one of the chains fell out, and the chain came loose. Without warning, Terasita was dumped out of the swing and plummeted to the ground with a large thump. Pain darted through both of her legs and one hip. It took six hours of surgery to repair her hip and place screws in both legs. During her long rehabilitation, Terasita decided never to go near a swing again.

A s discussed in the previous chapter, maintenance involves more than going out once a month and checking to make sure children's play areas are in good condition. It also involves more than just tightening a loose bolt or replacing a broken swing chain. Maintenance keeps all equipment working and all surfacing materials safe. Maintaining children's play areas takes time and dedication. But, the time and dedication is necessary when you consider who the users are. Maintenance is important for children because it ensures the equipment and surfacing are as safe as possible. Maintenance is also valuable to owners because it can extend the life span of the equipment.

The agency responsible for the maintenance of the playground environment has an important job. Child care centers, schools, and park departments need to be proactive, responding to problems before they occur.

In this chapter, we'll focus on implementing sound maintenance practices. Such practices start with playground planning and equipment installation, so that topic will come first. Next, we'll describe what a well-maintained area looks like. Finally, we'll consider specific items to check during a maintenance assessment.

In the Beginning

Maintenance considerations have to be part of the initial planning process. A poorly built playground is difficult to maintain. Providing good maintenance for a safe play environment begins with planning the total play environment. Factors to consider regarding maintenance during the planning stage include site location, materials used, and site management.

Site Location

Before creating the play area, a site analysis should take place to ensure that the location is compatible with the intended use. The purpose of site analysis is to find a place for a particular use or find a use for a particular place. During the site analysis, information about environmental characteristics, manufactured elements, and hazardous conditions that will affect the use and safety of the area is gathered and analyzed (Molnar and Rutledge, 1986).

Environmental Characteristics

Environmental characteristics to consider during the site analysis include soils and geology, drainage, topography, vegetation, wind, climate, and sun orientation, all of which may affect the ongoing maintenance of the site.

Soils and Geology   Soil type is important because it is directly related to drainage. The playground equipment should be installed on well-drained soil. A playground constructed on poor soil will be subject to pooling or standing water. The foundations of the equipment will also erode and create problems of equipment stability.

Drainage   In general, water should drain away from the playground. Thus, the site should be slightly elevated. Keep in mind that construction of the playground or surrounding areas may alter the patterns of water movement on the site. If you have questions about preventing or solving water problems, a good source of professional information is the local office of the Soil Conservation Service (SCS).

Topography   Topography concerns the lay of the land. As a general rule, slopes around and beneath playground equipment should conform to the following guidelines (Illinois Park and Recreation Association [IPRA], 1995):

- Slopes between 1 percent and 4 percent are most suitable for playgrounds; 1 percent slope falls 1 foot (.3 meter) for every 100 linear feet (30.5 linear meters).
- Slopes less than 1 percent may result in drainage problems.
- Slopes greater than 4 percent may require site modifications to install and level equipment.

In addition, slope is an important consideration in providing equal access to the playground regardless of physical capabilities. The accessible route into the playground must have a maximum slope of 5 percent—1 foot (.3 meter) of fall for every 20 linear feet (6.1 linear meters)—and a maximum cross slope of 2 percent.

Vegetation   Vegetation is another environmental consideration in terms of design and maintenance. Shade is an essential ingredient for every playground. If trees are not present, it may be necessary to provide a shade structure. Trees planted along a western and southern exposure may provide the necessary shade, but caution must be taken to ensure that overhanging limbs do not interfere with play activities (Thompson and Hudson, 2005). Limbs need to be pruned to at least 7 feet (2.1

meters) off the ground to prevent children from climbing the trees. In addition, avoid planting trees, shrubs, or flowers that contain residue or are likely to attract stinging insects such as bees.

Wind   The direction of the prevailing winds should also be determined. If at all possible, locate the playground upwind from open fields, farms, or areas like unpaved roads where dust will blow directly into the play area. In addition, if an area is susceptible to routine strong winds, some type of windbreak should be created. Wind can directly affect the type and maintenance of loose fill surfacing used.

Climate   Heat, cold, humidity, and precipitation can all affect playground equipment and surfacing. These factors directly influence the materials used for equipment and surfacing. For instance, sand is an inappropriate surfacing material in extremely cold climates because it will freeze if moisture is present. Likewise, metal equipment that comes into contact with bare skin may cause problems if temperatures are below freezing. Humidity will hasten the decomposition of organic surface materials, and most playground equipment becomes extremely slippery when wet. An area that receives constant precipitation may need to provide a cover over the equipment as well as excellent drainage.

Sun Orientation   Sun orientation is another factor that will affect the play area. Slide surfaces that tend to absorb heat should not be placed on a western exposure. The best orientation is north. However, if this is not possible, then provide natural or manufactured shade (see figure 9.1).

Figure 9.1   Large trees are a good source of shade.

Manufactured Elements

The second major factor to consider in the site analysis is manufactured elements. These include roads, buildings, adjacent land use, site accessibility, and utilities.

Roads   The play area should be located far enough away from roads and parking lots so that moving vehicles do not pose a hazard for children. A barrier surrounding the play area is recommended if children can inadvertently run into a street. Fences that are used for barriers should conform to applicable local building codes (CPSC, 1997). In addition, the ASTM has developed a specific standard for fencing around playgrounds (ASTM F2049).

Buildings   Proper use zones need to be maintained in relation to any buildings or structures present on the site. For example, a school playground should be located far enough away from the school buildings so that a child on a climbing structure is in no danger of falling off the play equipment into the building. In addition, close proximity of the play area to windows may encourage vandalism of the windows.

Adjacent Land Use   Uses of neighboring land need to be considered because they may affect or be affected by the play area. Railroads, freeways, landfills, streams, and rivers may all contribute to a hazardous environment for children. The long-term effects of some of these uses (e.g., waste dumps) may not be determined for years. On the other hand, the location of the play area itself may be seen as an undesirable element within the neighborhood. Some people may be upset by the perceived increase of noise, vandalism, and traffic that they assume a play area will attract.

Site Accessibility   Accessibility to and from the site is also a consideration. How will children get to the play area? Will they arrive on bicycles or walk? Will adults bring them by car? The answers to these questions will determine the need for bicycle racks, pathways, and parking lots. It will also determine the amount of maintenance needed for the total area.

Utilities   As a general rule, play areas should not be constructed under utility lines. Also, pay attention to unused utility easements. Some might be tempted to use these seemingly open areas, but nothing can stop a utility from using the easement for power lines at a later date. Another utility consideration is support structures that may be found near the play site. Power poles and towers can constitute an attractive nuisance in the play area. In addition, guide wires or other supporting cables on these utility structures can create a hazard for children.

Hazardous Conditions

The third element of site analysis is the consideration of hazardous conditions. These can include items related to visibility and security, crossings, and accessible water areas.

Visibility and Security   The ability to see children is of the utmost importance in providing a safe environment. Do not plant large shrubs above 4 feet (1.2 meters) in height around a playground because they inhibit the ability to observe children at play. In addition, as previously mentioned, maintenance personnel should remove low tree branches to prevent climbing. Any trees by the development of the play area should also be removed before they create a hazardous situation. Unfortunately, dead tree limbs have fallen and killed children in play areas.

Crossings Children should not be required to use unprotected street crossings to reach play areas. Fencing or natural barriers may be necessary if alternative solutions are not feasible (IPRA, 1995). Another traffic consideration involves schools and child care centers where delivery truck routes may pose a hazard for children going to and from the play area. Take special care to make certain that these routes do not intersect the play area and are not located nearby. In addition, take care in moving maintenance vehicles in and out of the area.

Open Water Areas Children are attracted to ponds, streams, and drainage ditches. Cement culverts or ditches are especially dangerous because their smooth sides may not allow for an easy escape in case of a flash flood. Signage alone will not stop children from trying to play in these areas. In addition, because standing water can breed mosquitoes and attract animals, special maintenance considerations need to be taken if standing water is on or near the play area.

Materials Used in Play Equipment

There is no such thing as a maintenance-free material when it comes to the development of a play area. Without good maintenance, wood will splinter, metal will rust, and plastic will crack (see figure 9.2). Equipment in public areas such as child care

Figure 9.2 At first, a wooden play area can look safe (a), but up close, the need for maintenance is clear (b).

centers, schools, and parks should be designed for public use, not home use. The equipment should be durable and meet requirements for insurance, standards, warranty, age appropriateness, and use. Any equipment should conform to both CPSC guidelines and ASTM standard F1487.

Playground equipment is usually made out of one of five types of materials: wood, steel, aluminum, plastic, or recycled materials. Each material has advantages and disadvantages with regard to durability and maintenance requirements.

Wood Products

Wood must be treated to prevent rotting due to weather or insects, especially when the wood is in direct contact with the ground. Any chemical wood preservative used must be approved for contact with humans. Since 2002, manufacturers have stopped using chromated copper arsenate (CCA) for treated wood. One of the prime ingredients of CCA is arsenic. As this type of treated wood deteriorates, minute particles of arsenic are released to the wood surface. In particular, young children are at risk of ingesting small portions of arsenic when they put their hands in their mouths after touching CCA-treated wood. Therefore, it is crucial to annually use a clear preservative to seal the wood of any wooden structure older than 2002. Not only will this clear preservative prevent CCA from escaping, it will also help to extend the life of the structure.

Wood is also subject to splitting, which may eventually weaken the total structure. Watch out for evidence of splitting in new wood, especially in support beams and poles. Sanding and other treatments may be required to avoid injuries from splinters. Although aesthetically pleasing, wooden pieces usually have a life span of only 10 years. This depends, of course, on the amount of preventive maintenance that is performed. The authors have seen wooden structures that are still very viable after 15 years and others that are extremely deteriorated after 5 years.

Steel Equipment

The 1950s saw an increase in steel play equipment across the United States, and many of those pieces can still be found today. However, most do not meet modern safety standards for playground equipment.

Steel equipment should be galvanized and given a protective coating that inhibits rust such as powder coating and painting. Never use paint that has lead as a component. Also, scratches and construction defects are subject to rust. Finally, steel can heat up to dangerous levels with direct exposure to sunlight. On the other hand, steel equipment is very durable and has a long life span.

Aluminum

Components made out of aluminum are rust resistant and offer lightweight installation. Because of the manufacturing process, aluminum is sometimes more costly at purchase; however, the reduced maintenance cost is often worth the extra money. Shipping charges will be reduced because of the lighter weight. Like steel, aluminum can heat up with direct exposure to sunlight.

Plastic

Plastic has become the material of choice in recent years because it can be molded, cut, or formed into a wide variety of shapes for playground use. However, most plastics do not have the strength of natural lumbers and metals and can sag and bend. It is recommended that ultraviolet (UV) light inhibitors be added to the plastic to extend life expectancy and color.

Plastic is also susceptible to vandalism. Knife cuts can create cracks in slide beds and heat can actually melt the play structure (see figure 9.3). In addition, plastic surfaces provide a tempting target for graffiti artists. Plastic is not maintenance free; it should be power washed occasionally to remove dirt, grime, and other things that might stick to its surface.

Recycled Materials

In recent years, recycled materials have become increasingly popular in playground equipment. Many people like the aesthetics of wood but not the upkeep, and recycled materials usually come from recycled plastic products such as milk jugs and can be manufactured to resemble wood beams. However, recycled materials are not as durable as wood, and many of the early pieces of equipment made from these materials have dips and bends in platforms. On the other hand, as technology improves, so will the durability of these products. Recycled materials require the same type of maintenance as plastics.

Site Management

Before developing a playground, you must decide how the area will be maintained. If you anticipate that there will be heavy use of the play area year round, then you

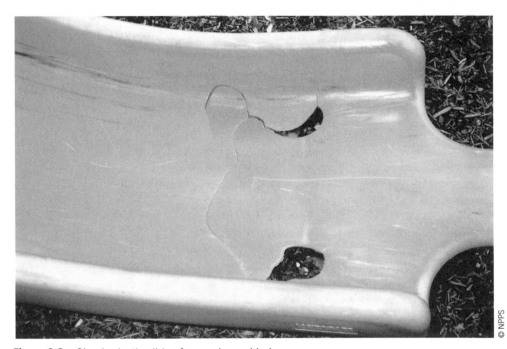

Figure 9.3 Check plastic slides for cracks and holes.

will need to develop a more frequent maintenance schedule. On the other hand, if the play area is in a more remote spot and will see infrequent use, a longer period of time can elapse between routine inspections. The worst-case scenario is to develop a play area that will demand frequent maintenance by an overextended agency that has too many areas to maintain already.

Practical considerations such as access to the site for maintenance personnel also need to be discussed. When a high-use play area is at the far end of several acres, trash barrels will not be emptied on a timely basis and loose fill surfacing will not be replaced as often as needed.

To avoid these types of problems, maintenance personnel need to be part of the initial planning team. When the play area becomes just one more place that needs attention, the maintenance tends to be haphazard at best.

Building a Firm Foundation

Equipment installation is as important to the total maintenance process as planning. Improper installation of equipment and surfacing will not only jeopardize the safety of the total play environment, it will compromise the ability to maintain the area. Three major factors to consider in the installation of equipment and surfacing include the manufacturer's instructions, the installer, and sign-off by the manufacturer.

Reading the Instructions

According to ASTM F1487, the manufacturer or designer must provide clear and concise instructions for the installation of each structure and a complete parts list. It is crucial to follow these procedures during the installation process. Afterward, file these instructions in case any liability issues arise concerning the proper installation of equipment and surfacing.

If the manufacturer installs the equipment and surfacing, the responsibility for proper installation lies with the company. If agency personnel do the installation, the agency assumes the liability and the burden of proof that they followed proper procedures.

Manufacturer's instructions should discuss the proper use-zone placement of equipment, the installation of the equipment at the proper depths, the correct method of mixing adhesives for surfacing materials, the correct mixing of cement in proportion with water, and the use of proper tools to lock structure joints.

In addition to the instructions, any recommendations by the manufacturer must also be followed. For example, in order to maintain the proper impact attenuation of a surface, the manufacturer may recommend that pea gravel used to enhance drainage be separated from wood products by a filter cloth. Once installed, it is the agency's responsibility to see that the separation continues. Other recommendations might be to check bushings on swings annually for wear or to cover wood products with a preservative on an annual basis. In each of these cases, it is imperative to follow the recommendations of the manufacturer.

The agency must also post any manufacturer's warnings that are included with materials. Many manufacturers now place labels on equipment that suggest ages for which the equipment is designed or the proper depth for loose fill materials. When warnings accompany playground equipment, the agency is responsible for replacing the warnings if they become illegible, are destroyed, or are removed. Diligence in posting warning labels will inform adults about ways to prevent children from being injured.

Selecting the Installer

The agency must decide who will install the equipment and surface. Usually it is possible to use an installer recommended by the company from whom the equipment or surfacing has been purchased. This installer should be trained by the company or be a certified installer of playground equipment and surfacing. A trained installer adds to the overall cost of the equipment; thus, many agencies decide to use in-house personnel to install the equipment and surface. If this installation method is selected, for liability protection it is important to have a company representative observe or direct the installation process.

A third method has come about in recent years—installation as a community project. In these instances, volunteers in the community get together, usually on a weekend, to build a playground for children (see figure 9.4). The playground then becomes a source of civic pride and involvement. Obviously, trying to coordinate a group of volunteers who have little knowledge of equipment installation is more difficult than simply having the company install the equipment. But, because this process helps to foster community involvement, it may be worth the extra effort required to coordinate this type of installation.

Similar to the in-house installation, care must be taken to ensure that both the agency and the community volunteers have liability protection. This means that all volunteers must be covered by liability insurance during the installation process and that the agency should investigate what might occur if a volunteer is hurt while installing the equipment. In addition, it is imperative that a company representative be present to ensure that instructions are followed.

The amount of time needed for the installation will influence the number of people involved in the actual installation process. It is necessary to determine whether the community will tolerate weekend installation or if the work must be done during usual work hours or evenings. If installation takes a period of days or weeks, preventing children from using partially built structures is a priority.

Signing Off

After the installation is completed, the agency should have the manufacturer's representative of both the equipment and surfacing sign off that both items were installed according to specifications. This process should include a playground audit.

A playground audit is a comprehensive first-time inspection of the playground that sets the baseline for future maintenance procedures. It should be based on the current CPSC guidelines and ASTM standards. The audit identifies all pieces that are on

© NPPS

Figure 9.4 Members of a community work together to build a new playground.

the playground, their current condition, and how they measure up to the guidelines and standards.

After the audit is completed, hold regularly scheduled inspections and compare the findings to those of the audit. This will help ensure that the playground equipment and surfacing remain in good condition, and it will help maintenance personnel make decisions about repairing and replacing worn and deteriorating parts of equipment.

Keeping a Well-Maintained Playground

Community playgrounds often remain empty, in part because they're poorly maintained. Parents are concerned when equipment is broken, worn, or vandalized. They fear that something dangerous could happen to their child.

The first visual impression that a maintained play area should give is that it is clean. Trash is picked up. There is no animal feces around. A maintained play area is free of broken, missing, and worn parts. The swing chains are not rusted. Pieces of equipment do not have worn paint or graffiti. Most important, there are children all over the playground, laughing, running, playing, and socializing with their friends.

You will also find parents, grandparents, and adults playing the role of caretaker. You will see adults walking around looking at equipment. As we all know, owners have challenging responsibilities because they cannot be at each play area during every second of the day. That is why adults need to be helpers. They need to be aware of ways to prevent unsafe situations from occurring. Adults need to be alert when they take their children to the play area. They can visually assess the equipment for safety problems and make sure that children do not play on any unsafe equipment.

Use the S.A.F.E. Model Checklist: Caregiver Quick Check in appendix C to assess the general safety of a playground. The checklist also appears on the CD-ROM for easy reproduction.

Adults can help keep play areas free from hazards. If you spot a problem that you can remedy yourself, such as picking up litter, go ahead and do it. However, if you observe safety problems that require professional attention, such as broken equipment, contact the organization responsible for the area.

Some situations might require you to use good judgment. For example, if you notice a broken piece of equipment that you think could cause injury or even death, you first should tell any children present not to play on that item. Immediately afterward, you should call the agency in charge of the play area to report the broken equipment and state your concerns. Give the agency at least two weeks to fix the problem. If they do nothing, you might need to go up the chain of command within that agency to get action. As a last resort, you could alert local media to the problem, but this might bring adverse publicity and make it more difficult for you to work with the agency in the future. The best solution is to try to get the problem fixed with the first phone call.

Of course, visiting adults can only do so much. The organization or agency in charge of a play area has the responsibility to maintain it. To do this effectively, they must understand maintenance needs and current safety guidelines.

One way an agency can stay on top of maintenance needs is to have extra parts on hand. Too often a playground is not repaired immediately because extra nuts and bolts need to be ordered from the manufacturer. Be sure to request extra parts when purchasing equipment. Never replace parts with materials from a local hardware store.

Using the S.A.F.E. Model
for Maintenance Assessment

Every day, park departments, schools, and child care centers struggle to manage day-to-day operations and sometimes overlook the outdoor environment. But children's playgrounds can't be ignored.

Use the six S.A.F.E. Model Checklists in appendix C to assess safety and identify needed repairs. You can customize the checklists by filling in the blanks to reflect your specific policies, procedures, management, and location details. The checklists also appear on the CD-ROM for easy reproduction.

These checklists are based on the S.A.F.E. model. Throughout this book, we've addressed the importance of a safe play environment and the four components of the model:

S = Supervision

A = Age-appropriate design

F = Fall surfacing

E = Equipment maintenance

Rather than presenting a laundry list of items to be addressed by a maintenance plan, it makes sense to organize them according to the S.A.F.E. model. In the following sections, we'll explore items related to each of the four components and then consider the general layout of the play environment.

Check for Supervision

Playground areas should be designed so that adults can be effective supervisors. For example, benches are often present in park playgrounds. Make sure that benches are stationed so that the adults can view the children (see figure 9.5). It does no good to install a bench that does not provide clear sight lines of the children's play area.

To make supervision more effective, ask three questions:

1. Are all areas in the play environment visible to supervisors?
2. Do enclosed spaces (i.e., crawl spaces, boxed areas, tunnels) have small openings or clear plastic to enable a supervisor to see if a child is inside?
3. Are all necessary signs or labels present?

Figure 9.5 Proper bench placement provides clear sight lines.

Supervisors need to see through vegetation and through equipment. This means that open sight lines need to be maintained by removing obstacles that might interfere with vision. It also means that items such as clear plastic bubbles and clear panels must be cleaned on a regular basis so that they do not become cloudy or covered with dirt. This can be accomplished by power washing the equipment on a yearly basis.

Signage and labels are especially important on community playgrounds. Many manufacturers include the suggestion for supervision on labels that are affixed to the equipment. As mentioned, the agency should maintain any label that the manufacturer has affixed to the equipment.

Check for Age-Appropriate Design

As we have learned, all children should play on developmentally appropriate equipment. There are a few questions that can guide maintenance personnel in this area.

1. For whom is the playground area intended?
2. Are there guardrails or protective barriers designed to prevent children from jumping off platforms?
3. Is equipment designed to prevent children from easily climbing outside of the equipment to heights over 3 feet (.9 meter)?

One of the determining factors concerning inspection frequency is the user. A preschool play area, for instance, may not need the same type of weekly maintenance as a community playground serving all ages. Multiple play areas for different grades may need to be inspected less frequently than a school play area that has only one structure serving 400 children. Thus, the intended user of the play space has a direct bearing on the frequency of maintenance and the overall wear and tear that will occur on a daily, weekly, monthly, and yearly basis.

The users' age will influence their play patterns and how they will use or misuse the equipment. Appropriate guardrails or protective barriers must be in place for any elevated surface that is more than 20 inches (51 centimeters) above the protective surfacing. In addition, there should be barriers designed to prevent attempts by children to climb outside the structure. Wear marks on supporting poles or plastic roofs are evidence that children are routinely using these structures in their play. In such instances, contact the agency administrator to report this misuse before an injury occurs. The administrator, in turn, should work with supervisory and maintenance staff to develop methods to stop misuse of the equipment.

Check Fall Surfacing

As mentioned in chapters 6 and 7, an important aspect of reducing playground injuries is cushioned surfaces beneath and around equipment at depths appropriate for equipment height. Surfaces such as asphalt, cement, dirt, and grass are not acceptable surfaces. Acceptable surfacing materials include wood products, shredded rubber, sand, pea gravel, poured-in-place rubber, and rubber tiles. Questions that guide maintenance in this area include the following:

1. Are appropriate surfacing materials present?
2. Is loose fill surfacing maintained at the appropriate depth?
3. Are unitary surfaces firmly attached to the underlying surface?
4. Are the use zones under and around equipment being maintained with proper surfacing?
5. Are concrete footings covered with suitable materials?
6. Is the surface free from foreign objects?
7. Is the surface free of water puddles, snow, or poor drainage?
8. Is the surface free of animal feces?

Due to the importance of surfacing in injury prevention, maintaining the surface under and around equipment needs to be a top priority for maintenance personnel. Loose fill surfacing requires a high degree of inspection and work in order for it to consistently provide safe cushioning that will help prevent injuries. This means that agencies that use loose fill materials should have at least weekly inspections to ensure that the materials are at the proper depths within the use zones of stationary equipment, swings, and slides. In addition, a weekly check will help to ensure that concrete footings are covered.

A check for animal contaminants and foreign objects should be part of a daily inspection by someone at schools and child care centers since these play areas are used every day. This check needs to be done at least weekly in community parks, perhaps more frequently during summer months when usage of these areas is high.

Water pooling on surfaces is an indication of poor drainage. With organic surface materials such as wood, water hastens the decomposition of the materials. In addition, weeds and other vegetation growing up through the materials is a sign that decomposition has taken place and that wood chips, fibers, or mulch should be completely replaced.

Unitary surfaces require less maintenance. Still, maintenance personnel or other adults should periodically sweep or blow the surfaces clean (see figure 9.6). This is especially true if other types of surface materials are present that can compromise the integrity of the unitary surface.

Check for Equipment Maintenance

This check is also a priority for maintenance personnel. While there are specific details they should look for on major equipment pieces, they should also frequently make broad observations. The following questions should guide general assessment in this area.

1. Is the equipment free of broken parts?
2. Is the equipment free of missing parts?
3. Is the equipment free of protruding bolts or fixtures?
4. Are equipment pieces free of noticeable gaps that can entangle drawstrings or entrap body parts?
5. Are equipment pieces free of places where head entrapment can occur?
6. Is metal equipment free of rust?

Figure 9.6 Keep unitary surfaces free of debris and foreign materials.

7. Is wooden equipment free of splinters?
8. Is plastic equipment free of cracks and holes?

Equipment should have no broken components. If damaged equipment is not repaired quickly, children will find alternative ways to use it that might cause physical injury, turn a minor repair into a major repair, or both. If a major piece of equipment has a broken or missing part, make sure it is off limits until personnel have a chance to replace or repair it. Don't simply wrap yellow caution tape around the affected part—that only entices children to investigate so they can see what's wrong. Instead, construct a more effective barrier. For example, you can block the entrance to a broken slide with a large sheet of wood, erect plastic fencing material around the damaged area, or even put up a chain-link fence around the play equipment.

Protruding bolts or fixtures can cause puncture wounds or entanglements. No protrusion should extend beyond two threads of a bolt head. When examining nuts and bolts, make sure they are tight, especially at the top of swings and other moving equipment. A loose bolt at the top of a swing can be disastrous, as shown in the cautionary tale at the beginning of this chapter.

Head entrapments on guardrails, protective barriers, platforms decks, and other elevated components can cause life-threatening injuries. These entrapments are especially prevalent in equipment manufactured before 1991. However, they can also be caused by faulty installation, so check new equipment as well to make sure that guardrails haven't shifted during use.

Although some materials are more durable than others, they all will develop problems over time (rust, splinters, and cracks). It is important to monitor the wear and tear of the equipment in order to keep it safe for children.

Check the General Layout

It is essential to examine the physical layout of the environment. In some play areas, children have been injured due to the lack of protection from the surrounding streets, parking lots, shade, and other factors (see the cautionary tale at the beginning of chapter 2). When considering the layout and environment, ask four basic questions.

1. Is the equipment located away from high traffic areas, ponds, and parking lots?
2. Is there a buffer area between the play structures and play zones such as zones for ball activities, sand and water play, tricycle paths, and so on?
3. Are swings located away from other equipment?
4. Is there adequate shade in the area?

The answers to these questions help determine what items should be part of a maintenance checklist. For instance, if the area is near a street or parking lot, make sure there is fencing or a buffer to prevent the children from running in front of cars and that it is maintained. Adequate closing mechanisms should work and no holes should be present along the fence line that will allow balls and children to easily escape. If vegetation (i.e., bushes) is used as a buffer, it needs to be trimmed periodically to provide visibility of the area.

In addition, equipment should be situated so that the clearance space allocated to one piece of equipment does not interfere with another piece of equipment. This is especially true at child care centers where equipment pieces are easily moved around. Use zones need to be maintained. If moveable pieces are on a unitary surface, the use zones for each piece of equipment can be outlined with tape so that maintenance personnel can easily move the pieces back into the proper use zone area after they sweep the surface.

Make sure children are aware of the location of swings and other moving equipment. This is especially important for young children who haven't learned the concept of cause and effect. They often run in front of swings because they do not realize that the swings will move forward and strike them.

Finally, if shade is provided, then part of the maintenance inspection should be to look up. No one wants a dead limb to come crashing down into the play area when people are present. In addition, periodically check shade frames to ensure that fasteners are tight and that there are no rips in canopies or fabric coverings.

Developing a Maintenance Checklist

In addition to the checklists in appendix C and on the CD-ROM, other such lists are available for maintenance personnel. The CPSC *Handbook for Public Playground Safety* (1997) includes a 10-item list in the back. The NPPS offers two assessment kits (one designed for child care centers and one designed for school playgrounds) that provide detailed information based on the CPSC guidelines and ASTM standards.

When using these or other checklists, remember these important points:

- Adapt the checklist to fit your particular site.
- Use the checklist to gather information to repair, replace, or retrofit equipment and surfacing to keep children safe.
- Keep documentation on file to protect your agency if a lawsuit is filed.

We all have a role in keeping play environments safe. By being vigilant about the condition of playgrounds through observation and inspections, we can help keep children safe.

 Success Story

Bob Porter, the safety coordinator of the Iowa City school district, has made it his personal crusade to reduce injuries in all of the play areas in the district. To that end, he's worked with school officials and the NPPS to develop guidelines that pertain to the purchase, installation, and maintenance of playground equipment within the district.

Not only are these guidelines based on the CPSC guidelines and the ASTM standards, but they also require all equipment and areas to be in compliance with the ADA. In the opening paragraph, the Iowa City guidelines state that the "selection and installation of playground equipment will be based with safety as a key design element" (Iowa City Community School District, 2006). Further, any equipment purchased must be in accordance with the age group of the children expected to use it.

Porter also knows the importance of documentation. The Iowa City guidelines require that "a file will be kept which includes a copy of the invoice, installation blueprints, the names and addresses of the manufacturer and the vendor, and the original contract documents." These records are stored at the district's physical plant.

In bringing the S.A.F.E. model to school playgrounds and educating others on supervision, surfacing, and other needs, Porter is an outstanding example of how one dedicated person can have a big effect. Thanks to his efforts, the children of the Iowa City school district can enjoy safe play areas today and in the future. One person really can make a difference.

Summary

In this chapter, we looked at the nuts and bolts of maintaining safe playgrounds. We learned that maintenance starts with the planning process and needs to be considered from the beginning, not as an afterthought. The manner in which structures are installed could affect the ability to maintain an area, and it's imperative to follow manufacturer directions. Appendix C provides checklists for maintenance and repairs, and we encourage you to adapt them to meet your particular needs.

This chapter marks the end of our study of the research and practical applications of the S.A.F.E. model, but it's not the end of our journey. In chapter 10, we'll offer recommendations on how you can implement these important lessons in your own community to help make play areas safe for children.

Toward a Safer World of Play

*A hundred years from now, it won't matter what
my bank account was, the sort of house I lived in,
or the kind of car I drove . . . but the world may be
different because I was important in the life of a child.*

Anonymous

In 1997, Lester Chuck, a facilities director for Hawaii public schools, attended the NPPS Safety School in Hawaii. Afterward, he returned to his job, determined to bring Hawaiian school playgrounds in line with the S.A.F.E. model.

First, he and his assistants assessed the existing elementary school playgrounds to see whether they met the CPSC guidelines. To their dismay, they found problems with all of them. Some didn't have the right type or proper amount of surfacing. Others had inadequate use zones. Still others had old, broken equipment with head entrapments.

Lester took the drastic action of closing 265 play areas. Then he invited the NPPS to provide a workshop for representatives of the public schools so they could learn how to build and renovate playgrounds according to the S.A.F.E. model. Community members were frustrated that so many play areas were closed, but they understood that something needed to be done to keep their children safe.

In addition, Lester had a good relationship with the Hawaii Board of Education and with several state legislators. He convinced the legislature to provide initial funding of $3 million to replace equipment that was deemed unsafe. One year later, the legislature allocated another $3 million to support continued efforts. Within five years, all equipment and surfacing had finally been replaced.

Lester has retired from his position as facilities director, but those who have taken his place continue to monitor and improve public school playgrounds in Hawaii. Among other initiatives, the district has instituted supervision training for all schools, which Lester came out of retirement to conduct.

Supervision, age-appropriate design, fall surfacing, and equipment maintenance are the four components of the S.A.F.E. model—the foundation for keeping children safe in any type of play environment. Although we have focused on outdoor play areas in this book, the same attention to safety is needed in gymnasiums, swimming pools, and a multitude of recreation facilities.

The absence of the four elements can also be considered risk factors. If you don't have proper supervision, age-appropriate equipment and design, proper surfacing, and equipment maintenance, there is a greater possibility that children will be injured. That's why we pointed out the difference between risk (the probability of loss or injury) and challenge (how individuals test themselves in completing a task) in the play environment. We also reviewed the history of playground safety, including the contributions of the CPSC and the ASTM.

In chapters 2 through 9, we studied each component of the S.A.F.E. model.

- For supervision, we considered the ABCs (anticipation, behavior, and context) of supervision and how to develop a supervision plan.

- For age-appropriate design, we showed how children of different ages have different developmental characteristics, requiring play areas designed to meet their specific needs.

- For surfacing, we looked at the relationship between fall height and injuries and presented a decision model for choosing appropriate materials.

- For equipment, we stressed the importance of keeping play areas in good repair, which involves an ongoing process of planning, documentation, and assessment.

Now that you've learned how to use the S.A.F.E. model to create, renovate, and maintain play areas, it's time to move forward and put this knowledge to work.

Ten Tips for Taking Action

We began *S.A.F.E. Play Areas: Creation, Maintenance, and Renovation* by debunking 10 common myths about fun and safety in play environments. Now, we conclude with 10 things you can do to keep children safe in your community. We hope these ideas will inspire you to create additional ways to take action.

Refer to appendix D to learn more about any of the NPPS resources mentioned in the following ways to take action.

1. Join a Planning Committee

Join a planning committee for a playground at a child care center, school, or park. You can lead or organize the committee, or perhaps serve as the contact person for a local business. In this way, you can directly affect the creation of the new playground, which might turn out to be one of the safest and most heavily used play areas in your town, county, or state.

2. Assess a Playground

Learn to assess the playgrounds in your community and teach others how to do the same. Use the reproducible forms on the CD-ROM to assess an existing playground, or obtain assessment kits from the NPPS and distribute them to child care centers, schools, or park agencies. Alternatively, if you're an employee of one of those agencies, you can ask businesses, service clubs, and other community organizations to provide the NPPS kits. Conduct the assessments before the beginning of the new school year so that problems and dangers can be addressed in time. Remember what Lester Chuck did for playgrounds in Hawaii!

3. Train Supervisors

Make sure that you understand the recommendations for safe, effective supervision of play areas, and then provide that training to others. If you're part of a child care center, school, or park agency, offer a workshop to your fellow employees. Again, you can obtain supervision kits from the NPPS or ask businesses and service clubs to supply the kits to local agencies.

4. Raise Funds

The safety of children trumps the costs of creating or renovating appropriate play areas, but the fact is that such efforts do come with some expense. Contribute funds directly, or help agencies raise funds in the community. Lead an effort to organize and publicize raffles, bake sales, pizza parties, or other methods of funding playgrounds.

5. Send Someone to Safety School

Do you know anyone in your community (perhaps even yourself) who would benefit from attending the NPPS Safety School? (See figure 10.1.) Solicit contributions to fund a scholarship, and ask your local school board or Parent–Teacher Association (PTA) to provide or match donations.

6. Sponsor Local Workshops

Sponsor one or more workshops on the S.A.F.E. model and its four components. The workshops might include online training available from the NPPS or showing children how to use the Kid Checker form on the NPPS Web site. Depending on community interest, you could offer training lasting anywhere from one to eight hours. Check the

Figure 10.1 Attendees of the NPPS Safety School learn to assess play equipment.

calendar and offer the workshops during National Playground Safety Week, which is always the last full week in April.

7. *Sponsor a State Bill*

Lead the effort to sponsor a bill to make public playgrounds in your state conform to the CPSC *Handbook for Public Playground Safety.* Visit the NPPS Web site for a list of states that have passed such a bill and for contact information of the people who made it happen. On the site, states that have adopted the CPSC handbook have higher grades than others, indicating that their playgrounds are safer.

8. *Sponsor a National Bill*

Lead an effort to sponsor a bill in the national legislature to make public playgrounds across the United States conform to the CPSC handbook. Start by talking to a politician in your state who might consider such an effort. All it takes is a leader who is willing to make the contacts and devote the time on behalf of children.

9. *Advocate Surfacing*

Insist that suitable surfacing be provided at an adequate depth at a child care center, school, or park in your neighborhood. Make the organization's board of directors aware of the importance of proper surfacing. Use the research and statistics in this book (or from your own community) to show how proper fall surfacing can reduce the risk of injury. Emphasize that taking preventative measures might absolve the organization of responsibility if lawsuits are brought by the families of children who suffer injuries.

10. *Develop a Maintenance Policy*

Follow the guidelines in this book to develop a maintenance policy for the playground equipment and surfacing at the child care center, school, or park where you work. More important, once the policy has been developed, make sure that everyone understands and follows it. If you're in charge of an agency, create a training schedule. In any case, encourage employees to view the new policy not as a chore to be avoided or rushed but as a critical part of keeping children safe.

Share Your Success Stories

Of course, there are many more than 10 ways to improve the safety of play areas. As you plan, assess, build, and repair playgrounds in your community, you'll undoubtedly generate other ideas. We want to hear how you're doing so we can include *your* success story in the next edition of *S.A.F.E. Play Areas: Creation, Maintenance, and Renovation.* You can find details about contacting us in appendix D.

We all play a role in providing safe playgrounds for our children!

Appendix A

Related Organizations

This appendix provides information and contact details for four types of organizations:

- Groups devoted to playground safety
- Groups involved in other aspects of safety
- Professional groups that have applied safety to playgrounds in relation to their other priorities
- Groups involved with playgrounds in general

If you have any concerns related to playground safety, please feel free to contact the appropriate organization.

National Playground Safety Organizations

This section presents information about three national organizations that focus on playground safety.

Consumer Product Safety Commission

Office of Information and Public Affairs
U.S. Consumer Product Safety Commission (CPSC)
Washington, D.C. 20207
Phone: 800-638-2772
E-mail: info@cpsc.gov
Web site: www.cpsc.gov

As you can see from the text, the CPSC has been very involved in keeping statistics of playground injuries, producing user-friendly handbooks, and providing research to make sure that the surfacing standard accurately measures impact attenuation. A new edition of the CPSC *Handbook for Public Playground Safety* will be produced in the future. In addition, the CPSC contributes technical information to ASTM standards and considers research projects that would benefit the safety of children on playgrounds.

National Program for Playground Safety

National Program for Playground Safety (NPPS)
School of Health, Physical Education, and Leisure Services
University of Northern Iowa
Cedar Falls, IA 50614-0618
Phone: 800-554-7529; 319-273-7529
E-mail: playground-safety@uni.edu
Web sites: www.playgroundsafety.org; www.playgroundsupervision.org; www.kidchecker.org

For information about the NPPS, please see appendix D.

National Playground Safety Institute

National Playground Safety Institute (NPSI)
National Recreation and Park Association
22377 Belmont Ridge Rd.
Ashburn, VA 20148
Phone: 800-626-6772; 703-858-0784
Web site: www.nrpa.org

The NPSI, created by the NRPA in 1990, has spent more than a decade training individuals to be playground safety inspectors. To date, it has held 334 two-day institutes to train over 7,000 people. The program focuses on playground equipment and surfacing found at schools and parks. There are trained NPSI inspectors in every state.

International Playground Safety Organizations

This section presents information about eight associations that publish standards about playground safety.

American Society for Testing and Materials

American Society for Testing and Materials (ASTM)
100 Barr Harbor Dr.
West Conshohocken, PA 19428
Phone: 610-832-9500
E-mail: service@astm.org
Web site: www.astm.org

Similar to the CPSC, the ASTM has made an enormous commitment to playground safety. In the ASTM, 534 members are involved in the six committees that create

13 playground equipment and surfacing standards. The standards committees have included representatives from manufacturers, users, and interested parties. The public-use playground equipment committee is one of the largest in the ASTM, boasting a membership of 170. Since standards must be revised every five years, the standards in the most recent edition reflect current use and interpretation.

Australian Standard—Playground Equipment for Parks, Schools, and Domestic Use (AS)

Standards Australia International, Ltd.
GPO Box 5420
Sydney, NSE 2001
Australia
Web site: www.standards.com.au

The *Australian Standard 1924, Part 2* was drafted but not published. It was later revised in 1981 and again in 1992. Its purpose is to provide safety standards for playground equipment for parks, schools, and homes. In 1982, the standard AS 2155, Australian Standard playgrounds guide to siting and to installation and maintenance of equipment, was adopted. AS 2155-1982 was revised, amalgamated, and designated as part of Playground Equipment Standards Number AS 4685, on playgrounds and playground equipment.

British Playground Equipment Standard

British Standards Institution
389 Chiswick High Road
London W4 4AL
United Kingdom
Phone: +44 (0)20 8996 9000
Fax: +44 (0)20 8996 7001
E-mail: cservices@bsi-global.com
Web site: www.bsi-global.com/index.xalter

Play Equipment Intended for Permanent Installation Outdoors was published in 1979 by the British Standards Institute (BSI). The standards were updated in 1986: BS 5696, part 1 (methods of test) and BS 5696, part 2 (specification for construction and performance). Their purpose is to increase the safety of playground equipment. The BSI has adopted EN 1176 as its base document as a member of EU (see European Standard for more details).

Canadian Playground Equipment Standard

Canadian Standards Association (CSA)
5060 Spectrum Way, Ste. 100
Mississauga, Ontario, L4W 5N6
Canada
Phone: 800-463-6727; 416-747-4044
E-mail: info@csagroup.org
Web site: www.csa.ca

A Guideline on Children's Play Spaces and Equipment was the standard published by the Canadian Standards Association (CSA) in 1991. It was revised in 1998 and 2003.

Playground equipment purchased by Canadians must comply with this standard. In 2003 it was renamed: *Children's Play Spaces and Equipment: A National Standard of Canada.*

European Norm: Playground Equipment Standards Number EN 1176-1, A1 and A2

European Committee for Standardization (CEN)
Management Centre
reu de Stassart 36
B-1050 Brussels
Belgium

The EN 1176 European safety documents (parts 1 through 7) were approved in May of 1998 by the European Committee for Standardization as the European norm for playground equipment and other items. The documents include descriptors, playgrounds, recreation facilities, toys, communal equipment, safety requirements, accident prevention, specifications, tests, design, verification, maintenance, marketing, technical information, and notices. These documents have been adopted by members of the European Common Market. It is an effort to combine standards and is widely used in Europe. This standard exists in three official versions (English, French, and German). A version in any other language translated under the responsibility of an ECM member into its own language and notified to the Central Secretariat has the same status as the official versions. Each country has the authority to add or supersede requirements of EN 1176. For example, Germany issues DIN EN 1176 which contains an "A-deviation" based on a legal requirement that conflicts with some parts of EN 1176, and in France, there are decrees (laws) that effectively amend EN 1176. Other countries do the same.

German Equipment Standard

Richter Spielgeräte GmbH
Postfach 54, 83110 Frasdorf
Phone: +49 (0)8052/17980
Fax: +49 (0)8052/4180
Web site: www.spielgeraete-richter.de

The German standard (DIN) was published by the German government in 1985 in several parts: DIN 7926, part 1 *(Playground Equipment for Children: Concepts, Safety Requirements, Testing)*; DIN 7926, part 2 *(Playground Equipment for Children: Swings)*; DIN 7926, part 3 *(Playground Equipment for Children: Slides)*; DIN 7926, part 4 *(Playground Equipment for Children: Cable Railways)*; and DIN 7926, part 5 *(Playground Equipment for Children: Carousels)*. They are known as the DIN standard and were widely used in Europe prior to the creation of the European Standard. As a member of the EU, the German DIN has adopted EN 1176 as its base document.

International Playground Contractors Association

International Playground Contractors Association (NPCAI)
P.O. Box 2364
Salt Lake City, UT 84110-2364
Phone: 888-908-9519
E-mail: npca@playground-contractors.org
Web site: www.playground-contractors.org

The NPCAI began in 1997. Its founders were Curtis Stoddard, David Antonacci, Mike Egan, Michael Baker, and Paul Cullins. Its purpose is to advance the playground-building industry by promoting playground installation as a legitimate contracting profession within the playground industry. In 2005 they began a certification program for installers.

International Play Equipment Manufacturers Association

International Play Equipment Manufacturers Association (IPEMA)
4305 N. 6th St., Ste. A
Harrisburg, PA 17110
Phone: 888-944-7362
E-mail: info@ipema.org
Web site: www.ipema.org

The IPEMA was created in 1995 to provide a check for equipment created by manufacturers in relation to the ASTM standards. It now includes surfacing manufacturers as well. It requires manufacturers to have their products tested by an independent laboratory to determine whether or not the product passes the applicable standard. When a product passes, it is IPEMA certified. When that information appears about a product in a catalog, however, it simply means that the product is certified, not necessarily that all of the products in the catalog are certified. For a complete listing of companies that participate in the certification program and what products are certified, consult the IPEMA Web site. A company may be a member of IPEMA but not necessarily participate in the certification program.

Safety-Related Organizations

This section provides information about four organizations that indirectly work in the area of playground safety.

American Academy of Pediatrics

American Academy of Pediatrics (AAP)
141 Northwest Point Blvd.
Elk Grove Village, IL 60007
Phone: 847-434-4000
Web site: www.aap.org

The AAP has published the *National Health and Safety Performance Standards: Guidelines for Out-of-Home Child Care* (2002) and *Stepping Stones to Caring for Our Children* (2003). One section of that standard deals with playground equipment. In addition, the association just published the sixth edition of *School Health: Policy and Practice* (2004), which includes a chapter about playground safety. Periodically, the AAP also contributes financially to community playgrounds.

American Academy of Orthopaedic Surgeons

American Academy of Orthopaedic Surgeons (AAOS)
630 N. River Rd.
Rosemont, IL 60018-4262
Phone: 847-823-7186
Web site: www.aaos.org

In 1999, the AAOS was responsible for analyzing NEISS data and drew the conclusion that over 569,000 children under the age of 15 are injured on playgrounds annually at a cost of $9.9 billion in 1998.

Consumer Federation of America

Consumer Federation of America (CFA)
1620 I Street NW, Ste. 200
Washington, D.C. 20006
Phone: 202-387-6121
E-mail: cfa@consumerfed.org
Web site: www.consumerfed.org

The CFA has published several editions of the *Report and Model Law on Public Play Equipment* (Morrison and Fise, 1998). In addition, the CFA assesses playgrounds on a periodic basis and draws generalizations from the assessments. Unfortunately, the generalizations are not based on a random sample so the conclusions are inaccurate, which can be confusing to the public.

Safe Kids Worldwide

Safe Kids Worldwide
1301 Pennsylvania Ave., Ste. 1000
Washington, D.C. 20004-1707
Phone: 202-662-0600
Web site: www.safekids.org

Safe Kids Worldwide originated in 1991 with a grant from Johnson and Johnson. Its purpose is to make the environment safer for children in the United States. They have made significant progress regarding the wearing of helmets by bicycle riders and the use of car seats for children. Periodically they include playground safety information at their annual convention for their representatives. State representatives have been productive in getting their governors to proclaim National Playground Safety Week in their states.

Professional Organizations

These organizations have major purposes for existing other than emphasizing playground safety. However, many do provide presentations about playground safety at their conventions and articles about playground safety in their journals.

American Association for the Child's Right to Play

American Association for the Child's Right to Play (AACRP)
Web site: www.ipausa.org

The AACRP was established in 1983 as a subset of the International Play Association (IPA). The group's primary purpose is to encourage opportunities for children to play, and they have advocated the inclusion of recess in schools. Rhonda Clements has been the primary driver of the association's goals. The group holds conferences on a regular basis and includes presentations about playground safety.

American Association for Leisure and Recreation

American Association for Physical Activity and Recreation (AAPAR)
1900 Association Dr.
Reston, VA 20191
Phone: 800-213-7193; 910-321-0789
E-mail: info@aahperd.org
Web site: www.aahperd.org

This association was subsumed under the American Association for Physical Activity and Recreation (AAPAR) in 2006. Concern about playground injuries in the United States caused the AALR to undertake the first large survey of playgrounds from 1985 to 1989. They looked at 206 elementary school playgrounds, reported in *Where Our Children Play: Elementary School Playground Equipment* (Bruya and Langendorfer, 1988); 198 community park playgrounds, reported in *Where Our Children Play: Community Park Playground Equipment* (Thompson and Bowers, 1989); and 349 child care playgrounds, reported in *Playgrounds for Young Children: National Survey and Perspectives* (Wortham and Frost, 1990). They concluded that major contributors to children's injuries include climbing equipment, slides, swings, and surfacing.

Community Built Playground Association

Community Built Playground Association
144 Back Canaan Rd.
Strafford, NH 03884
Phone: 800-533-1553; 603-664-5490
E-mail: info@learningstructures.com
Web site: www.learningstructures.com

The Community Built Playground Association was created in 1989 by Bob Leathers of Leathers and Associates, Kit Clews of Learning Structures, and John Palms of the

Chicago Public Art Group in order to further the theory and practice of involving volunteers in the design, organization, and creation of community projects that reshape the physical environment, including playgrounds. The group has a firm belief in volunteerism, empowerment, and the value of community, and they encourage artistic endeavors in the environments they build.

Environmental Design Research Association

Environmental Design Research Association (EDRA)
P.O. Box 7146
Edmond, OK 73083-7146
Phone: 405-330-4863
E-mail: edra@edra.org
Web site: www.edra.org

The EDRA primarily consists of architects and psychologists. In the 1970s they had a subdivision called Childhood City whose purpose was to study and influence architects who design areas where children spend time, including play areas. Their influence led to child-sized designs, which help create a safer environment for children.

International Play Association

International Play Association (IPA)
Web site: ipaworld.org

The IPA was formed in 1975. Its purpose is to encourage appropriate environments that provide opportunities for children to play. In 1987, they provided a tour of playgrounds in Denmark and Sweden. Periodically their conventions include presentations about playground safety.

National Association for the Education of Young Children

National Association for the Education of Young Children (NAEYC)
1313 L St. NW, Ste. 500
Washington, D.C. 20005
Phone: 800-424-2460
E-mail: naeyc@naeyc.org
Web site: www.naeyc.org

The NAEYC is the largest professional association for the child care industry. They have regularly included presentations about playground safety at their national convention. In addition, they have published articles about playground safety in their national journal. Most recently, they included information about playground safety in their national standards.

Other Playground-Related Organizations

These organizations either build playgrounds or provide information about a specific facet of playgrounds. Each has a different emphasis.

KaBOOM!

KaBOOM!
4455 Connecticut Ave., Ste. 100
Washington, D.C. 20037
Phone: 202-659-0215
Web site: www.kaboom.org

KaBOOM! was created in 1996 by Darrell Hammond and Dawn Hutchinson. Its purpose is to encourage people in communities to communicate better with one another by having adults build playgrounds for children. Over the last 10 years, KaBOOM! has built over 700 new playgrounds and renovated more than 1,300 playgrounds. Over half are at schools and parks. Whether or not this has increased communication is not clear since the organization has not done much follow-up after the playgrounds have been built. However, it has built playgrounds that conform to ASTM standards.

National Center for Boundless Playgrounds

National Center for Boundless Playgrounds
45 Wintonbury Ave.
Bloomfield, CT 06002
Phone: 877-268-6353; 860-243-8315
Web site: www.boundlessplaygrounds.org

Boundless Playgrounds was created in 1998 by Amy Barzach and Jean Schappet. Its purpose is to design fully integrated, universally accessible playgrounds for children of all abilities (Schappet, Malkusak, and Bruya, 2003). The inspiration for its creation was Amy's son, Jonathan, who died from spinal muscular atrophy (Barzach and Greenberg, 2001). In addition, the association wished to respond to the ADA law in order to provide playgrounds for all children. The Hasboro Foundation has partially supported this association. Boundless Playgrounds has built over 71 playgrounds in 20 states and one in a Canadian province since the organization's inception.

National Children's Center for Rural and Agricultural Health and Safety

National Children's Center for Rural and Agricultural Health and Safety
Marshfield Clinic Research Foundation
National Farm Medicine Center
1000 N. Oak Ave.
Marshfield, WI 54449-5777
Phone: 800-662-6900
E-mail: nccrahs@mcrf.mfldclin.edu
Web sites: www.marshfieldclinic.org/nfmc

The National Children's Center for Rural and Agricultural Health and Safety was established in 1981. It focuses on the evolving injury problems on farms, including playground injuries. The program has published a book called *Creating Safe Play Areas on Farms* (2003). They have also sponsored a three-day interactive demonstration to teach parents to build safe play areas on farms.

Peaceful Playgrounds

Peaceful Playgrounds
Phone: 877-444-9888
Web site: www.peacefulplaygrounds.com

Peaceful Playgrounds was created in 1998 by Melinda Bossenmeyer. Its purpose is to make playgrounds peaceful. Bossenmeyer has created games and spaces where children can play peacefully based on research about the way children play, the intercession of adults, and the kinds of spaces that are appropriate for children of different ages. In addition, Peaceful Playgrounds provides a monthly newsletter about various topics including potential grants for playgrounds. The organization is able to substantiate that its designs and training have reduced injuries (Bossenmeyer and Owens, 2004), increased children's activity levels (Bossenmeyer and Blackman, 2005), and reduced bullying (Beissenger et al., 2003).

Slyde, the Playground Hound

Slyde, the Playground Hound
P.O. Box 603
Ashton, ID 83420
Phone: 800-388-2196
E-mail: playgroundhound@ida.net
Web site: www.playgroundhound.com

Slyde, the Playground Hound, an association dedicated to promoting playground safety awareness, was begun in 2000 by Curtis Stoddard. Slyde is being promoted as the U.S. mascot for playground safety for children, much like Smokey the Bear is the mascot for fire safety. The group provides a number of products to promote their goals.

Appendix B

Student Injury Report

This appendix contains an injury report form you can use to document injuries that are severe enough to cause a child to miss school or receive medical attention. In addition, you might need to use the form to document other injuries; check the policy of your organization or school district.

The form also appears on the CD-ROM as a PDF file for easy printing and reproduction.

How to Fill Out the Injury Report Form

This form is to be completed immediately following the occurrence of any injury that is severe enough to

- cause the loss of one-half day or more of school,
- warrant medical attention and treatment (i.e., school nurse, MD, ER, etc.), and/or
- require reporting according to organization or school district policy.

Sections	Explanation
1-6	Record basic information about the incident.
7	Record the number of days missed. If the child will be absent for an extended period of time, use the parent's estimate of days missed. If no school is missed, mark "Less than ½."
8-11	Record the type of first aid given, the body part injured, the suspected type of injury, and the action taken. Record the amount of time the child spent in the nurse's office, using "h" and "m" to indicate hours and minutes (example: 1h 40m).
12	Mark the cause of the injury:

- *Collision with person:* incidental or intentional contact with another person
- *Hit with object:* struck by an object (such as a ball, backpack, etc.)
- *Fall:* fell from equipment or fell while running; also record the height of the fall
- *Collision with obstacle:* ran into an object (such as equipment, a fence, etc.)
- *Injury to self:* injured due to action carried out by the child
- *Other:* write in any reason not covered above

13	Mark the location where the injury occurred.
14	Describe the surface on which the injury occurred.
15	In the small box, record the number that corresponds to the child's activity at the time of the injury. If you record "22," be sure to write in the explanation.
16	Document the extent to which equipment was involved in the injury.
17	Briefly explain how the injury occurred, giving specific details. Include the names of all witnesses present. If additional space is needed, continue on another sheet of paper and attach it to the form.

From *S.A.F.E. Play Areas: Creation, Maintenance, and Renovation* by Donna Thompson, Susan D. Hudson, and Heather M. Olsen, 2007, Champaign, IL: Human Kinetics.

Injury Report Form

1. Child's name _____ 3. Grade _____ 5. ( ) Male ( ) Female

2. School name _____ 4. Date of injury _____ 6. Time of injury _____

7. Days absent: ___Less than ½   ___½   ___1   ___1 ½ to 2   ___2 ½ to 3   ___Other: _____

8. First aid: _____ Observed   _____ Kept immobile   _____ Washed wound   _____ Stopped bleeding
   _____ Applied ice   _____ Applied dressing   _____ Applied splint   _____ Other

   Explain: _____

9. Body part injured:

Head	Trunk	Extremities		Other
___Ear	___Abdomen	___Ankle	___Lower arm	
___Eye	___Back	___Elbow	___Lower leg	
___Face	___Chest	___Finger	___Thumb	
___Head	___Groin	___Foot	___Toes	
___Neck	___Shoulder	___Hand	___Upper arm	
___Scalp	___Trunk	___Hip	___Upper leg	
		___Knee	___Wrist	

10. Type of injury suspected:
    _____Bruise/contusion   _____Burn   _____Concussion
    _____Dislocation   _____Fracture   _____Laceration/abrasion
    _____Sprain/strain   _____Surface cut/scratch
    _____Other: _____

11. Action taken: _____Returned to class   _____Called 911   _____Transferred to hospital
    _____Parent took home   _____Parent took to doctor   _____Parent took to ER
    _____Other: _____   _____Time spent in nurse's office

12. Cause of injury: _____Collision with person   _____Collision with obstacle
    _____Hit with object   _____Injury to self
    _____Fall   _____Height of fall   _____Other _____

13. Accident location: _____Assembly   _____Bus   _____Classroom   _____Gym   _____Hallway
    _____P.E. class   _____Playground   _____Stairs   _____Other: _____

14. Surface: _____Blacktop   _____Carpet   _____Concrete   _____Dirt   _____Grass
    _____Ice/snow   _____Mats   _____Pea gravel   _____Rubber tile   _____Sand
    _____Synthetic surface   _____Wood products
    _____Other: _____
    _____Depth of loose fill material

15. Activity:

1. Baseball/softball	6. Fighting	11. Playing on bars	16. Soccer	21. Walking
2. Basketball	7. Football (flag/touch)	12. Running	17. Swinging	22. Other: _____
3. Bicycling	8. Jumping	13. Rough-housing	18. Throwing objects	_____
4. Climbing	9. Kickball	14. Sliding	19. Track/field	_____
5. Dodge ball	10. Playground equipment	15. Sliding on ice	20. Volleyball	_____

16. Equipment: Was playground equipment involved in injury?   ___Yes ___No

IF YES:

(a) Which piece?   ___Arch climber   ___Cargo net   ___Chinning bar   ___Horizontal ladder   ___Seesaw
    ___Slide   ___Sliding pole   ___Swing   ___Track ride
    ___Other: _____

(b) Did equipment appear to be used appropriately?   ___Yes ___No

(c) Did equipment appear to malfunction?   ___Yes ___No

17. Description: Explain specifically how the injury occurred. _____
_____
_____
_____
_____

Signed: _____   Signed: _____
(Person filing report)   (Principal/Director)

From *S.A.F.E. Play Areas: Creation, Maintenance, and Renovation* by Donna Thompson, Susan D. Hudson, and Heather M. Olsen, 2007, Champaign, IL: Human Kinetics.
Adapted from and © 2005 National Program for Playground Safety.

Appendix C

Safety and Maintenance Checklists

This appendix contains six checklists that can be used to assess the safety of a play area and identify items that need maintenance or repair.

- S.A.F.E. Model Checklist: Play Environment—Use this to check the overall conditions of the physical environment of the play area.
- S.A.F.E. Model Checklist: Surfacing Materials—Use this to check the conditions of loose fill and unitary surfacing materials.
- S.A.F.E. Model Checklist: General Equipment Issues—Use this to check the overall condition of all equipment in the play area.
- S.A.F.E. Model Checklist: Specific Equipment Issues—Use this to check the condition of specific pieces of equipment in the play area.
- S.A.F.E. Model Checklist: Daily Maintenance Quick Check—Use this frequently to identify maintenance needs resulting from recent use, abuse, or environmental conditions.
- S.A.F.E. Model Checklist: Caregiver Quick Check—Use this to determine whether a play area is safe for children under your care.

You can customize the checklists to include items or issues specific to your particular play area. Use the numbered blank lines to add simple checks, and use the back of the page to sketch a diagram of the area, mark hazards, draw sight lines, and so on.

Each checklist also appears on the CD-ROM as a PDF file for easy printing and reproduction.

S.A.F.E. Model Checklist: Play Environment

Use this checklist to assess the overall conditions of the physical environment of the play area.

1. Y ❑ N ❑ N/A ❑ Is the area, equipment, and surfacing free of foreign objects, such as (but not limited to) debris, sticks, loose rocks, and toys?

2. Y ❑ N ❑ N/A ❑ Are surfaces (including equipment surfaces) free of algae, mold, and other fungi?

3. Y ❑ N ❑ N/A ❑ Are plant materials pruned so that branches do not present a hazard to children or adults?

4. Y ❑ N ❑ N/A ❑ Are plant materials located so as not to create visual obstructions that prevent supervision of the play area?

5. Y ❑ N ❑ N/A ❑ Are plant materials free of thorns, berries, and sticky sap?

6. Y ❑ N ❑ N/A ❑ Is the area free of insect and rodent infestation?

7. Y ❑ N ❑ N/A ❑ Is the area free of standing water?

8. Y ❑ N ❑ N/A ❑ Are drainage grates securely attached or locked?

9. Y ❑ N ❑ N/A ❑ Are utility boxes locked and located away from the play area?

10. Y ❑ N ❑ N/A ❑ Does fencing separate the play area from adjacent hazards, such as streets, parking lots, railroads, streams, and so on?

11. Y ❑ N ❑ N/A ❑ Are benches, tables, and other site amenities in good condition and located out of the playground equipment use zone?

12. Y ❑ N ❑ N/A ❑ Is the play area (including hard surface areas) free of trip hazards, such as rocks, protruding tree roots, exposed concrete footers, sudden drop offs, and abrupt changes in pavement surfaces?

13. Y ❑ N ❑ N/A ❑ Are pavement surfaces (including pathways and pavement game areas) free of wood mulch, pea stone, sand, and other debris that might create a trip or slipping hazard?

14. Y ❑ N ❑ N/A ❑ Is the play environment free of broken or missing parts?

15. Y ❑ N ❑ N/A ❑ Is the play environment free of sharp edges?

16. Y ❑ N ❑ N/A ❑ _____

17. Y ❑ N ❑ N/A ❑ _____

18. Y ❑ N ❑ N/A ❑ _____

19. Y ❑ N ❑ N/A ❑ _____

From *S.A.F.E. Play Areas: Creation, Maintenance, and Renovation* by Donna Thompson, Susan D. Hudson, and Heather M. Olsen, 2007, Champaign, IL: Human Kinetics.

S.A.F.E. Model Checklist: Surfacing Materials

Use this checklist to inspect loose fill or unitary surfacing materials in a play area.

Loose Fill Materials

1. **Y** ☐ **N** ☐ **N/A** ☐   Is the surfacing material at least 12 inches (30.5 centimeters) deep throughout the entire play area?

2. **Y** ☐ **N** ☐ **N/A** ☐   Has the surfacing material been prevented from compacting too much?

3. **Y** ☐ **N** ☐ **N/A** ☐   Has the sand been sifted and aerated at least once a year?

4. **Y** ☐ **N** ☐ **N/A** ☐   Is the surfacing material maintained on a regular basis?

5. **Y** ☐ **N** ☐ **N/A** ☐   Is the surfacing material free of foreign materials, such as debris, toys, animal feces, broken glass, sticks, and stones?

6. **Y** ☐ **N** ☐ **N/A** ☐   Is the resilient surfacing area draining well?

7. **Y** ☐ **N** ☐ **N/A** ☐   Is the play area closed when the surfacing material is frozen due to cold weather?

8. **Y** ☐ **N** ☐ **N/A** ☐   _____
_____

9. **Y** ☐ **N** ☐ **N/A** ☐   _____
_____

Unitary Materials

1. **Y** ☐ **N** ☐ **N/A** ☐   Is the surfacing material free of foreign materials, such as debris, toys, animal feces, broken glass, sticks, and stones?

2. **Y** ☐ **N** ☐ **N/A** ☐   Is the resilient surfacing area draining well?

3. **Y** ☐ **N** ☐ **N/A** ☐   Is the surface uniform, with no separation of tiles or abrupt elevation changes?

4. **Y** ☐ **N** ☐ **N/A** ☐   Are tile systems free of exposed anchoring devices?

5. **Y** ☐ **N** ☐ **N/A** ☐   If tiles are used as surfacing material, is the area between the edges of tiles free of grass, weeds, and other plant growth?

6. **Y** ☐ **N** ☐ **N/A** ☐   If the surfacing is a poured-in-place material, is the surfacing free of holes?

7. **Y** ☐ **N** ☐ **N/A** ☐   Are unitary surface materials free of cracks and holes?

8. **Y** ☐ **N** ☐ **N/A** ☐   _____
_____

9. **Y** ☐ **N** ☐ **N/A** ☐   _____
_____

From *S.A.F.E. Play Areas: Creation, Maintenance, and Renovation* by Donna Thompson, Susan D. Hudson, and Heather M. Olsen, 2007, Champaign, IL: Human Kinetics.

S.A.F.E. Model Checklist: General Equipment Issues

Use this checklist to assess the general conditions of equipment in the play area.

1. Y ❏   N ❏   N/A ❏   Is all equipment stable, with no loose parts or loose footings? (Periodically, expose the footers and check the stability of equipment at a point where it goes into the footer. This is especially important for wood equipment.)

2. Y ❏   N ❏   N/A ❏   Is all equipment (including hardware) free of missing or broken parts?

3. Y ❏   N ❏   N/A ❏   Is all equipment free of pinch, crush, or shear points?

4. Y ❏   N ❏   N/A ❏   Do handholds stay in place when grasped?

5. Y ❏   N ❏   N/A ❏   Is all hardware tight and free of gaps or spaces that might create entanglement?

6. Y ❏   N ❏   N/A ❏   Are all equipment parts free of excessive wear or degradation?

7. Y ❏   N ❏   N/A ❏   Are all equipment parts in their original configuration, without having become shifted or bent?

8. Y ❏   N ❏   N/A ❏   Are all parts designed so as not to create protrusion hazards?

9. Y ❏   N ❏   N/A ❏   Is all wood equipment free of warping, splinters, rough edges, and sharp edges?

10. Y ❏   N ❏   N/A ❏   Is all metal equipment free of rust, sharp edges, and chipping paint?

11. Y ❏   N ❏   N/A ❏   Are all plastic parts free of warping and separation (especially at the seams)?

12. Y ❏   N ❏   N/A ❏   Are the ends of all pieces of tubing protected by caps or plugs?

13. Y ❏   N ❏   N/A ❏   Are all openings designed so as to prevent head entrapments?

14. Y ❏   N ❏   N/A ❏   Are all moving parts lubricated and free of wear?

15. Y ❏   N ❏   N/A ❏   Are all S hooks closed?

16. Y ❏   N ❏   N/A ❏   Are signs or warning labels still legible?

17. Y ❏   N ❏   N/A ❏   _____

18. Y ❏   N ❏   N/A ❏   _____

19. Y ❏   N ❏   N/A ❏   _____

20. Y ❏   N ❏   N/A ❏   _____

From *S.A.F.E. Play Areas: Creation, Maintenance, and Renovation* by Donna Thompson, Susan D. Hudson, and Heather M. Olsen, 2007, Champaign, IL: Human Kinetics.

S.A.F.E. Model Checklist: Specific Equipment Issues

Use this checklist to inspect balance beams, climbers, merry-go-rounds, seesaws, slides, swings, and other specific pieces of equipment in the play area.

Balance Beam

1. Y ❑   N ❑   N/A ❑   Is the beam secured and stable?
2. Y ❑   N ❑   N/A ❑   Is the beam free of rough edges, splinters, or rough surfaces?
3. Y ❑   N ❑   N/A ❑   Is the beam free of corrosion or visible rotting?

Climber (Stationary)

Stationary climbers are those that do not move.

1. Y ❑   N ❑   N/A ❑   Do handholds stay in place when grasped?
2. Y ❑   N ❑   N/A ❑   Is the climber free of sharp edges, splinters, or rough surfaces?
3. Y ❑   N ❑   N/A ❑   Are nuts, bolts, and screws recessed, covered, or sanded smooth?
4. Y ❑   N ❑   N/A ❑   Are all nuts and bolts tight?
5. Y ❑   N ❑   N/A ❑   Is the climber free of wear and deterioration?
6. Y ❑   N ❑   N/A ❑   Is the climber in its original configuration, without having become shifted or bent?
7. Y ❑   N ❑   N/A ❑   Is the climber free of rust or chipping paint?
8. Y ❑   N ❑   N/A ❑   Does the climber have all of its parts?
9. Y ❑   N ❑   N/A ❑   Is the climber free of broken parts?

Climber (Flexible)

Flexible climbers are those that move, such as climbers made of chain.

1. Y ❑   N ❑   N/A ❑   Are cables, chains, or ropes fixed tightly at both ends so children cannot become entrapped?
2. Y ❑   N ❑   N/A ❑   Are anchoring devices located below the playing surface?
3. Y ❑   N ❑   N/A ❑   Is the climber free of pinch, crush, and shear points?
4. Y ❑   N ❑   N/A ❑   Are all nuts and bolts tight?
5. Y ❑   N ❑   N/A ❑   Are connecting S hooks closed?

Merry-Go-Round

1. Y ❑   N ❑   N/A ❑   Is the platform parallel to the ground?
2. Y ❑   N ❑   N/A ❑   Is there a minimum clearance of 9 inches (23 centimeters) between the protective surface and the underside of the platform?
3. Y ❑   N ❑   N/A ❑   Is the equipment free of corrosion or rust?

(continued)

From *S.A.F.E. Play Areas: Creation, Maintenance, and Renovation* by Donna Thompson, Susan D. Hudson, and Heather M. Olsen, 2007, Champaign, IL: Human Kinetics.

4. **Y** ❑ **N** ❑ **N/A** ❑ Does the equipment have a continuous circular movement?

Seesaw

1. **Y** ❑ **N** ❑ **N/A** ❑ Does each seat rise to a maximum of 5 feet (1.5 meters)?
2. **Y** ❑ **N** ❑ **N/A** ❑ Is the fulcrum fixed and enclosed?
3. **Y** ❑ **N** ❑ **N/A** ❑ Are the handgrips secure?
4. **Y** ❑ **N** ❑ **N/A** ❑ Are shock-absorbing materials embedded in the ground beneath the seats?

Slide

1. **Y** ❑ **N** ❑ **N/A** ❑ Are all steps present and evenly spaced?
2. **Y** ❑ **N** ❑ **N/A** ❑ For slides at least 4 feet (1.2 meters) tall, is the exit region between 7 inches (17.8 centimeters) and 15 inches (38 centimeters)?
3. **Y** ❑ **N** ❑ **N/A** ❑ For slides less than 4 feet (1.2 meters) tall, is the exit region no more than 11 inches (28 centimeters)?
4. **Y** ❑ **N** ❑ **N/A** ❑ Is the sliding surface free of gaps or rough edges?

Swing

1. **Y** ❑ **N** ❑ **N/A** ❑ Is there an absence of animal figure swings, multiple occupancy swings, and rope swings?
2. **Y** ❑ **N** ❑ **N/A** ❑ Are all S hooks closed?
3. **Y** ❑ **N** ❑ **N/A** ❑ Are all seats level?
4. **Y** ❑ **N** ❑ **N/A** ❑ Does each bay have no more than two swings?
5. **Y** ❑ **N** ❑ **N/A** ❑ Are there at least 12 inches (30.5 centimeters) between the swing seat and the surfacing materials beneath?
6. **Y** ❑ **N** ❑ **N/A** ❑ Do tire swings have adequate drainage?
7. **Y** ❑ **N** ❑ **N/A** ❑ Are swing chains free of wear and tear?
8. **Y** ❑ **N** ❑ **N/A** ❑ Are chain fasteners secure and free of wear?

Other Equipment

1. **Y** ❑ **N** ❑ **N/A** ❑ _____

2. **Y** ❑ **N** ❑ **N/A** ❑ _____

3. **Y** ❑ **N** ❑ **N/A** ❑ _____

4. **Y** ❑ **N** ❑ **N/A** ❑ _____

From *S.A.F.E. Play Areas: Creation, Maintenance, and Renovation* by Donna Thompson, Susan D. Hudson, and Heather M. Olsen, 2007, Champaign, IL: Human Kinetics.

S.A.F.E. Model Checklist:
Daily Maintenance Quick Check

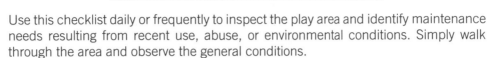

Use this checklist daily or frequently to inspect the play area and identify maintenance needs resulting from recent use, abuse, or environmental conditions. Simply walk through the area and observe the general conditions.

1. **Y** ❏ **N** ❏ **N/A** ❏ Is all equipment free of damage resulting from vandalism, such as graffiti, broken glass, trash, and so on?
2. **Y** ❏ **N** ❏ **N/A** ❏ Does each piece of equipment have all of its parts?
3. **Y** ❏ **N** ❏ **N/A** ❏ Are all parts on each piece of equipment still tight and secure?
4. **Y** ❏ **N** ❏ **N/A** ❏ Is all equipment free of exposed footers?
5. **Y** ❏ **N** ❏ **N/A** ❏ Is all wooden equipment intact, with no splitting or splintering?
6. **Y** ❏ **N** ❏ **N/A** ❏ Do swing chains hang freely, without being kinked, twisted, or wrapped around the top rail?
7. **Y** ❏ **N** ❏ **N/A** ❏ Are swing seats intact, with no splitting or cracking?
8. **Y** ❏ **N** ❏ **N/A** ❏ Is the climber free of wear and deterioration?
9. **Y** ❏ **N** ❏ **N/A** ❏ Is the surfacing material free of trash and other foreign objects?
10. **Y** ❏ **N** ❏ **N/A** ❏ Is the general area free of trash and other foreign objects?
11. **Y** ❏ **N** ❏ **N/A** ❏ Are walkways, steps, and platforms free of trash and other foreign objects?
12. **Y** ❏ **N** ❏ **N/A** ❏ Have trash cans been emptied?
13. **Y** ❏ **N** ❏ **N/A** ❏ Is the general area free of standing water?
14. **Y** ❏ **N** ❏ **N/A** ❏ Are restrooms and water fountains clean and functional?

15. **Y** ❏ **N** ❏ **N/A** ❏ _____

_____

16. **Y** ❏ **N** ❏ **N/A** ❏ _____

_____

17. **Y** ❏ **N** ❏ **N/A** ❏ _____

_____

18. **Y** ❏ **N** ❏ **N/A** ❏ _____

From *S.A.F.E. Play Areas: Creation, Maintenance, and Renovation* by Donna Thompson, Susan D. Hudson, and Heather M. Olsen, 2007, Champaign, IL: Human Kinetics. Reprinted, by permission, from NPPS, 2005, Nuts and bolts. In *National Program for Playground Safety school curriculum manual*, edited by S.D. Hudson (Cedar Falls, IA: National Program for Playground Safety), 21.

S.A.F.E. Model Checklist:
Caregiver Quick Check

Parents, guardians, and other adults should use this checklist to determine whether a play area is safe for children under their care.

1. **Y** ❑ **N** ❑ **N/A** ❑   Are you prepared to supervise your children at the playground?

2. **Y** ❑ **N** ❑ **N/A** ❑   Is there age-appropriate equipment for the children to play on?

3. **Y** ❑ **N** ❑ **N/A** ❑   Is the equipment in good condition?

4. **Y** ❑ **N** ❑ **N/A** ❑   Is the equipment located away from high traffic areas, ponds, and parking lots?

5. **Y** ❑ **N** ❑ **N/A** ❑   Does the play area have appropriate surfacing materials?

6. **Y** ❑ **N** ❑ **N/A** ❑   Are all spaces and gaps less than 3.5 inches (9 centimeters) wide or greater than 9 inches (23 centimeters) wide to prevent head entrapments?

7. **Y** ❑ **N** ❑ **N/A** ❑   Are all spaces and gaps closed?

8. **Y** ❑ **N** ❑ **N/A** ❑   Are surfaces on all equipment smooth?

9. **Y** ❑ **N** ❑ **N/A** ❑   Are surfaces on all equipment cool enough to touch safely?

10. **Y** ❑ **N** ❑ **N/A** ❑   Is the play area clean and free of trash and other foreign objects?

11. **Y** ❑ **N** ❑ **N/A** ❑   _____

_____

12. **Y** ❑ **N** ❑ **N/A** ❑   _____

_____

13. **Y** ❑ **N** ❑ **N/A** ❑   _____

_____

14. **Y** ❑ **N** ❑ **N/A** ❑   _____

_____

From *S.A.F.E. Play Areas: Creation, Maintenance, and Renovation* by Donna Thompson, Susan D. Hudson, and Heather M. Olsen, 2007, Champaign, IL: Human Kinetics.

Appendix D

The National Program for Playground Safety

The mission of the National Program for Playground Safety (NPPS) is to be the leader in research and training for the development of play areas that follow the S.A.F.E. model. The organization strives to help the public create safe and developmentally appropriate play environments for children.

About the NPPS

Established in 1995 at the University of Northern Iowa, the NPPS was created with funding from the CDC. As the premier nonprofit organization in the United States delivering training and services about outdoor play and safety, the NPPS believes that every child has the right to play; that all children need to learn to play and play to learn; and that every child is entitled to a safe, positive, nurturing, and fun experience in the play environment.

The organization puts these beliefs into practice in a number of ways.

- It serves as a child advocate on playground safety issues before government and regulatory agencies.
- It helps the public create, renovate, and maintain safe and developmentally appropriate play environments for children by providing products, services, and programs that are professional, well-researched, highly informative, and user friendly.
- It serves as a national resource for the latest educational and research information about playground safety.

The NPPS has developed the largest and most comprehensive clearinghouse of information and resources about outdoor play area safety in the United States. The NPPS offers research, training, and educational resources. For a summary of NPPS accomplishments, see pages 199 to 201.

Contacting the NPPS

National Program for Playground Safety (NPPS)
School of Health, Physical Education, and Leisure Services
University of Northern Iowa
Cedar Falls, IA 50614-0618
Phone: 800-554-7529
Fax: 319-273-7308
E-mail: playground-safety@uni.edu
Web sites: www.playgroundsafety.org; www.kidchecker.org; www.playgroundsupervision.org

National Program for Playground Safety:
12 Years of Excellence

Summary of Accomplishments (October 1995-September 2006)

Education

- Distributed over 100,000 national action plans for the prevention of playground injuries
- Created 25 informational brochures and pamphlets (4 in Spanish)
- Developed a clearinghouse containing more than 5,000 citations (1984 to present)
- Conducted 32 sessions of the NPPS Safety School, including schools held in Germany, Hawaii, Indiana, Massachusetts, New Mexico, Ohio, and Kentucky
- Published the following:
  - 19 books and monographs
  - 21 book chapters
  - 150 professional articles
  - 18 technical reports
- Produced the following:
  - 13 public service announcements
  - 8 videos
  - 2 CD-ROMS
- Provided 300 presentations across the country at professional conferences and before professional groups
- Developed a playground safety supervision kit
- Developed the Kid Checker program as an assessment tool
- Developed a school assessment kit
- Developed a child care assessment kit

Research

- Received grants and contracts for research and assessment projects
- Conducted four studies on surfacing
  - Loose fill surfacing (led to changes in the ASTM F1292 protocol)
  - Impact attenuation of common surfaces found in the inside play environment
  - Iowa Safe Surfacing Initiative (2003-2004)
  - Iowa Safe Surfacing Initiative (2004-2005)
  - Iowa Safe Surfacing Initiative (2005-2006)
  - Iowa Safe Surfacing Initiative (2006-2007)

(continued)

- Conducted two comprehensive studies regarding the risk factors found on playgrounds
  - First study (1998-2000)
  - Second study (2003-2004)
- Assessed 65 child care and school-age sites for the U.S. Air Force
- Developed three theoretical models
  - S.A.F.E. model
  - Risk–challenge model
  - S.A.F.E. surfacing decision model
- Participated with the University of Northern Colorado in a study of playground safety on American Indian school sites in Wyoming
- Assessed airport playgrounds for the Iowa Air Space Consortium
- Conducted a study concerning supervision practices at elementary schools in Iowa
- Analyzed CPSC NEISS data for the years of 1990 to 1994
- Conducted research regarding the use of informational signs on playgrounds

Advocacy

- Received over 2 million Web site visits; fielded over 44,000 phone calls on its toll-free line
- Generated over $130 million of public relations value
- Made seven major TV appearances on ABC, CBS, CNN, FOX, and NBC
- Created National Playground Safety Week
- Participated in advocacy efforts in Hawaii, Indiana, Iowa, Missouri, Montana, Ohio, Nevada, Texas, Virginia, and Wisconsin
- Participated in the following ASTM standards committees:
  - Committee for play equipment for children under the age of 2
  - Committee on public-use playground equipment
  - Committee on surfacing under and around playground equipment
  - Committee on ssoft contained playground equipment
  - Committee on home playground equipment
- Provided information for the revision of the CPSC *Handbook for Public Playground Safety,* 1997 version
- Involved in the revision of the CPSC *Handbook for Public Playgrounds*, 2007 version

Educational Opportunities

- Workshops
  - Supervision
  - Planning
  - Design of age-appropriate playgrounds
  - Selection and provision of surfacing
  - Maintaining safe playgrounds

- National Playground Safety Schools
- Online training
- Consultation
- Assessment of playgrounds
  - Child care agencies
  - Schools
  - Parks

Products

- Videos
  - *ABCs of Supervision*
  - *Nuts and Bolts of Playground Maintenance*
  - *Planning S.A.F.E. Playgrounds*
  - *S.A.F.E. Playgrounds*
  - *S.A.F.E. Surfaces*
  - *Sammy's Playground Pointers*
- CD-ROMS
  - *Applying CPSC Guidelines for the Development of S.A.F.E. Playgrounds*
  - *Planning Accessible S.A.F.E. Playgrounds Using the Americans with Disabilities Act*
- Kits
  - S.A.F.E. Playground Supervision Kit
  - Child Care Assessment Kit
  - School-Age Assessment Kit
- Brochures
  - *Working to Make America's Playgrounds S.A.F.E.*
  - *Inspection Guide for Public Playgrounds*
  - *Planning a Play Area for Children*
  - *Tips for Playground Fundraising*
  - *Selecting Playground Surfacing Material*
  - *S.A.F.E. Set*
- Books and Monographs
  - *National Action Plan for the Prevention of Playground Injuries*
  - *Playground Safety Lesson Plans*
  - *S.A.F.E. Playground Handbook*
- Other products
  - Lapel pins
  - Hats
  - T-shirts
  - Magnets
  - Safety travel pack
  - Signs

Glossary

adventure playground—A playground that children build under the supervision of adults. Adventure playgrounds were popular in the 1960s, especially in Europe.

attractive nuisance—A hazardous object or condition of property that can be expected to attract children to play.

auditory awareness—The ability to pay attention to the environment by using the sense of hearing.

behavioral cards—Note cards that supervisors can use to document positive or negative behaviors.

blind spot—A place in the playground where adults cannot see children. Blind spots can be created by vegetation and solid pieces of equipment, and they may also be corners and alleyways.

challenge—A task that is stimulating and arousal seeking; a test of strength or endurance.

critical height—The fall height below which a life-threatening head injury would not be expected to occur; the height from which measurement is taken to determine the appropriate depth of surfacing under and around playground equipment.

direct supervision—Watching and directing children's activities within an outdoor play area and responding to each child's needs.

ego—The self; the individual as self-aware.

egocentric—Focusing on the self; self-centered.

emotional (affective) characteristic—Feelings and emotions; one of four main characteristics of human beings.

fall height—See *critical height*.

figure-ground perception—The ability to discern between an item and its background.

gap—A narrow opening, such as the area between a slide platform and the slide itself, in which clothing strings can get caught.

hazard—A source of danger that the user cannot see and evaluate.

head entrapment—An opening of a distance between any interior opposing surfaces greater than 3.5 inches (9 centimeters) and less than 9 inches (23 centimeters).

id—The source of psychic energy dominated by the pleasure principle; its impulses are controlled by the ego and superego.

impact attenuation—The ability of a surface system to reduce and dissipate the energy of a falling body.

intellectual (cognitive) characteristic—The ability to use reasoning powers to solve problems; one of the four main characteristics of human beings.

loose fill material—Surfacing consisting of small, independent, movable components such as sand, gravel, wood chips, or shredded rubber.

model—A symbolic representation of a concept or physical being.

movement awareness (kinesthetic awareness)—The ability to know, through observation, the placement of one's body in space.

negligence—The omission to do something that a reasonable person, guided by ordinary considerations, would do, or the doing of something that a reasonable and prudent person would not do.

parallel play—An activity where children play next to one another but do not interact. They share the immediate play space but do not share the objects of play.

perceptual motor development—The ability to receive stimulation and then move as a result.

periodic inspection—An inspection that is done on a regular, designated basis.

PESI model—Model that describes the four main characteristics of human beings (physical, emotional, social, and intellectual). Also sometimes referred to as *PIES*.

physical (psychomotor) characteristic—The body as opposed to the mind; one of the four main characteristics of human beings.

play facilitator—An adult who helps children play. This person is not a playground supervisor.

play value—The level of developmental challenge in the interaction of a child with an event or object.

play zone (zone of play)—The space in which one expects specific play activities to occur in the play area.

playground audit—The first inspection of a playground after it is built; also, the first inspection of a playground after a disaster (i.e., tornado, hurricane, earthquake) occurs.

playground supervisor—An adult who supervises children when they play on a playground. Supervisors should be trained to perform that task.

quality of use—See *play value.*

risk—The probability of loss or injury. In play areas, the higher the risk, the higher the probability of injury.

routine inspection—A playground inspection that occurs on a regular basis.

S.A.F.E. model—NPPS model that describes four aspects of safe playgrounds: supervision, age-appropriate design, fall surfacing, and equipment maintenance.

sight line—The vision line of a supervisor in a play area. Good sight lines provide the ability to see 360 degrees without any obstructions.

site analysis—Analysis of the physical environment to determine its safety or appropriateness for a particular use by particular individuals.

social characteristic—The ability of individuals to get along with others; one of four main characteristics of human beings.

soft contained play equipment—Equipment usually found indoors at fast food restaurants; includes items such as bubble pits, enclosed slides, and tubes over rubber matting.

spatial orientation—The ability to know where you are in relation to the space and objects around you.

standard of care—Procedures accepted by an association or by the courts as normal and appropriate in relation to safety.

superego—The part of the psyche that controls the ego, enforces moral standards, and blocks unacceptable impulses of the id.

supervise—To oversee, direct, or manage (work, children, or adults).

supervision—Active yet unobtrusive monitoring of the play environment.

trigger—In the case of playgrounds, something that precipitates an injury or other problems.

unitary surface (unitary material)—A surface system consisting of one or more components bound together; for example, foam components, urethane, or rubber tiles.

unreasonable risk—Knowingly creating a situation where the probability of injury is high; for example, installing playground equipment over concrete.

use zone—The surface under and around a piece of equipment onto which a child falling from the equipment would be expected to land.

vestibular stimulation apparatus—Nerves in the ears that are activated by sound to provide information to the brain about the movements of the head.

Bibliography

American Academy of Orthopaedic Surgeons (AAOS). (1999, May 3). 10 common questions about playground safety. [News release.] Rosemont, IL: Author.

American Academy of Pediatrics (AAP). (2004). *School health: Policy and practice* (6th ed.). Elk Grove Village, IL: Author.

American Academy of Pediatrics (AAP), American Public Health Association (APHA), & National Resource Center for Health and Safety in Child Care. (2002). *Caring for our children: National health and safety performance standards: Guidelines for out-of-home child care* (2nd ed.). Elk Grove Village, IL: Authors.

American Academy of Pediatrics (AAP), American Public Health Association (APHA), & National Resource Center for Health and Safety in Child Care. (2003). *Stepping stones to caring for our children: National health and safety performance standards* (2nd ed.). Elk Grove Village, IL: Authors.

American Society for Testing and Materials (ASTM). (1988). *F1148: Standard consumer safety performance specification for home playground equipment.* Philadelphia: Author.

American Society for Testing and Materials (ASTM). (1991). *F1292: Standard test method for shock-absorbing properties of playing surface systems and materials.* Philadelphia: Author.

American Society for Testing and Materials (ASTM). (1993). *F1487: Standard consumer safety performance specification for playground equipment for public use.* Philadelphia: Author.

American Society for Testing and Materials (ASTM). (1994). *F355: Standard test method for shock-absorbing properties for playing surface systems and materials.* West Conshohocken, PA: Author.

American Society for Testing and Materials (ASTM). (1997). *F1816: Standard for safety specification on children's upper outerwear.* West Conshohocken, PA: Author.

American Society for Testing and Materials (ASTM). (1998). *F1918: Standard safety performance specification for soft contained play equipment.* West Conshohocken, PA: Author.

American Society for Testing and Materials (ASTM). (1999). *F1951: Standard specification for determination of accessibility of surfacing systems under and around playground equipment.* West Conshohocken, PA: Author.

American Society for Testing and Materials (ASTM). (2000). *F2049: Standard guide for fences/barriers for public, commercial, and multi-family residential use outdoor play areas.* West Conshohocken, PA: Author.

American Society for Testing and Materials (ASTM). (2001a). *F2088: Standard consumer specification for infant swings.* West Conshohocken, PA: Author.

American Society for Testing and Materials (ASTM). (2001b). *F2075: Standard specification for engineered wood fiber for use as a playground safety surface under and around playground equipment.* West Conshohocken, PA: Author.

American Society for Testing and Materials (ASTM). (2004a). *F1292: Standard test method for shock-absorbing properties of playing surface systems and materials.* Philadelphia: Author.

American Society for Testing and Materials (ASTM). (2004b). *F2223: Standard guide for ASTM playground surfacing.* West Conshohocken, PA: Author.

American Society for Testing and Materials (ASTM). (2005). *F2373: Standard consumer specification for public use play equipment for children 6 months to 23 months.* West Conshohocken, PA: Author.

Augustus v. Joseph A. Craig Elementary School, 459 So.2d 665 (La. App., 1984).

Barzach, A.J., & Greenberg, S.T. (2001). *Accidental courage, boundless playgrounds.* West Hartford, CT: Aurora.

Bauer, H. (2001). *School playground supervision practices in the state of Iowa.* Unpublished master's thesis, University of Northern Iowa, Cedar Falls, IA.

Beckwith, J. (1988). Negligence: Safety from falls overlooked. In L. Bruya & S. Langendorfer (Eds.), *Where our children play: Elementary school playground equipment* (pp. 223-226). Reston, VA: American Alliance for Health, Physical Education and Recreation.

Beissenger, O., Webster, A., Hogan, S., & Vega, J. (2003). *Customer satisfaction report of findings: Peaceful playgrounds.* Los Angeles: Bissell & Associates.

Bertenthal, B.I., Campos, J.J., & Caplovitz, K.S. (1983). Self-produced locomotion: An organizer of emotional, cognitive, and social development in infancy. In R.N. Emde & R. Harmon (Eds.), *Communities and discontinuities in development* (pp. 175-220). New York: Plenum.

Bossenmeyer, M., & Blackman, M. (2005, January). *Physical activity: A healthy movement on school campuses.* Paper presented at the meeting of the California Obesity Conference, San Diego.

Bossenmeyer, M., & Owens, K. (2004). *Peaceful playgrounds: A program to reduce playground injuries in school settings.* Unpublished manuscript, International University, San Diego.

Boulton, M.J. (1999). Concurrent and longitudinal relations between children's playground behavior and social preference, victimization and bullying. *Child Development, 70* (4), 944-954.

Bowers, L. (2003). *A research study of comparisons of physical activity on a play structure between age groups over twenty weeks.* Philadelphia: American Alliance for Health, Physical Education, Recreation and Dance.

British Standards Institute (BSI). (1979). *Play equipment intended for permanent installation outdoors, part 2: Recommendations for minimizing hazards in equipment.* London: Author.

Brown, V.R. (1978). *Human factors analysis of injuries associated with public playground equipment.* Washington, D.C.: Consumer Product Safety Commission.

Bruya, L.D. (1998a). *Play spaces for children: A new beginning.* Reston, VA: American Alliance for Health, Physical Education, Recreation and Dance.

Bruya, L.D. (1998b). *Supervision on the elementary school playground.* Unpublished master's thesis, Gonzaga University, Spokane, WA.

Bruya, L.D., & Bruya, L. (2000, March). Risk factor one: Supervision on a safe playground. *Journal of Physical Education, Recreation, & Dance, 71* (3), 20.

Bruya, L., Hudson, S., Olsen, H., Thompson, D., & Bruya, L. (2002). *S.A.F.E. playground supervision manual.* Cedar Falls, IA: National Program for Playground Safety.

Bruya, L.D., & Langendorfer, S.J. (Eds.). (1988). *Where our children play: Elementary school playground equipment.* Reston, VA: American Alliance for Health, Physical Education and Recreation.

Bruya, L.D., & Wood, G.S. (1998). Achieving a safe ratio on the playground. *Parks and Recreation, 33* (4), 74-77.

Burgeson, C.R., Wechsler, H., Brener, N.D., Young, J.C., & Spain, C.G. (2001). Physical education and activity: Results from school health policies and programs study 2000. *Journal of School Health, 71,* 279-293.

Butler, G.D. (1938). *The new play areas: Their design and equipment.* New York: Barnes.

Butwinick, E. (1974). *Petition to the Consumer Product Safety Commission.* Washington, D.C.: Author.

California Playground Regulations. (2000). *Supervisor.* Retrieved November 21, 2006, from www.safety-policy.org/play-reg/play-reg.htm.

Campos, J.J., Bertenthal, B.I., & Kermonian, R. (1992). Early experience and emotional development: The emergence of wariness of heights. *Psychological Science, 3* (1), 61-64.

Canadian Standards Association (CSA). (1991). *A guideline on children's play spaces and equipment.* Ottawa, ON: Author.

Chalmers, D.J., Marshall, S.W., Langley, J.D., Evans, M.J., Brunton, C.R., Kelly, A.M., & Pickering, A.F. (1996). Height and surfacing as risk factors for injury in falls from playground equipment: A case-control study. *Injury Prevention, 2,* 98-104.

Clapperton, A., & Cassell, E. (2005). Consumer product-related injury (1): Playground equipment and trampolines. *Hazard, 61,* 1-21.

Clements, R.L., & Fiorentino, L. (2004). *The child's right to play: A global approach.* Westport, CT: Praeger.

Colvin, G., Sugai, G., Good, R.H., & Lee, Y. (1997). Using active supervision and precorrection to improve transition behaviors in an elementary school. *School Psychology Quarterly, 12,* 344-363.

Consumer Product Safety Commission (CPSC). (1981a). *A handbook for public playground safety, Volume I: General guidelines for new and existing playgrounds.* Washington, D.C.: Author.

Consumer Product Safety Commission (CPSC). (1981b). *A handbook for public playground safety, Volume II: Technical guidelines for equipment and surfacing.* Washington, D.C.: Author.

Consumer Product Safety Commission (CPSC). (1991). *Handbook for public playground safety.* Washington, D.C.: U.S. Government Printing Office.

Consumer Product Safety Commission (CPSC). (1994). *Handbook for public playground safety.* Washington, D.C.: U.S. Government Printing Office.

Consumer Product Safety Commission (CPSC). (1997). *Handbook for public playground safety.* Washington, D.C.: U.S. Government Printing Office.

Consumer Product Safety Commission (CPSC)/EPHA. (1999). *National Electronic Injury Surveillance System (NEISS) data* (11/1/98-10/1/99). Washington, D.C.: Author.

Cremen, L.A. (1961). *The transformation of the school.* New York: Author.

Curtis, H. (1912, July-August). Neighbor center. *American City, 7,* 14-17.

Curtis, H.S. (1917). *The play movement and its significance.* Washington, D.C.: McGrath.

Curtis, H., Hill, A., & Woodruff, R. (1906). *Letters pertaining to the first meeting and organization of the Playground Association of America.* Arlington, VA: NRPA Archives.

DeMary, J.L., & Ramnarain, A.K. (2003). *From playgrounds to play/learning environments.* Richmond, VA: Department of Education, HSB, NRPA.

Dewey, J. (1899). *The school and society* (reprinted 2001). Mineola, NY: Dover Publications.

Dickerson, J.G. (1985). *The development of the playground movement in the United States: A historical study.* Unpublished dissertation, New York University.

Dunklee, D.R., & Thompson, T. (1990, November). People management on the playground. *School Business Affairs, 56* (11), 34-35.

Edginton, C.R., Hudson, S.D., & Lankford, S.V. (2000). *Managing recreation, parks, and leisure services.* Champaign, IL: Sagamore.

Edginton, C.R., Hudson, S.D., & Scholl, K. (2005). *Leisure recreation, parks, and leisure services* (3rd ed.). Champaign, IL: Sagamore.

Edmondson v. Brooks County Board of Education, 423 S.E.2d 413 (Georgia, 1992).

Eisenberg, A., Murkoff, H.E., & Hathaway, S.E. (1994). *What to expect: The toddler years.* New York: Workman.

Eisenberg, A., Murkoff, H.E., & Hathaway, S.E. (1996). *What to expect the first year.* New York: Workman.

Elledge v. Richland/Lexington School Dist. Five, 573 S.E.2d 789 S.C. (2002).

Evans, R. (1993). The human face of reform. *Educational Leadership, 51,* 19.

Fiissel, D., Pattison, G., & Howard, A. (2005). Severity of playground fractures: Play equipment versus standing height falls. *Injury Prevention, 11,* 337-339.

Freud, S. (1918). *Totem and taboo.* New York: New Republic.

Frost, J.L. (1992). *Play and playscapes.* Albany, NY: Delmar.

Frost, J.L. (Ed.). (2001). *Children and injuries.* Tucson, AZ: Lawyers & Judges.

Frost, J.L., Brown, P., Sutterby, J.A., & Thornton, C.D. (2004). *The developmental benefits of playgrounds.* Olney, MD: Association for Childhood Education International.

Frost, J.L., & Klein, B.L. (1979). *Children's play and playgrounds.* Boston: Allyn & Bacon.

Frost, J.L., Wortham, S., & Reifel, S. (2001). *Play and child development.* Upper Saddle River, NJ: Prentice Hall.

Gabbard, C. (1992). *Lifelong motor development.* Dubuque, IA: Brown.

Gallahue, D.L. (1976). *Motor development and movement experiences of young children.* New York: Wiley.

Gallahue, D.L. (1993). Child development. In B. Spodek (Ed.), *Handbook of research on the education of young children* (p. 32). New York: Macmillan.

German Institute for Norms. (1985). *Playground equipment for children, concepts, safety requirements, testing.* Berlin: Author.

Gottlieb, G. (1983). The psychobiological approach to development issues. In P. Mussen (Ed.), *Handbook of child psychology* (Vol. II, pp. 1-26). New York: Wiley.

Gottlieb, G. (1991). Experiential canalization of behavioral development: Theory. *Developmental Psychology, 27,* 4-13.

Gulick, L. (1920). *A philosophy of play.* New York: Associated Press.

Hendy, T. (1997). The National Playground Safety Institute: The most commonly asked questions, answered. *Parks and Recreation, 23* (4), 102-105.

Hendy, T. (2004). The nuts and bolts of playground maintenance. In S. Hudson (Ed.), *The S.A.F.E. playground handbook* (2nd ed.) (pp. 77-86). Cedar Falls, IA: National Program for Playground Safety.

Henzy, E. (2001). *Press release: CT offers playground safety advice.* Hartford, CT: Connecticut Children's Medical Center.

Hudson, S., Mack, M., & Thompson, D. (2000). *How safe are America's playgrounds? A national profile of childcare, school and park playgrounds.* Cedar Falls, IA: National Program for Playground Safety.

Hudson, S., Olsen, H., & Thompson, D. (2004). *How safe are America's playgrounds? A national profile of childcare, school, and park playgrounds: An update.* Cedar Falls, IA: National Program for Playground Safety.

Hudson, S., & Thompson, D. (1999). Reducing risk in playgrounds. In M. Guddemi, T. Jambor, & A. Skrupskelis (Eds.), *Play in a changing society: Research, risk and application* (p. 61). Little Rock, AR: Southern Early Childhood Association.

Hudson, S., & Thompson, D. (2000). Is your playground safe? *Journal of Physical Education, Recreation, & Dance, 71* (3), 9.

Hudson, S., & Thompson, D. (2004). Overview of playground safety. In S. Hudson (Ed.), *The S.A.F.E. playground handbook* (pp. 1-8). Cedar Falls, IA. National Program for Playground Safety.

Hudson, S., Thompson, D., & Mack, M. (1999). *Selecting playground surface materials.* Cedar Falls, IA: National Program for Playground Safety.

Hudson, S., Thompson, D., & Olsen, H. (2004). *Nine years of excellence.* Cedar Falls, IA: National Program for Playground Safety.

Hunter v. Caddo Parish School Board, 25, 283-CA (Louisiana, 1993).

Illinois Park and Recreation Association (IPRA). (1995). *A guide to playground planning.* Winfield, IL: Author.

Iowa City Community School District. (2006, March 30). *Playground guidelines.* Iowa City, IA: Author.

King, S. (1995). A study of maintenance procedures in 900 parks department. Delano, MN: Unpublished study, Landscape Structures.

Kitzes, W.F. (2001). Standards, regulations and safety guidelines to protect children from injury. In J.L. Frost (Ed.), *Children and injuries* (pp. 107-151). Tucson, AZ: Lawyers & Judges.

Knapp, R., & Hartsoe, C. (1979). *Play for America, 1906-1965.* Arlington, VA: National Recreation and Park Association.

Kutska, K. (1996). Playgrounds: Are yours safe? In M. Christiansen (Ed.), *Points about playgrounds* (pp. 9-17). Arlington, VA: National Recreation and Park Association.

LaForest, S., Robitaille, Y., Lesage, D., & Dorval, D. (2001). Surface characteristics, equipment height and the occurrence and severity of playground injuries. *Injury Prevention, 7,* 35-40.

Leff, S.S., Kupersmidt, J.B., Patterson, C., & Power, T.J. (1999). Factors influencing teacher predictions of peer bullying and victimization. *School Psychology Review, 28,* 505-517.

Macarthur, C., Hu, X., Wesson, D.E., & Parkin, P.C. (2000). Risk factors for severe injuries associated with falls from playground equipment. *Accident Analysis & Prevention, 32* (3), 377-382.

Mack, M., Hudson, S., & Thompson, D. (1997). A descriptive analysis of children's playground injuries in the United States 1990-1994. *Injury Prevention, 3* (2), 100-103.

Mack, M., Sacks, J., Hudson, S., & Thompson, D. (2001). The impact attenuation performance of materials used under indoor playground equipment at child care centers. *Injury Control and Safety Promotion, 8* (1), 45-47.

Mack, M., Thompson, D., & Hudson, S. (1997, December). An analysis of playground surface injuries. *Research Quarterly for Exercise and Sport, 68* (4), 368-372.

Marks, I. (1987). The development of normal fear: A review. *Journal of Child Psychology, 28* (5), 667-697.

Marsh, C.J., & Willis, G. (2003). *Curriculum: Alternative approaches, ongoing issues.* Columbus, OH: Merrill Prentice Hall.

Mero, E. (1908). *American playgrounds.* Boston: Dale Association.

Miller, N.P., & Robinson, D.M. (1963). *The leisure age.* Belmont, CA: Wadsworth.

Mittelstaedt, A. (2004, December). Playgrounds and fencing. *Landscape Architect and Specifier News, 28,* 72-73.

Molnar, D., & Rutledge, A. (1986). *Anatomy of a park* (2nd ed.). New York: McGraw-Hill.

Morrison, M.L., & Fise, M.E. (1998). *Report and model law on public play equipment and areas* (3rd ed.). Washington, D.C.: Consumer Federation of America.

Mott, A., Rolfe, K., James, R., Evans, R., Kemp, A., Dunstan, F., Kemp, K., & Sibert, J. (1997). Safety of surfaces and equipment for children in playgrounds. *Lancet, 349* (9069), 1874-1876.

Nansel, T.R., Overpeck, M., Pill, R.S., Ruan, W.J., Simons-Morton, B., & Scheidt, P. (2001). Bullying behaviors among U.S. youth: Prevalence and association with psychological adjustment. *Journal of the American Medical Association, 285,* 2094-2100.

National Association for the Education of Young Children (NAEYC). (2005). Accreditation criteria and procedures of NAEYC. Retrieved July 26, 2005, from www.naeyc.org/academy/criteria.

National Children's Center for Rural and Agricultural Health and Safety. (2003). *Creating safe play areas on farms.* Marshfield, WI: Marshfield Clinic.

National Program for Playground Safety (NPPS). (1996). *National action plan for the prevention of playground injuries.* Cedar Falls, IA: Author.

National Program for Playground Safety (NPPS). (2001). *Safe surfacing selection guide.* Cedar Falls, IA: Author.

National Program for Playground Safety (NPPS). (2004a). Age-appropriate equipment [Brochure]. Cedar Falls, IA: Author.

National Program for Playground Safety (NPPS). (2004b). Supervision means [Brochure]. Cedar Falls, IA: Author.

National Program for Playground Safety (NPPS). (2004c). *The S.A.F.E. playground handbook.* Cedar Falls, IA: Author.

National Program for Playground Safety (NPPS). (2005). *National action plan for the prevention of playground injuries.* Cedar Falls, IA: Author.

National Program for Playground Safety (NPPS). (2006). Research results from the Iowa Safe Surfacing Initiative, 2003-2006. Retrieved February 10, 2006, from www.playgroundsafety.org/issi/Research_Results_from_the_Iowa_Safe_Surfacing_Initiative-University_of_NorthernIowa.pdf.

National Recreation and Park Association (NRPA). (1976). *Proposed safety standard for public playground equipment.* Arlington, VA: Author.

National Recreation and Park Association (NRPA). (1992). *Playground equipment for public use: Continuum of skills and size differences of children age two to twelve.* Arlington, VA: Author.

National Recreation Association (NRA). (1907, June). NRA board minutes, April 12, 1906. *Recreation,* pp. 13-15.

National Recreation Association (NRA). (1931). *Report of committee on standards in playground apparatus* (Bulletin 2170). New York: Author.

National SAFE KIDS Campaign. (2003, May). *Report to the nation: Trends in unintentional childhood injury mortality, 1987-2000.* Washington, D.C.: Author.

Olsen, H., Hudson, S., & Thompson, D. (2002, August). What your school board should know about playground supervision and safety: Child's play. *American School Board Journal, 189* (8), 22-24.

Olweus, D. (1995). *Bullying at school: What we know and what we can do.* Oxford: Blackwell.

Owens, K. (1997). The developmentally appropriate designed playground. In S. Hudson (Ed.), *The S.A.F.E. playground handbook* (pp. 50-59). Cedar Falls, IA: National Program for Playground Safety.

Parten, M.B. (1932). Social participation among preschool children. *Journal of Abnormal and Social Psychology, 27,* 243-262.

Pellegrini, A.D. (1995). *School recess and playground behavior.* Albany, NY: State University of New York Press.

Piaget, J. (1962). *Play, dreams and imitation in childhood.* New York: Norton.

Playground and Recreation Association of America (PRAA). (1928). *Play areas: Their design and equipment.* New York: Barnes.

Rivkin, M.S. (1995). *The great outdoors: Restoring children's right to play outside.* Washington, D.C.: National Association for the Education of Young Children.

Roderick, C., Pitchford, M., & Miller, A. (1997). Reducing aggressive playground behavior by means of a school-wide raffle. *Educational Psychology in Practice, 13,* 57-63.

Rollins v. Concordia Parish School Board, 465 So.2d 213 (La.App.3d Cir. 1985).

Schappet, J., Malkusak, A., & Bruya, L.D. (2003). *High expectations: Playgrounds for children of all abilities, early childhood edition.* Bloomfield, CT: National Center for Boundless Playgrounds.

School District of Stanley-Boyd vs. Auman, 635 WI. N.W.2d 762 (Wisconsin, 2001).

Siefert, K.L., & Hoffnung, R.J. (1991). *Child and adolescent development* (2nd ed.). Boston: Houghton Mifflin.

Shoop, J., & Dunklee, R.D. (1992). *School law for the principal.* Boston: Allyn & Bacon.

Standards Australia International. (1981). *Australian standard 1924, part 1-1981, playground equipment for parks, schools and domestic use, part 1: General requirements.* Melbourne: Author.

Sweeney, T. (1974). *Petition to the Consumer Product Safety Commission.* Cleveland Heights, OH: Author.

Thompson, D. (2005). Development of age-appropriate playgrounds. In S. Hudson (Ed.), *National Playground Safety School curriculum* (pp. 35-49). Cedar Falls, IA: National Program for Playground Safety.

Thompson, D., & Bowers, L. (Eds.). (1989). *Where our children play: Community park playground equipment.* Reston, VA: American Alliance for Health, Physical Education and Recreation.

Thompson, D., & Hudson, S. (1996). *National action plan for the prevention of playground injuries.* Cedar Falls, IA: National Program for Playground Safety.

Thompson, D., & Hudson, S. (2005). Playgrounds. In T. Sawyer (Ed.), *Facility design and management for health, fitness, physical activity, recreation, and sports facility development* (11th ed.) (pp. 313-328). Champaign, IL: Sagamore.

Thompson, D., Hudson, S.D., & Mack, M.G. (1999, March/April). Matching children and play equipment: A developmental approach. *Early Childhood News, 11* (2), 14-25.

Thompson, T., & McClintock, H. (1998). *Demonstrating your program's worth: A primer on evaluation for programs to prevent unintentional injury.* Atlanta: National Center for Injury Prevention and Control.

Tinsworth, D.K., & McDonald, J.E. (2001). *Special study: Injuries and deaths associated with children's playground equipment.* Washington, D.C.: Consumer Product Safety Commission.

University of Michigan. (1975, May 31). *Physical characteristics of children as related to death and injury for consumer product design and use* (UM-HSRI-BI-75-5). East Lansing, MI: Author.

University of Michigan. (1977, May 31). *Anthropometry of infants, children, and youths to age 18 for product safety design* (UM-HRSI-77-17). East Lansing, MI: Author.

University of Michigan. (1986, January). *Size and shape of the head and neck from birth to four years* (UMTRI-86-2). East Lansing, MI: Author.

U.S. Congress, Office of Technology Assessment. (1995). *Risks to children in school.* Washington, D.C.: U.S. Government Printing Office.

U.S. Department of Health and Human Services (DHHS). (2003). *Bullying is not a fact of life.* Washington, D.C.: U.S. Government Printing Office.

van der Smissen, B. (1990). *Legal liability and risk management for public and private entities* (vol. 2). Cincinnati: Anderson.

van der Smissen, B. (2003). Elements of negligence. In D. Cotten & J.T. Wolohan (Eds.), *Law for recreation and sports managers* (3rd ed.) (pp. 56-65). Dubuque, IA: Kendall/Hunt.

Vogelsong, H., & Christiansen, M. (1996). *Play it safe: An anthology of playground safety* (2nd ed.). Arlington, VA: National Recreation and Park Association.

Wade, M.G. (1971). *Biorythms in children during free play.* Unpublished dissertation, University of Illinois, Champaign, Illinois.

Wallach, F. (1997a). Playground safety update. *Parks & Recreation, 32,* 95-99.

Wallach, F. (1997b). Playground hazard identification. In H. Vogelsong & M. Christiansen (Eds.), *Play it safe: An anthology of playground safety* (2nd ed.) (pp. 119-132). Reston, VA: National Recreation and Park Association.

Whitall, J. (2003). Developing of locomotor coordination and control in children. In G. Savelsbergh, K. Davids, J. van der Kamp, & S.J. Bennett, *Development of movement coordination in children* (pp. 81-90). New York: Routledge.

Wortham, S.C., & Frost, J.L. (Eds.). (1990). *Playgrounds for young children: National survey and perspectives.* Reston, VA: American Alliance for Health, Physical Education and Recreation.

Index

Note: The letters *f* and *t* after page numbers indicate figures and tables, respectively.

About the Authors

Donna Thompson, PhD, is an acknowledged national and international expert in the field of playground development and safety, and she is the executive director of the National Program for Playground Safety. She has more than 30 years of experience in teaching, writing, and researching about playgrounds. She has given numerous presentations on playground development, including television interviews on ABC's "Good Morning America," CBS' "Early Edition," "CNN Headline News," and NBC's "Today" program. She has served as consultant for numerous groups planning playgrounds and has been called as an expert witness on playground safety. Dr. Thompson is recognized by early childhood educators, physical educators, elementary principals, park and recreation professionals, and parents for her expertise in playground safety.

Susan D. Hudson, PhD, is a nationally acknowledged expert in the area of playground safety and the education director of the National Program for Playground Safety. She has made presentations both nationally and internationally on playground design and safety and is the author or coauthor of more than 175 articles concerning playgrounds. As the education director, she has spearheaded major research projects for NPPS. Dr. Hudson has held numerous leadership and committee assignments in national professional organizations, including the American Association for Health, Physical Education, Recreation and Dance and the National

Recreation and Park Association. She holds an endowed professorship at the University of Northern Iowa in Cedar Falls.

Heather M. Olsen, MA, is the operations director for the National Program for Playground Safety at the University of Northern Iowa in Cedar Falls. She has been associated with the development of playgrounds and educating the public about maintenance, supervision, and age appropriateness; has given presentations throughout the country about the design of safe playgrounds; and has written many articles on creating playgrounds for children. She is also the major developer of the new online training program for NPPS. Ms. Olsen is a NPPS playground safety school instructor and a member of the Iowa Playground Safety Network and the Black Hawk County Safe Kids Coalition.

How to Use the CD-ROM

Minimum System Requirements

Microsoft® Windows®

- IBM PC compatible with Pentium® processor
- Windows® 98/2000/ME/XP (2000 or XP recommended)
- Adobe Acrobat Reader®
- 16 MB RAM (32 MB recommended)
- At least 6 MB hard drive space recommended for installation
- Microsoft® PowerPoint® Viewer 97 (included)
- 4x CD-ROM drive
- High color display setting (true color recommended)
- Mouse

Macintosh®

- Power Mac® required
- System 9.x/10.x
- 16 MB RAM (32 MB recommended)
- Adobe Acrobat Reader®
- At least 6 MB hard drive space recommended for installation
- Microsoft® PowerPoint® Viewer OS9 or OS10 (included)
- 4x CD-ROM drive (or faster)
- High color display setting (true color recommended)
- Mouse

Installing the Presentation Package

Note: You may open files directly from the CD-ROM without installing them to your hard drive. The following instructions should be used if you wish to edit the files.

Microsoft® Windows®

1. Insert the CD-ROM into the CD-ROM drive.
2. Select the Windows® "Start" button.
3. Select the "Run..." option.
4. Type "X:\setup.exe" (X being the letter corresponding to your CD-ROM drive).
5. Select the "OK" button.
6. Follow the on-screen instructions to install the software.

Macintosh®

1. Insert the CD-ROM into the CD-ROM drive.
2. Double-click the "Thompson PP" icon on the desktop.
3. Open the "Macintosh Installers" folder.
4. Double-click the "Thompson PP Installer" icon. This action launches a hybrid installer that works on both OS X and earlier operating systems.
5. Follow the on-screen instructions to install the software.

Installing the Microsoft® PowerPoint® Viewer 97 for Windows® (for display of content from PowerPoint® 97, 2000, and 2002)

1. Insert the CD-ROM into the CD-ROM drive.
2. Select the Windows® "Start" button.
3. Select the "Run..." option.
4. Type "X:\PPView97.exe" (X being the letter corresponding to your CD-ROM drive).
5. Select the "OK" button.
6. Follow the on-screen instructions to install the software.

Installing the Microsoft® PowerPoint® Viewer 98 for Macintosh® OS 9.x or OS 10.x

1. Insert the CD-ROM into the CD-ROM drive.
2. Double-click the CD-ROM icon on your desktop.
3. Open the "Macintosh Installer" folder.
4. Drag either "PPViewerOS9.hqx" or "PPViewerOS10.hqx" to your desktop or a preferred place on your hard drive.

5. Double-click the ".hqx" file.
6. The installation creates a "Microsoft®
PowerPoint® Viewer" folder in the location

you selected. The Viewer will be inside that folder.

Opening the Presentation Package from within the Microsoft® PowerPoint® 98 Viewer (for Mac OS 9.x users only)

1. Locate the Microsoft® PowerPoint® 98 Viewer folder at the location you installed it to and open the folder.
2. Double-click the Microsoft® PowerPoint® 98 Viewer icon.

3. Select the "Thompson Presentation Package" in the directory listing.
4. Select the "Show" button to begin presentation.

Navigating Within the Presentation Package

NOTE: To manipulate the presentation content, you must have the full version of Microsoft® PowerPoint® 97 or higher.

The following includes instructions for some common tasks you might want to perform within the presentation package (from within the full version of Microsoft® PowerPoint®)

How to Delete a Slide

1. Use the full version of Microsoft® PowerPoint® to open the chapter file that you wish to delete a slide from.
2. In the left nav bar, click on the slide you want to delete.
3. The slide number will be highlighted in black.
4. Hit the Delete key.
5. A pop-up box will confirm that you really want to delete a slide and all of its contents. If you click OK, the slide goes away forever. Click Cancel and your slide will stay put.

How to Edit an Existing Slide

1. Use the full version of Microsoft® PowerPoint® to open the chapter file where you wish to edit a slide.
2. In the left nav bar area, put your cursor wherever you want to adjust text.
3. Edit however you like. PowerPoint will automatically adjust the spacing and scale of subsequent items to fit the space on the slide.

How to Add a New Slide

1. Use the full version of Microsoft® PowerPoint® to open the chapter file where you wish to add a slide.
2. Over on the left nav bar, move your cursor to the place where you want your new slide to go. (It will insert in the spot above your cursor.)
3. Click on Insert/New Slide...
4. A pop-up will come up with an assortment of "template" slide types. PowerPoint calls these "AutoLayouts." The ones we use most

commonly in HK presentations are called "Bulleted List," "Table," and "Object." The Object slide is basically a title at the top and then an image box—where there's the opportunity to import an image file (a piece of art, a photo, some other design element, for example).

5. On-screen instructions are pretty intuitive once the AutoLayout has been selected. Users can see PowerPoint's Help feature for more details.

How to Change the Order of Slides

1. Use the full version of Microsoft(R) PowerPoint(R) to open the chapter file where you wish to reorder the slides.
2. On the left nav bar, click on the number of the slide you want to move.
3. Hit Control-X.
4. On the left nav bar, move your cursor to the new location where you want the slide to go.
5. Hit Control-V and the slide will insert in the spot above the cursor.

This presentation package is an ancillary to the textbook *S.A.F.E. Play Areas: Creation, Maintenance, and Renovation,* published by Human Kinetics. If you need technical support for the *S.A.F.E. Play Areas: Creation, Maintenance, and Renovation Presentation Package* software, please call 217-351-5076, ext. 2970 Monday through Friday (excluding holidays) between 7 a.m. and 7 p.m. (CST). Or, e-mail us at support@hkusa.com.

When you call or e-mail, please provide the following information:
- The type of hardware you are using
- The version of the software you are currently using
- The exact wording of error messages or the message numbers appearing on screen
- A complete description of what happened and what you were doing when the error message appeared
- An explanation of how you tried to solve the problem